Beyond Innocence

On a global platform we are witnessing the increased visibility of the people we call children and teenagers as political activists.

Meanwhile, across the contemporary performance landscape, children are participating as performers and collaborators in ways that resonate with this figure of the child activist. *Beyond Innocence: Children in Performance* proposes that performance has the ability to offer alternatives to hegemonic perceptions of the child as innocent, in need of protection, and apolitical. Through an in-depth analysis of selected performances shown in the UK within the past decade, alongside newly gathered documentation on children's participation in professional performance in their own words, this book considers how performance might offer more capacious representations of and encounters with children beyond the nostalgic and protective adult gaze elicited within mainstream contexts. Motivated by recent collaborations with children on stage that reimagine the figure of the child, the book offers a new approach to both reading age in performance and also doing research *with* children rather than *on* or *about* them. By redressing the current imbalance between the way that we read children and adults' bodies in performance and taking seriously children's cultures and experiences, *Beyond Innocence* asks what strategies contemporary performance has to offer both children and adults in order to foster shared spaces for social and political change. As such, the book develops an approach to analysing performance that not only recognises children as makers of meaning but also as historically, politically, and culturally situated subjects *and* bodies with lived experiences that far exceed the familiar narratives of innocence and inexperience that children often have to bear.

Adele Senior is a Reader in Theatre and Performance at Leeds Beckett University.

Routledge Advances in Theatre & Performance Studies

This series is our home for cutting-edge, upper-level scholarly studies and edited collections. Considering theatre and performance alongside topics such as religion, politics, gender, race, ecology, and the avant-garde, titles are characterised by dynamic interventions into established subjects and innovative studies on emerging topics.

Performing the Transition to Democracy
Theater and Performance in 1970s Spain
David Rodríguez-Solás

Dressaged Animality
Human and Animal Actors in Contemporary Performance
Lisa Moravec

Giving Voice
The Power of Theatre for Positive Change
Carol J Maples

Beyond Innocence
Children in Performance
Adele Senior

Archaeology of the Political Unconscious
Theatre and Opera in East Berlin, 1967–1977
Jennifer Williams

Post-choreography
Jérôme Bel's Choreography and Movement in Malfunction
Shuntaro Yoshida

For more information about this series, please visit: www.routledge.com/Routledge-Advances-in-Theatre--Performance-Studies/book-series/RATPS

Beyond Innocence

Children in Performance

Adele Senior

Routledge
Taylor & Francis Group
LONDON AND NEW YORK

First published 2025
by Routledge
4 Park Square, Milton Park, Abingdon, Oxon OX14 4RN

and by Routledge
605 Third Avenue, New York, NY 10158

Routledge is an imprint of the Taylor & Francis Group, an informa business

British Library Cataloguing-in-Publication Data
A catalogue record for this book is available from the British Library

ISBN: 978-0-367-48835-2 (hbk)
ISBN: 978-1-032-84848-8 (pbk)
ISBN: 978-1-003-04307-2 (ebk)

DOI: 10.4324/9781003043072

Typeset in Times New Roman
by KnowledgeWorks Global Ltd.

For Arthur and Samuel

Contents

Part I

Performing Children

1 The Problem Child of Contemporary Performance

The house lights come down. Two girls, aged about four or five, take to the stage dressed in well-worn, shaggy sheep costumes. They look at each other and awkwardly shuffle to the spot where they have been told to stand under a sparkling sign that reads *Hey Ewe*, the title of the show. These 'curious sheep', as the script frames them, gaze out into the crowd looking for their parents, their curiosity somewhat undermined by the adult direction that evidently ghosts their movements. A small boy enters dressed in emperor attire and tells us in a booming voice that he has 'decided to conduct a census'. Quiet laughter ripples through the audience. I fail to catch the rest of his speech but his mumbled lines nevertheless carefully communicate a great sense of import about the news he is delivering. The emperor has spoken, the choir stands and the tinkling of bells can be heard as the band, donning bow ties over their white PE t-shirts, ready their instruments.

Hustle bustle, let's get busy, planning for our journey.
Hustle bustle, let's get busy, must be on our way.
Caesar has decreed a law we all must heed:
We must travel to the place of our birth.[1]

Decreed. An adult word that is jarring as it leaves the mouths of babes. I make a mental note to ask my son who stands in the choir what he thinks that means once we get home (postscript: he doesn't know), but I'm swiftly pulled away from my thoughts by the two extremely confident and well-rehearsed sheep that occupy centre stage. They have left their nerves at the school assembly door and are here to move the narrative forward, knowingly and with a surprisingly large number of lines to learn and perform for children of reception age. The remaining acts of the play follow as many nativities do, with plenty of yawning, nose-picking, waving, and the occasional line prompts from the teachers who occupy the edge of the playing space. More songs, a few obligatory contemporary references, and a dressage-inspired haughty donkey later, and the animal-led storytelling of Jesus' birth draws to a close.

The tradition of the nativity is not just many children's primary theatrical encounter but often a parent's first experience of their child in performance proper. As such, this annual ritual undoubtedly paves the way for how the people we call

DOI: 10.4324/9781003043072-2

children are to be seen and experienced on stage during the juvenile years that follow: scripted, choreographed, and directed. As a cultural phenomenon in many schools and churches across the globe, the nativity serves to shore up dominant perceptions of the child as innocent, in need of protection, and, perhaps most significantly, as not yet fully developed. We forgive the childish distractions; throw supportive glances at the fumbling of lines; and look on with encouragement when the nerves outwardly declare themselves. We celebrate the child who memorises well and we gaze adoringly at the 'cute' kids, whilst perhaps nostalgically recalling our own experience of stepping onto the school stage in our youth. The child of the nativity is offered to the audience as unknowing or knowing too much, in need of adult direction or well-rehearsed, but nevertheless, still very much a subject in formation. Not yet ready.

These prevailing narratives of the child in mainstream performances such as the nativity inevitably foreclose more complex, alternative discursive means of describing, understanding, and encountering the people we call children. This is not to say that a richer perspective on the child is not available in mainstream or popular performance practices.[2] In relation to professional musical theatre, Helen Freshwater argues that the Royal Shakespeare Company's 2010 adaptation of Roald Dahl's novel *Matilda* challenges 'the residual, yet still powerful, fantasies of childhood innocence and vulnerability that continue to circulate on Broadway and in the popular cultural imaginary' (2017: n.p.). However, the focus of our attention as audience members is nevertheless often towards appreciating children's development, innocence, and experience or lack thereof in popular forms rather than creating space for adults to widen their perspectives on the young performers who take to the stage in front of them. At the same time, more nuanced and complicated iterations of the figure of the child are emerging, particularly at the turn of the 21st century, and specifically within the field of contemporary performance that is made with the people we call children. As spectators, we undoubtedly bring the same narratives of innocence and inexperience to bear on these child figures but, as this book attests, many iterations of the child within the contemporary performances cited here deliberately resist hegemonic representations of the child or play with the nostalgic or protective adult gaze that occupies more mainstream forms.

Whilst the contemporary performance landscape is offering alternative images of the child, on a global platform we are also witnessing the increased visibility of the people we call children and teenagers as political activists, which, despite many historical antecedents[3] have garnered extensive news media attention recently, almost as if children have suddenly become politicised over the past few years. Paul Amar reminds us of a wealth of examples not just of individual action but also of collective organisation at the global scale in recent times:

> In 2014 [...] preadolescents from El Salvador and Honduras—many between six and nine years old—confronted immigration enforcement officers at the US southern border (Park 2014) [...] In the Middle East, children continued to take to the streets on their own terms: preteen protesters flooded the streets of Palestine and Yemen by the thousands, hurling their bodies against police barriers and security perimeters (Frykberg 2015). In Brazil prepubescent black

> favelado residents launched the "rolezinho" movement, challenging the forces of militarization, exclusivism, and eviction around World Cup and Olympic developments by strolling, dragging themselves in carefree ways, and dancing en masse through elite shopping malls and gated communities [...]
>
> (2016: 569)

In the context of North America, the image of the child and young person as a political activist has been particularly prevalent following the protest actions of the teenage survivors of the Stoneman Douglas High School shooting in Florida in 2018. Referred to widely as 'crisis actors' – a derogatory term used to suggest that they are working secretly on behalf of gun control campaign groups and have received FBI (The Federal Bureau of Investigation) coaching – these young activists have been both lauded and treated with suspicion by various commentators, from politicians to journalists to pro-gun lobbyists (Sharman 2018). In this context, school-age children who have direct lived experience of gun violence have been personally and publicly verbally attacked, framed as performers or puppets carrying out the agenda of adult anti-firearms activists in their bid to reform gun laws in the United States (Stanglin and Hayes 2018). Many of the adult commentators responding to their protests have utilised the discourse of children's so-called inexperience, immaturity, innocence (and implied the potential for evil therefore), as well as their on-going social development in an attempt to underplay the significance of their political action. This has included describing them in dismissive terms such as 'misguided youth' (Jesse Hughes cited in BBC 2018). After lawmakers voted on a bill to ban assault weapons, teenage activists were similarly patronised on Twitter: 'worst news since their parents told them to get summer jobs' (Dinesh D'Souza cited in Sharman 2018).

Yet, at the same time the symbolic and material actions of these young people in the form of protests, sit-ins, and informed cultural references made during news media interviews, counters hegemonic perceptions of children as passive and apolitical. In particular, the close relationship of their activism to theatre and performance has played an important role in creating both an image of these young activists as more complex subjects and conversely providing those who oppose their political actions with an opportunity to employ an antitheatrical discourse, such as labelling them 'crisis actors', to undermine their attempts to affect change (Senior 2018). Given this wider political context and its relationships to performance, the book asks: what is the contemporary performance landscape doing to facilitate more capacious representations, readings of, and encounters with the people we call children? What strategies can contemporary performance offer the people we call children in order to facilitate spaces for future practice towards social and political change? Furthermore, how can we develop approaches to both making and analysing performance in a way that not only recognises children as makers and carriers of meaning but also as historically, politically, and culturally situated subjects *and* bodies with their own important lived experiences. By asking these questions, I echo Cindy Katz who suggests that 'when it comes to children, we seem able to see them as innocent, unformed, as savage, as "good" or as vulnerable without historicizing, locating, or specifying their much more complicated unstable and contingent subjectivity' (2008: 8).

To begin acknowledging both the situatedness of children's complex subjectivities and responding to the questions above, I suggest, demands a paradigm shift within the study of theatre and performance. That is, young people deserve the same analytical attention that is ordinarily directed towards adult bodies in performance but has previously been denied to the diverse bodies of the people we call children.

In parallel with this global context of young people's activism – a context which is imbricated in the world of performance through their performative actions and where the people we call children or 'youth' are defiantly visible as politically and historically situated subjects – this book focuses on the ways in which prevailing and often reductive narratives of the child are simultaneously being challenged or disrupted within professional contemporary performance. In particular, I examine how contemporary performance that has been developed and seen predominantly by UK and European audiences offers and reflects new narratives of the figure of the child and the people we call children beyond the dominant notion of the child as pure, uncorrupted, and not-yet adult who demands adult protection. Whilst the book discusses practice across different disciplinary platforms including theatre, dance, film, and live art, it is important to note that it is not a comprehensive history of the appearance of children in contemporary UK and European performance. Neither is its focus on children's participation in theatre for young audiences, applied theatre, or drama education settings. Instead, it offers an in-depth analysis of selected 21st century professional contemporary performance works that have mainly taken place on a theatre stage over the last decade and which have largely been made with children for adult audiences. As such, a detailed analysis of key projects that have taken place outside of the UK theatrical context but have been fundamental in shaping the wider landscape of contemporary performance and live art with children–such as the work of Theatre of Research at Fundus Theatre and Mammalian Diving Reflex based in Germany and Canada, respectively–is not within the scope of this study.[4] Similarly, a history of children's participation in experimental performance in relation to wider political activism, such as the emerging historical archive of children's appearance within the Happenings of the 1960s that is currently being mapped by Heike Roms (2022), is also out of scope. *Beyond Innocence* instead focuses on mining particular case studies in order to develop a catalogue of performance strategies, context-specific readings of performance, and novel approaches to both performance analysis and practice research that challenge dominant narratives of the child and interrogate how these works intersect with the various gazes that are referenced or elicited by performance itself. It is my hope that the performance works discussed within these pages open up different discursive possibilities for how both adults and the people we call children – who will be the next generation of academics, artists, and audiences – perceive, experience, and encounter young people in performance, performance research, and cultural life more generally. In doing so, I want to draw attention to contemporary performance as one of the potential 'mechanism[s] and practices by which social actors branded as children challenge the regime of infantilization' (Amar 2016: 597).

The book has a three-part structure. This part, *Part I Performing Children*, sets the scene by mapping hegemonic discourses of the child whilst also problematising terminology such as the child, children, and childhood as it is used within majority culture. This first part also situates the challenges of 'reading' children against the backdrop of this wider context of responses to young people's increased participation in public activist practice, raising questions about the specific meanings that are created by the appearance and labour of the people called children within the context of theatrical performance of the past. *Part II Reading Children* identifies specific strategies through which contemporary performance navigates dominant representations of the child and child/adult relations through a close analysis of two stage productions with children and female-identifying teenagers respectively: Milo Rau's *Five Easy Pieces* (2016) and HETPALEIS & Lies Pauwels' *The Hamilton Complex* (2016). In response to the spectatorial challenges thrown up by what I am coining the trans*-age practices in these performances, Part II offers a new model for reading 'age' in performance that accounts for the complexities of reading the bodies of the people we call children, specifically when they play people called adults.

Part III Experiencing Children moves beyond the ocularcentrism of both mainstream and much contemporary performance practice with children. Instead, it considers alternative ways that we might encounter young people in both professional performance and performance research in order to resist the dominant discourses of the child that often marginalise their experiences. To this end, Part III attends to the lived, relational, and embodied experiences of the people we call children as performers and as archivists of their own experiences. It does so by adopting queer phenomenology as a means of attending to the specific relationality of the embodied and intimate encounter available to an audience member of Britt Hatzius' *Blind Cinema* (2017) and by queering existing approaches to research with children that ordinarily maintain adult privilege. In particular, I put into practice Kathryn Bond Stockton's notion of 'growing sideways' as a methodological approach for researching *alongside* (rather than on/about) the young people who participated in London-based Fevered Sleep's *Men and Girls Dance* (2016) and *We Are Not Finished* (2019) and the Manchester-based cast of Andy Field and Beckie Darlington's *News News News* (2022). By creating space for young performers to become co-researchers, archivists, and authors who self-represent in these post-performance contexts, Part III attempts to address the inequity of the lack of space and time given to documenting the voices and experiences of the people we call children within the current contemporary performance and performance studies scene.

In order to shed light on the multifarious representations and perceptions of the child emerging in the current UK and European contemporary performance context, let us begin by turning our attention to those dominant discourses of the child that continue to shape our understanding and reception of children. Following Mary Kehily (2004), I categorise these discourses of the child in terms of three interrelated and yet distinct visions of childhood: romantic, tabula rasa, and Puritan. That is, the child as innocent, the child as 'blank slate' who awaits socialisation, and the child as potentially evil and capable of deviating from the norm of the inherently 'good' child. The persistence of these images of the child are evident in the very same iterations of the child we see operating in both the news media that broadcasted confrontational verbal attacks on the children of Stoneman Douglas and in mainstream performance forms such as the school nativity, pantomime, or musical theatre. Whilst these perceptions and representations of the people we call children might be considered unproblematic in the context of viewing mainstream performance, the discursive conditions established by these often reductive ways of viewing young people are the same as those that lead to a disregard for their knowledges, insights, subjectivities, and embodied experiences.

The remainder of this part, Part I, is organised in five sections, with the first three sections setting the stage for dominant discourses of the child, the fourth section problematising the category of the child, and the final section offering a synopsis of the book. THE INNOCENT CHILD section considers some of the historical foundations for the prevalence of the concept of the innocent child within romantic discourse. It starts with Jean-Jacques Rousseau's writing on the pure and natural child ([1762] 1947) and situates the child as an innocent figure in relation to the largely European context within which the contemporary performances discussed throughout are made and experienced by audiences. Since theatre as an institution also has its own complex historical associations with the notion of childhood innocence, I look back at a key moment in the child performer's relationship to theatrical labour and spectatorship during the social and legal reforms of the 19th century. The questions raised about eroticising children, perceptions of their lack of agency, responsibility, and unequal power relations with adults in this historic moment then help to signal the backdrop against which some contemporary performances are working when they resist the romantic discourse of the innocent child.

In the next section, THE CHILD AS BLANK SLATE, I outline the idea derived from John Locke of the tabula rasa child who gains knowledge through experience. This blank slate child is a figure we see returning again and again in reviews of child performers in mainstream theatrical practice as well as in public responses to more contemporary experimental work. It is this hegemonic perspective on children as adults-in-the-making rather than autonomous agents that arguably renders them 'incomplete' subjects, who lack knowledge and experience. The third section explores the innocent child's deferred other, THE EVIL CHILD, which we inherit from the 17th century writing of the Puritan Thomas Hobbes. This section charts a brief history of the evil child from Saint Augustine's *Confessions* to more recent examples of the demonisation of children in the UK news media, to highlight the way in which the child is often marked as Other through reference to this discursive category. This context is important because whilst this 'adult-child' (Jenks 2005a) is often seen as a problematic composite creature, we see the same ambiguous, marginalised child presumed to be an 'evil' figure that is refused the status of 'child', recurring subversively in various guises in contemporary performance practice. The methodological complexities of researching the people we call children in performance are then discussed in the fourth section, WHAT IS A CHILD?, where the unstable and problematic categories of the child, childhood, and children begin to be unpacked. The final section of the chapter, CHILDREN ON STAGE, brings us to a synopsis of the book. It offers some thoughts on how the current artistic and political climate demands a serious and careful consideration of children and young people in contemporary performance practice in order to understand the role that performance is playing and might play in future child-led activism.

Outside of the wealth of literature on working with children in applied drama and pedagogical settings, a full-length study of children in performance is long overdue, given the increased concentration of professional contemporary experimental work with children in the UK and Europe at the turn of the 21st century.

By laying out dominant discourses of the child and opening them up to scrutiny in Part I, I want to foreground how they continue to dictate our modes of viewing children both within and beyond the world of contemporary performance, even whilst these discourses may be challenged, resisted, or problematised in the practice itself and/or a spectator's engagement with it. The remaining two parts of the book will then take on the task of addressing and identifying the ways in which these prevailing approaches to encountering children are often dismantled or disrupted in the performances and performance research discussed, and how these encounters subsequently operate to reimagine the homogenised and hegemonic figure of the child. By the end of this book, it is my hope that scholars, artists, and those interested in (problematising) discursive categories of the child will have gained new insights into two main areas: firstly, the various performance strategies related (mainly) to age, gender, and the body that are adopted in artistic practice to unsettle normative representations of the child; and secondly, the methodological challenges and opportunities that these strategies present to those invested in the analytical work of researching children in performance or researching in/with/about children in other disciplinary contexts.

THE INNOCENT CHILD

The romantic discourse of the child mobilises a perspective that children are innately innocent and pure. The figure of the innocent child as a concept can largely be attributed to the work of Genevan philosopher Jean-Jacques Rousseau during the 18th century. Whilst we can also observe romantic images of children conjured in the poetry of Blake and Wordsworth, Rousseau's well-known text *Emile*, or *On Education* ([1762] 1947) champions an understanding of the child as naturally wholesome; an idea of childhood purity that has persisted throughout the ages. When he says 'God makes all things good; man meddles with them and they become evil' (1955: 5), Rousseau is framing the child as one of God's creations and, therefore, as inherently innocent; a figure of absolute purity until they are corrupted by societal experiences.

The prevailing discourse of innocence we inherit from Rousseau[5] in many Western cultural contexts has subsequently shaped assumptions about children in practices and policies relating to them and in doing so has undoubtedly influenced legal, educational, and other socio-political matters concerning young people up to the present day. The Romantic vision of the child, for example, has been adopted to manufacture a perception of children as essentially vulnerable in a way that worked in the favour of social reformers of the 19th century, who sought to protect children from the perils of child labour (see Hendrick 1990, Jenks 2005a). This image of the child as vulnerable and needing protection has persisted into the contemporary context with charity adverts, mass media, and government rhetoric deliberately operating to position the child as a 'passive victim of abuse, neglect and poverty' (Jenks 2005a: 125; see also Burman 1994). So, whilst 'innocence' as a concept has arguably had some benefits for children's lives, it has also worked (and continues to work) against the lives of real, material human beings under the age of 18 by framing them in terms of victim rhetoric that justifies power over the people we call children in the name of offering them protection. Childhood innocence also plays a significant role in consumerism, with corporate culture's appropriation of childhood innocence functioning to 'commodify and sexualize children's bodies, desires, and identities in the interests of turning a profit' (Giroux 2000: 17).[6] Paradoxically, innocence has been eroticised for the viewing pleasures of adults in ways that fetishize, idealise, and ultimately objectify the bodies of the people we call children (Kincaid 1998). Contemporary performance's representations of the child, as we shall see, operate within and sometimes against the context of the historical development of this erotic gaze towards the innocent child.

However, Allison James *et al.* remind us that Rousseau 'opened up the question of the child's particularity' and in doing so has elevated the child to 'the status of person, a specific class of being with needs and desires and even rights' (1998: 13). So, although Rousseau's image of the child invites sentimentality, eroticisation, and has been appropriated to work both for and against the well-being of actual children, Rousseau acknowledges children as a distinct but important part of his wider agenda to recognise humans' individual freedom (see for example *The Social Contract* 1762). His attention towards childhood as a process rather than (just) a product (Robertson [1974] 2006: 407) is thus tied up in Enlightenment thinking and ultimately advocates a kind of freedom for children as part of a demand for progress. By recognising the child as a person with individual needs rather than as an adult-in-waiting, Rousseau foregrounds the responsibility of adults and particularly education in addressing those needs through guidance and support.[7] His seemingly contradictory claim of children's freedom alongside the call for more responsibility from adults, parallels recent concerns in journalistic and public responses to contemporary performance around what kinds of freedoms children are able to exercise (see Gardner 2008).

The performance practices discussed throughout this book share this European historical context of Enlightenment thinking about the child, even whilst some of these performances resist the notion of the innocent child in terms of both form and content. All of the performances and projects I foreground in the chapters that follow include within them people we call children or teenagers and are either made in the UK and Europe or exhibited predominantly in the UK and/or European countries (and in many cases, both). As mentioned, these include *Five Easy Pieces* by Milo Rau (Switzerland/Belgium), *The Hamilton Complex* by HETPALEIS (Belgium), *Blind Cinema* by Britt Hatzius (Belgium/Germany), *Men and Girls Dance* and *We Are Not Finished* by Fevered Sleep (London, UK), and *News News News* by Andy Field and Beckie Darlington (Manchester, UK). We can therefore assume that performance makers and collaborators – sometimes both adults and children – who are working in this area have, to some degree, inherited the discourse and effects of Rousseau's innocent child, even whilst they might simultaneously reject the romantic image of the child. The persistence of this discourse of innocence is evident in the way these works speak directly or indirectly to the themes and questions that emerge from attributing innocence to the people we call children. Such themes have become of increasing concern to the disciplines of critical pedagogy and childhood studies over the last few decades and more recently performance studies (Senior *et al.* 2018); namely, issues of adult responsibility, the nostalgic gaze, children's autonomy and freedom, the child's well-being, passivity, and inexperience. We can also assume that the reception of these performances, how they are perceived and received, is affected by the prevalence of the idea of the romantic child within European cultural contexts, as attested by the critical reviews, online comments from audience members, and scholarly responses that I cite throughout.

The pervasive 18th century image of the child as innocent informs the more recent conflicting, ambiguous, and shifting adult-child relationships in contemporary Europe which inform this study. In the field of performance, Bridget Escolme has noted a trend that still pervades into the 2020s:

> [c]hildren in Europe are a sensitive issue. Child abuse and pornography are both a genuine problem and a tabloid mainstay: we must protect our children from the real-life monsters that lurk around every corner. Delinquency and disruption hold equal pride of place in popular mythology: we must control and punish our children more effectively, they are the twenty-first century's real-life monsters.
>
> (2006: 164)

These antagonistic relationships with children are echoed in social media and news media responses to the participation of young people in political activism. They are to be protected yet feared, controlled yet free (at least within the boundaries of the adults who are setting the terms). These antagonisms are, at least in part, a consequence of the discourse of innocence inherited from Rousseau and his contemporaries. That is, if we assume the child is vulnerable, we recognise that they need support and protection and if we accept that they need to be protected we also acknowledge innocence's supposed binary opposition, that is, the Puritan-informed idea that children are also capable of being and doing 'evil'.

The purpose of drawing attention to the prevailing notion of the innocent child is not to homogenise conceptions of 'the child' across different geographical contexts within the UK and Europe. One needs to only look at the vast differences in the minimum age at which young people can be criminally prosecuted across various European countries to gain a sense of the multiple perspectives concerning when the people we call children should be held legally responsible for their actions. For example, young people can be held criminally liable at the age of 10 in England and Wales, whilst in Portugal the minimum age that a person can be criminally prosecuted is much older, at 16 years of age. This suggests that perceptions of young people's socialisation, rationality, culpability, and awareness of their own decisions and intentions vary across different legal and social contexts. In other words, to generalise across different European contexts would be problematic. However, we can observe some similarities in the concerns of artists, practitioners, companies, and performance makers working in this field which is also indicative of a shared cultural milieu in which dominant perceptions of children in the UK and Europe exist: complex adult-child relationships are explored in Fevered Sleep's *Men and Girls Dance* (2016) and Tim Etchells and Victoria's *That Night Follows Day* (2007); the voyeuristic gaze of the adult and the bodies of female-identifying teenagers are the focus of works such as Hetpaelis' *The Hamilton Complex* (2016) and Ontroerend Goed's *Once and For All We're Gonna Tell You Who We Are So Shut Up and Listen* (2008); both Boris Charmatz's *Enfant* (2011) and *Nightwalks with Teenagers* (2015) by Mammalian Diving Reflex consider control, responsibility, ownership, and freedom through an exploration of physicality and site respectively. The recurrence of these themes in different geographical performance-making and sharing contexts across the UK and Europe thus suggests some common concerns relating to children, childhood, and children's bodies. What also marks both the creation and reception of all of these performances, whether subtly or explicitly, is a rich history of the notion of the child performer and their historical presence to which we will now turn as it undoubtedly informs performance's relationship to the conceptualisation of the innocent child in our contemporary context.

Childhood Innocence and Theatre

The theatrical institution has its own specific and complex historical relationship to the discourse of childhood innocence; a history that cannot be ignored in a study that interrogates the ways in which we experience and work with children either onstage or in performance more generally. Questions of exploitation are abundant when children participate in performance and this is certainly the case when an economic exchange is anticipated, whereby an audience pays and/or the child does/does not receive payment for their work. Questions of the exploitation of children's work and labour are not new. Theatre producers, managers, and parents of the theatrical past have been regularly accused of taking advantage of children, although these arguments are often couched in terms of their presumed inherent vulnerability rather than material attempts to remove systemic barriers to children's access to economic power. Theatre history, particularly in reference to the UK context in which the performances discussed in this book were encountered, is subsequently littered with accounts of children being ill-treated (Barlee 1884, Fawcett 1889). Indeed, the care and protection of child performers continue to be a subject of controversy and concern in contemporary practice (Department for Education 2012, Holehouse 2014).[8] Although a complete history of theatre's relationship with notions of childhood innocence is beyond the scope of this book, the socio-legal interventions to improve the lives of so-called juvenile performers in the latter part of the 19th century have had a significant impact on the way we think about children onstage now. Indeed, changes to child labour practices and an intense period of educational reform during the Victorian era continue to shape current expectations around the thorny relationship between children's employment within 'entertainment industries' and their right to an education.

Towards the end of the nineteenth century, the child's life onstage and backstage was beginning to shift with the introduction of a number of Acts in Britain that arguably capitalised on Rousseau's notion of childhood innocence. In 1879, for example, the Children's Dangerous Performance Act was passed in response to the number of children engaged in physically demanding activities such as trapeze and acrobatic work in Victorian public entertainment. The Act prohibited the employment of children under the age of fourteen in entertainment work that was perceived to potentially endanger or fatally injure them, although children under the age of 5 were not protected by this law. A few years later, the publication of Ellen Barlee's book, *Pantomime Waifs*, in 1884 cited 'late hours, unsatisfactory working conditions and [the] moral dangers to which children were exposed' in British Theatre (Horn 1996: 38). Barlee's attention towards protecting children's innocence was foregrounded in her call to safeguard predominantly female child performers from 'a new and erotic attention' directed towards them from male adult audience members (cited in Horn 1996: 38). Notably, the figure of the innocent child was being used and appropriated in this Victorian context to regulate male adult behaviour and – as a theme that we will see recurring in contemporary works such as *The Hamilton Complex* and *Men and Girls Dance* – attests to the way innocence is always defined in relation to supposedly oppositional adult attributes. As Kincaid suggests, innocence and purity are 'negative inversions', that is, things that adults have that children do not possess such as sinfulness, experience, rationality, and so on (2004: 10).

By conflating the need to protect children's innocence with the demand to police adult males' 'immoral' behaviour, Barlee's plea offers an indication of the way in which assumptions of innocence might be ascribed to children for a purpose other than to solely protect the young performers in question. Indeed, we can see a contemporary parallel to Barlee's campaign in the current right-wing agenda to police drag performance in the UK and more fervently in some states in North America, which is framed as protecting innocent children from the 'deceptions' of drag storytime performers (Ellis 2022). The current weaponisation of children's so-called innocence by Conservative Christian, far-right, and anti-LGBTQA+ groups to regulate non-conforming gender performance within drag practice and the way innocence is being employed as a sleight of hand for concealing homophobic and/or transphobic perspectives make a discussion about the historical theatrical trend towards 'protecting children's innocence' all the more urgent.

Furthermore, part of the driving force for social reform that took place towards the end of the 19th century was the claim that children were being deceived into theatrical employment as a cover for child prostitution (Horn 1996: 41), again placing children's perceived innocence at the forefront of legal reform and flagging up the entertainment industry as an area of work that posed a severe threat to children's well-being. Organisations such as the Moral Reform Union and the National Vigilance Association fronted by Millicent Garrett Fawcett – who is well-known for her campaign work around women's suffrage – focused their attention on both the physical and moral harm done to young performers. Such organisations were not only concerned that children might be encouraged into prostitution during their time in the theatre but also for their fate after employment 'when they reached the age of thirteen or fourteen and were no longer wanted in the pantomime' (Horn 1996: 41). Whilst the entertainment industry had been somewhat overlooked in the Education Act of 1876 (Davis 1986: 130), the efforts of Fawcett and her fellow campaigners eventually contributed to the regulation of children's employment in entertainment in the 1889 Prevention of Cruelty to Children bill. This law meant that children under the age of 10 were no longer allowed to perform on stage.

The Act was later amended after it received strong opposition, most notably from key figures such as Lyceum and Drury Lane managers, Henry Irving and Augustus Harris, respectively. The revised law instead allowed children from the age of 7 to perform, provided they had obtained the necessary license, whilst children under the age of 7 were still prohibited. A few years later, the upper age limit for child performers requiring a license rose to 11 and 16 years old if they were working in more 'dangerous' professions, such as the circus. This meant that children or adolescents who 'looked young' but were above 11 were often cast to fulfil the roles of younger child characters in order to circumvent the need for a license (Horn 1996: 50). Stricter child employment regulations, along with the introduction of compulsory school attendance from 1880 onwards thus resulted in a significant decline in the number of child performers in the theatre in the first two decades of the 20th century in comparison with 1880 (Horn 1996: 52).

The celebration of childhood innocence, however, was still highly contradictory in the Victorian era, given the continued exploitative practices of child labour both within and outside of the theatre industry before and during this period of reform. Citing the public debate that emerged surrounding the all-child productions of *The Children's Pinafore* debuting in 1879 in the US and later in the UK, Marah Gubar suggests that 'anglo-american culture remained ambivalent about the idea that all children, regardless of class, were innocent "others" entitled to enjoy a protected period of dependence and development' (2012: 417). Yet, stories of 'philanthropic [theatre] managers rescuing children from the gutter' continued to circulate (Davis 1986: 122). Meanwhile, on the other side of the debate, 19th-century campaigns against child labour were likewise drawing on the discourse of innocence by using emotive language to suggest their 'helplessness', which is exemplified in one account of campaigners of the time describing teenagers hyperbolically as 'infants' (Cunningham 1991: 88). Victorians' contradictory relationship to children in the context of theatrical employment can be seen in a leading article called 'Children and the Theatre' in *The Stage* published in November of 1888:

> ... mere baby figures ought never to be allowed or tolerated on the stage for any length of time beyond a minute or two ... Theoretically these little ones should be snugly tucked in bed, though actually they are too often playing about in the gutter ... The children employed by the managers in large

> numbers at Christmas time are almost exclusively drawn from this class … They are not badly used; they are kept with clean skins; they are drilled in certain evolutions; they are taught to have their wits about them and generally exercise their intelligence.
>
> (The Stage, 1888: 8)

The take-home message of this piece, which is a direct response to the efforts of reformers such as Fawcett *et al.*, is that the theatre is morally enriching for children but not all children: babies should be protected and lower-class children benefit intellectually and physically from theatre work. This suggests that innocence, or lack thereof, was often perceived in relation to age and class. Furthermore, although the article goes on to state that '[i]t is right enough to say that boys and girls should not have to work', the author paradoxically celebrates the opportunities pantomime offers to young people from lower-class backgrounds who would otherwise be 'prowling' about, in the evening, drawing a clear parallel between economically deprived children and non-human animals. This connection between children and non-human animals, and how it has been put to work to imply children's closeness to nature, on the one hand, and children's inherent animalistic, irrational, and primitive qualities, on the other, still continues to dictate contemporary modes of perceiving children, which in turn excludes them from many rights of citizenship (Donaldson and Kymlicka 2018).

The Victorian investment in, and contradictory relationship to the idea of childhood innocence, was reflected as much on the stage itself as it was in the children's backstage conditions of employment. We might, therefore, look to the kinds of roles children were performing within this context of legislative changes in order to gain a sense of how children's so-called innocence was being negotiated in theatrical representation. Rather than being cast in child parts, for example, many young performers of the era were actually employed in more passive roles such as stage props, furniture, and 'costumed as elves, sprites, and woodland animals' (Steedman 1995: 143). Unlike earlier in the century where children, predominantly from stage families, were often seen playing in traditional dramas, the children of the mid to late Victorian period were thought to be mostly employed in non-speaking parts (ibid.). However, more recent research (Gubar 2008) suggests that children occupied a variety of roles and that scholarly readings of them (Rose 1992: 102, Steedman 1995: 143–4, 134) as simply 'muted', background furniture gives weight to the problematic assumption that Victorians were only interested in suspending child performers in time as 'icons of innocence' (Gubar 2008: 64). Instead, Gubar reminds us, this is a particularly rich time for children in theatre history where we see the emergence of all-child productions of Gilbert and Sullivan that began life in the US and became internationally very popular (2012: 413). These all-child productions continued an already well-established appearance of child dance troupes from the 1840s onwards such as the Viennoise children and the Marsh juvenile troupe (Gubar 2012, Vey n.d.). In addition to playing animals, fictional creatures, and in all-child operettas then, the mid-Victorian period also witnessed children from non-theatrical families 'playing themselves' in 'low' art forms such as music hall, circus, and pantomime, where they demonstrated dance, acrobatics, and some acting skills (Gubar 2012: 130).[9]

The multiple roles that the people called children occupied on the Victorian stage and the way in which these performers were regarded in terms of their skilfulness and not just in terms of their perceived innocence, demonstrates an uncertainty and perhaps even signals anxiety towards childhood innocence that arguably still endures in contemporary performance cultures. The fact that children were playing or impersonating adults is of particular importance to recognising the complex viewing habits of Victorian audiences which we see echoed in contemporary audiences' relationship to children and childhood innocence as I discuss in the next part of the book in terms of 'age transvestism', that is, children playing adults (or vice versa):

> [...] the presence of literally hundreds of professional children onstage acting like adults reflects how conflicted nineteenth-century anglo-american culture still was about how to define childhood: as originally sinful or originally innocent, as totally other or really quite similar to adulthood, as competent or incompetent, and so on.
>
> (Gubar 2012: 411)

Undoubtedly there was an investment in childhood innocence amongst Victorian spectators, as Jacqueline Rose (1992) and James Kincaid (2000) have suggested, but as evidenced by reviews such as Walt Whitman's 1846 account of the Viennoise Children as 'sweet-budding thoughtless ones' (cited in Bergman *et al.* 2003: 148) the attendant sexualisation of childhood innocence in his account (Gubar 2008: 422) is a stark reminder of the widespread contradictory relationship to innocence that contemporary performance still comments on, resonates with or otherwise intentionally deliberates in and through practice. Alongside acknowledging the voyeuristic invitation of 'childhood innocence' to the historical theatre spectator, let us briefly consider recent scholarship in other fields, which can offer further insights into what contemporary performance might be doing when it works intentionally or not 'against innocence' to dismantle the figure of the innocent child.

Against Innocence

If 'childhood innocence is an adult ideal, something which adults would like childhood to be' (Kehily and Montgomery 2004: 71) rather than an instinctual or inherent quality that children possess, then it is useful to consider in detail some of the current arguments that have been articulated *against* innocence across different disciplinary contexts. Such arguments are key to thinking about what is at stake in performance practices that either reinscribe or resist attempts to characterise the people we call children as a homogenised figure who is innocent and in need of protection. For one of the key theorists of critical pedagogy, Henry Giroux (2000), there are two main problems with ascribing innocence to children. One issue is that by defining children as pure and needing protection, they are actually 'denied a sense of agency and autonomy' (ibid.: 2). He suggests that the myth of childhood innocence paradoxically limits rather than sustains the welfare of actual children. Whilst the discourse of innocence has been acknowledged as elevating the child to the status of a person and foregrounds the responsibility of the adult (James *et al.* 1998), Giroux conversely argues that in the contemporary context:

> [c]hildhood innocence no longer aspires adults to fight for the rights of children, enact reforms that invest in their future, or provide them with the tools to realize their own political agendas or participate in the production of their own culture.
>
> (2000: 19)

This co-opting of innocence to disempower the people we call children relates to his second concern that 'innocence largely permits adults to not assume responsibility' instead, suggesting that children have been 'abandon[ed] to the dictates of marketplace mentalities that remove the supportive and nurturing networks that provide young people with adequate healthcare, food, housing, and educational opportunities' (Giroux 2000: 2). So, the adult is essentially denying their responsibility to and for the child because the child is predominantly perceived in relation to innocence and not as a historically, socially, and politically-situated subject who is ideologically embroiled in unequal power relations. If what is at stake in this more recent appropriation of childhood innocence by corporate culture is the child's agency and autonomy alongside adults' diminished responsibility, as Giroux argues, then my book asks how contemporary performance speaks to and interrogates this paradox of innocence, especially across different disciplines and forms such as theatre, live art, contemporary dance, and other media that are haunted by the theatrical institution's complex historical issues of adult accountability and children's ability to self-govern. In particular, I ask: how is contemporary performance that is made with the people we call children for predominantly adult audiences, navigating innocence in a way that considers other material harms beyond those proposed by Giroux over two decades ago, namely those related to gender, age, and race-specific expectations surrounding innocence?

Giroux's argument echoes that of cultural theorist Marina Warner who a few years earlier had argued that children are considered 'innocent because they're outside of society, pre-historical, pre-social, instinctual, creatures of unreason, primitive, kin to unspoiled nature' (1995: 56). Building on Warner's argument, Giroux demonstrates how developments in child psychology (Elkind 1998) have situated children outside of the political sphere by blaming the 'loss of childhood innocence' on the changing nature of the (American) family (Giroux 2000: 13) rather than on children's actual political circumstances in the face of the widespread problem of child poverty. Furthermore, he argues that cultural commentators such as Neil Postman who in *The Disappearance of Childhood* (1994) attributes the loss of innocence to new technologies and popular culture have failed to recognise how corporations have sexualised innocence and positioned the child as both the object and the subject of consumerism. In the context of performance, Giroux's provocations, therefore, invite us to consider: how the people we call children in performance might appear (or not) to the spectator as political agents; how we might instead utilise rather than fear new technologies and popular culture to further understand and give space to children's cultures and their own political agendas; and how performance making and scholarship could mobilise opportunities for adult responsibilities towards affecting material, political changes *for* children *alongside* children. The book addresses these considerations throughout and offers some future thoughts in the final chapter concerning how contemporary performance and performance research might create more space for child-authored activism.

In addition to the challenge that the romantic discourse poses for perceptions of children's agency and perpetuates the idea of the child as not-yet culturally and historically contingent subjects, there is the related problem that 'innocence' is a specifically white, heteronormative discursive tool. As Henry Jenkins suggests: 'the most persistent image of the innocent child is that of a white, blond-haired, blue-eyed boy… and the markers of middleclassness, whiteness, and masculinity are read as standing in for all children' (1998: 13). In other words, 'innocence' brings with it assumptions about class, gender, race, ability, ethnicity, and sexuality that reproduce a hegemonic model that centres whiteness, normative masculinity, and wealth. In *No Future: Queer Theory and the Death Drive* (2004) Lee Edelman takes up this problem of the child as a symbolic placeholder for a hegemonic future, *the* future, that is positioned as the biological result of a heterosexual union. The repercussions of the child as a signifier for a heteronormative future are detrimental, shaping our very understanding of the political as grounded in 'reproductive futurism' to the exclusion of 'queerness' Edelman argues (ibid.: 3).

Whilst Edelman is careful not to confuse this 'image' of the child 'with the lived experiences of any historical children' (ibid.: 11), performance as an embodied and bodily practice can explore this 'confusion' without reducing actual children to theoretical servants. Responding to the tension in Edelman's theory here, performance scholar Alan Read asks a key question that addresses the issue of the child being used as a polemical device: 'Have children not laboured enough without doing the bidding of such theoretical reductionism on behalf of adults' identitarian claims?' (Read 2018: 6). Whilst one would not be hard-pressed to find examples of Edelman's symbolic child in practice, the performances discussed here instead work to disrupt – or at least to some extent problematise – the notion of the child as a discursive marker of heternormativity, precisely because they include *actual* children that undermine this framework. Strategies, not unfamiliar to the 'adult' world of contemporary performance, such as playing a persona or version of themselves and co-creating the work with reference to their gender(s), sexuality, or class are employed to resist the normative perception of the innocent child. Instead of, and sometimes in relation to, the figure of the innocent child, audiences are confronted with bodies; bodies that un/intentionally reference class, race, gender etc. and that often 'queer' (Stockton 2009) the normative image of the child or recognise the child as already queer. Yet, the entrenched convention of seeing the bodies of the people we call children as unfinished and still in progress carries with it another persistent discourse of the child as tabula rasa, to which we will now turn.

THE CHILD AS BLANK SLATE

Seventeenth century English philosopher John Locke's influential and enduring take on children is not that they are innately innocent as Rousseau would have it, but rather innocent because they lack experience and knowledge. This distinction is important since it presumes that children are not born pure but rather that they are like empty vessels waiting to be filled up with knowledge, which they gain through their sensory experiences of being in the world. This notion of the child is often referred to using the Latin term 'tabula rasa', frequently translated as a 'blank slate' upon which knowledge is inscribed through experience. Locke develops this idea in his famous work *An Essay Concerning Human Understanding* ([1689] 1836), where he explores how knowledge is acquired:

> Let us then suppose the mind to be, as we say, white paper, void of all characters, without any ideas; how comes it to be furnished?… Whence has it all the materials of reason and knowledge? To this I answer in one word, from experience.
>
> (Book 2, ch. 1, sec 2)

Despite coming from a Puritan family, Locke's observation of the child as a blank slate is not a negative admission but instead he recognises the child as heading towards reason and knowledge because they are capable of being able to perceive and sense (James *et al.* 1998: 16). Furthermore, for Locke, who later focuses specifically on young people's learning in *Some Thoughts Concerning Education* (1693), education is key to developing the appropriate environment for the child to thrive and become a rational citizen who is capable of exercising reason and making decisions. Pedagogues in the form of parents and teachers, are thus responsible for guiding and shaping the child towards 'full' development within Lockean thought.

The idea of the child as a blank slate has significantly influenced a number of disciplines including philosophy (Hegel [1826] 2006), behavioural psychology (see Skinner [1957] 2014), and sociology (see Parsons 1955). It has played a polemical role in Foucault's idea that 'the body is the inscribed surface of events' (Foucault [1971] 1998) as well as feminist scholarship that draws on Foucauldian theory (Butler 1989: 603) and it has supported the growth of the child-centred movement in education in Western contexts (Archard 1993). The influence of Locke's claim has not escaped psychoanalysis either. In *Principles of Psychoanalysis* (1921) Abraham Brill captures the importance of Locke's thinking to the development of the field by arguing that for Sigmund Freud the child is the Lockean tabula rasa, although John Forrester (1990) later challenges Brill's claim, to argue that Freud did not actually consider the child as a passive blank slate. Whilst the influence of Locke's thinking is undeniable, in a review of the appropriation of the term 'tabula rasa' across different academic disciplines, Robert Duschinsky (2012) has contested the idea that tabula rasa originates with Locke and takes issue with the assumption that this concept means that the child's mind is formless.

Instead, Duschinsky traces the image of the blank slate back to Aristotle where he argues it is indicative of the possibility and potentiality of the human rather than – as it has often been interpreted in the academy – signalling the child's purity. He suggests that for Locke 'tabula rasa is not an image of cognitive formlessness, but of a state that requires correct instruction in order to form representations of true moral principles' (2012: 515). However, this conceptualisation of the child as requiring 'correct instruction' still privileges the assumption that there is an adult doing the instructing in order to shape the child's morality.

Whilst Duschinsky's analysis is convincing in its suggestion that tabula rasa has been used by theoreticians of philosophy and psychology as a 'rhetorically useful whipping post' against which a more nuanced idea of the human mind can be developed, I want to focus less on disciplinary interpretations of the concept and more on the way in which the idea of the child as pre-socialised or as a subject-in-formation informs both strategies used within contemporary performance and approaches to reading the people we call children in it. Specifically, I am interested in the way in which the idea of the child as a blank slate is put to work as a discursive category, whilst acknowledging that this and other dominant discourses of the child inevitably affect the material conditions of children. In other words, given that the prevailing idea of the child as a blank slate emphasises the child's socialisation and training towards 'rational' adulthood (Kehily 2004), how does performance negotiate the idea of the child as a blank slate with all of its attendant ambiguities? Does the recognition of the child as a blank slate in the production and reception of the performance works discussed here, translate as the human potentiality of the child or the child who is inexperienced and in need of adult instruction? How does performance reinscribe or challenge the idea of the child as lacking knowledge, understanding, and experience and, therefore, as a figure who is in need of protection, training, and moulding?

These questions are vital since the reception of the people we call children onstage often maps onto the Lockean-inspired notion that children are not yet fully formed and are in need of guidance in their development towards complete maturation. As discussed earlier, perceptions of the child performer often reflect the notion that the people we call children are *in the process of becoming subjects* and we can observe this in audience responses from the humble nativity to professional theatre reviews. Parents, grandparents, and other family members who leave the assembly hall discussing how 'talented' the kids were, 'that one looked like a pro', and 'didn't they do well' reveal adult expectations that these young performers are 'just learning' and 'not quite there' whilst also foregrounding an investment in children's precociousness. Similarly, theatre reviews of professional child performers in mainstream theatre and sometimes contemporary performances have tended towards describing their work in ways that would read very strange for their adult equivalents. These include: describing their practice in rather general terms such as 'terrific' (Gardner 2011, Spencer 2011); commenting on how child performers seem to be experiencing their own work, for example, 'everyone is having a good time' (Gardner 2011); and making a direct reference to the leading actor's age (Spencer 2009) although we also see this in ageist reviews about adult performers and celebrities. In general, professional adult performers are usually afforded a more nuanced critique of their work beyond 'this 32 year old's performance was terrific and he was having a really good time'. Unless the performer's age is relevant to the content of the performance it would be unusual to read about their age in a theatre review or, indeed, the critic's perception of whether they were enjoying their work or not. These examples offer some indication that child performers are still considered not-yet-adults even when they are on the payroll.

This reception of children 'in the process of becoming' is not new within theatrical practice. Whilst theatre historians have argued that spectators of Victorian theatre were predominantly invested in childhood innocence (Kincaid 2000, Rose 1992), Marah Gubar emphasises that the child's personal and professional 'knowingness' and skill was actually the basis of the audience's interest in these young performers (Gubar 2008: 67). Drawing on evidence from critic reviews and marketing materials, Gubar observes that spectators were fascinated not only with their so-called innocence but with the skills of children onstage:

> Far from functioning as voiceless embodiments of purity, child performers appealed to diverse audiences by exhibiting extreme precocity. Their prematurely developed skills and much-vaunted versatility enabled them to blur the line between child and adult, innocence and experience.
>
> (Gubar 2008: 64)

Like the contemporary reviews cited above, the performer's age was often foregrounded in Victorian theatre (ibid.: 66), presumably to emphasise the surprising maturity of skill that they demonstrated. Along with appreciating their skill, some reviews, however, also celebrated child performers' professionalism, intelligence, and autonomy (Gubar 2008: 67). Within this historical context and the current mainstream theatrical environment these latter qualities would not usually be publicly commented upon in a review of an adult performer's work and this, indeed, attests to the assumption that I am speculating still guides our spectatorship: that children are 'in development'. In other words, the admission that these Victorian child performers' talents are 'prematurely developed' assumes that they are heading towards full development, albeit early for their age.

For Gubar such reviews troubled rather than – as advocates of the Victorian era's 'cult of the child' would like to believe – shored up the perceived differences between adults and children at the time. By recognising the child performer's skill, these reviews gave rise to the child as a 'liminal figure' (Gubar 2012: 416) that is at once 'part child, part adult' and were indicative of Victorian culture's ambiguous relationship to the child. The presence of this liminal figure can be felt in different guises in contemporary performance too, namely through the strategy of 'age transvestism', a term I borrow from Lucy Munro (2005) to discuss the phenomenon of children 'playing' adults onstage. In contemporary performance, however, this liminal figure does not necessarily function to reinstate the child performer's innocence nor to celebrate their precocity, although it can do so. Rather, moving beyond age transvestism, the book identifies and reflects on a wider variety of strategies that I am calling trans*-age play in contemporary performance that have the potential to destabilise the tabula rasa discourse of the child as we will see.

Nevertheless, the idea of the child as a blank slate still persists in theatrical reception, as suggested by negative responses to contemporary performance which is specifically performed 'by children for adults'. For example, in response to Lyn Gardner's piece in *The Guardian* 'Theatre for adults is child's play' (2008) which discusses the performances *That Night Follows Day* by Tim Etchells and Victoria and *Once and For All We're Gonna Tell You Who We Are So Shut Up and Listen* by Ontroerend Goed, one respondent in the comments section writes:

> Neither of these shows is the authentic voice of young people; they consist of young people being used by adults to entertain other adults and, in this case, to titillate them with scenes of underage sex.
>
> (Cited in Gardner 2008: np)

Here the tabula rasa discourse is being used to mobilise the idea that these young performers are unaware of what they are doing and are being manipulated by the adult directors/collaborators. Whilst the makers of these works offer convincing responses against this position in the same comments section, attending to this discourse is an important reminder that the child as a blank slate is being negotiated not only (and sometimes intentionally) in the performance material itself, but also in the rehearsal room; in perceptions of the adult playwright/creator's relationship to the child performers; in the relationship between child performers and adult audience members; as well as in spectator responses. As with the discourse of childhood innocence, there are contradictions in the appropriation of the blank slate that suggests, on the one hand, that children are being manipulated because of their lack of understanding or, on the other hand, that children are too 'knowing' or precocious. We can observe this as far back as Barlee's campaign against the employment of children in the Victorian pantomime and specifically 'her perception that stage children were not only knowing but had knowledge of their own knowingness' (Steedman 1995: 136). Given this context for the blank slate discourse, my analysis intends to shed light on what meanings are created in contemporary performance when this idea that children are accustomed 'to seeing themselves as objects of someone else's contemplation' (ibid.) is *part of the work itself*, as in *The Hamilton Complex,* rather than being used in a campaign to censor children's appearance in theatre.

If the notion of the child as always in the process of socialisation has had some positive influences on the recognition of children as a 'vulnerable' group to be safeguarded – particularly in relation to beneficial reforms to children's theatrical labour – why might reinscribing the discourse of the child as tabula rasa be so problematic? As with the problems of ascribing innocence to the child, the conceptualisation of the child as always *in development* suggests that the people we call children are lacking. This presumption intersects with the idea of the innocent child who demonstrates 'a lack of guilt, sinfulness, knowingness, experience' (Stockton 2009: 12). Again, the child is defined in relation to an imagined adult figure, rather than on their own terms. This persistent discourse of the child as developmentally immature or as Kathryn Bond Stockton would say always in the process of 'growing up' is, she argues, a 'short-sighted, limited rendering of human growth, one that oddly would imply an end to growth when full stature (or reproduction) is achieved' (2009: 11). Instead, she wonders about the possibility of 'growing sideways' in a way that 'suggests the width of a person's experience or ideas, their motives or their motions, may pertain to any age, bringing "adults" and "children" into lateral contact' (ibid.). By attending to the idea of the child as a blank slate, we can identify in contemporary performance moments of horizontal as opposed to vertical growth. In particular, we can extend Isis Germano's (2018) convincing application of Stockton's idea of 'growing sideways' to consider the non-linear dramaturgy of *The Hamilton Complex*, to think about how other elements of performance practice with children, break with the assumption of upward growth implied by the child as tabula rasa. In a later chapter, for example, I consider how Britt Hatzius' *Blind Cinema* situates child performers spatially in 'lateral contact' with adult audience members to deny a reading of these children in terms of vertical growth and instead to foreground them as living, breathing, relational bodies.

Furthermore, since theatre and performance studies are historically concerned with issues of training and discipline, to think of the child as a blank slate in this context is to frame children in relation to debates around the trained/untrained, disciplined/undisciplined body. Again, the Victorian reformist debates concerning the cruelty of child theatrical labour practices have undoubtedly contributed to long-held anxieties over the effects of both the act of performing on the professional child performer's schooling as well as training regimes on young bodies (Steedman 1995: 102–3). Michel Foucault's writing on the disciplined subject provides a useful theoretical grounding for negotiating how contemporary performance produces or otherwise works against institutions and discursive regimes that render the child's body a docile body: a 'body that is manipulated, shaped, trained, which obeys, responds, becomes skilful and increases its forces' (1977: 136). This book, however, is not concerned with looking at how the processes of creating performance generate or resist treating children as docile bodies. Rather it considers a close analysis of how performances might themselves perpetuate or challenge the gaze that reads the body of child performers as either trained/untrained, disciplined/undisciplined, and considers how regulatory regimes within a theatrical tradition may be being signposted in performance in relationship to, and at the intersection of, age, gender, race, and ability.

Considering how the discourse of the child as a blank slate operates in relation to contemporary performance practice, prompts us to reflect on the presumption that the child in performance is in the process of becoming an adult and helps to identify the generalised assumptions that are often made about children's supposed lack of understanding, experience, and socialisation. If the child is reduced by the blank slate discourse to 'not-yet-adult', with the implication being that children are 'not-yet-human', then it follows that children's material circumstances can too often be ignored, disregarded, or marginalised. We can even see the effects of this marginalisation in theatrical scholarship, where child performers *as a workforce* have largely been overlooked until recently (Coclough 2016, Vey n.d.). Responding to their overlooked status, Part III creates space for the people we call children and teenagers – as collaborators, archivists, researchers, and authors of their own manifesto on making performances with children – to discuss their often-marginalised circumstances and experiences. By creating this space, Part III builds on the performance strategies identified in Part II that offer an alternative view of the people we call children in which spectators, makers, and commentators are confronted not with cultures and experiences that are 'lacking' but that are shown to deserve the equivalent attention as their adult counterparts.

THE EVIL CHILD

If Foucault was right that disciplinary regimes of social control in the modern world intend to create docile bodies (1976), then I would also agree with Jenks (2005b) that what is specifically being controlled by ensuring the docility of the people we call children is, in part, their presumed potential for 'evilness'. The image of the evil child has its antecedents in the much earlier 'doctrine of Adamic original sin', which perpetuates an assumption that the child is inherently evil and corrupt (Jenks 2005a: 62–63). This Christian idea can be traced back to Saint Augustine in *Confessions* (AD 397–400) where he argued that the act of creation meant that sin was passed down from one generation to the next and that 'no man is free from sin, not even a child who has lived only a day on the earth' (cited in Heywood 2001: 33). According to this position, the child is seen largely as a wilful figure to be managed and restrained. This image of the evil child re-emerged during the Protestant Reformation of the 16th century and can be observed in Luther's reassertion of the Augustinian claim that children possessed as much original sin as adults, except that paradoxically Luther also framed children up to the age of five or six as somewhat innocent (ibid.). In *A History of Childhood: Children and Childhood in the West from Medieval to Modern Times*, Colin Heywood offers a picture of this perception of the child as evil through his reference to a German sermon in the 1520s which characterised children as yearning 'adultery, fornication, impure desires, lewdness, idol worship, belief in magic, hostility, quarrelling, passion, anger, strife, dissension, factiousness, hatred, murder, drunkenness, [and] gluttony' (2001: 34). Like their Protestant equivalents, Catholic Puritans were also suspicious of children's capacity for evil but by recognising children to be incapable of acting on this innate evilness, somewhat ironically, children were also deemed to be model Christians (ibid.).

The discourse of the evil child continued to gain force from the 16th century onwards. During this time, children were widely perceived as being weak – in the sense of being easily led rather than vulnerable (Jenks 2005a: 63) – and therefore inclined towards evil (Ariès 1962). Applying moralistic judgments to children in this way emerges partly in response to the practice of 'coddling', which was heavily criticised by moralists and theorists of the time who felt that the widespread trend for caressing babies was to be discouraged in favour of training and disciplining children (Corsaro 2005: 63). Accounts of strict childrearing practices were justified 'for the child's own good' and formed the basis for Puritan reformation in the 16th and 17th centuries (James *et al.* 1998: 12). Puritan morality subsequently perpetuated a perceived need for excessive control and constraint on the child in the later centuries, the results of which we have seen discussed above in the moralising aspects of the campaigns against children's employment in theatre in the 19th century. Literature of the time also makes reference to this regulatory relationship towards the child, which can most readily be observed in the novels of Charles Dickens where 'institutionalized violence towards the young is depicted as a moral constraint' (ibid.: 12–13).[10]

The notion of the evil child during this period in history has often been attributed to the English philosopher Thomas Hobbes, whose educational background was in the Puritan tradition (James *et al.* 1998: 11). For Hobbes, children are not yet fully developed and so they should be entirely under the power and control of their parents and other care-giving adults. In his 1650 text *Elements of Law* (1839–45) Hobbes suggests:

> Children … whether they be brought up and preserved by the father, or by the mother, or by whomsoever, are in most absolute subjection to him or her, that so bringeth them up, or preserveth them.
>
> (Cited in King 1998: 65)

Like a slave to master, the child should be entirely in servitude to their parents according to Hobbes. In other words, the child does not have any rights and is obliged to obey the adult carer's every command. He proposes, however, that if adults choose to treat children as subjects rather than servants then it is the parents' prerogative rather than a right deserved by the child (ibid.). Hobbes' work thus emphasises the adult as a regulating force, rendering 'children [as] demonic, harbourers of potentially dark forces which risk being mobilized if […] the adult world allows them to veer away from the "straight and narrow" path that civilization has bequeathed to them' (James *et al.* 1998: 10).

Hobbes' writing and the wider Puritan discourse of the evil child have subsequently sown the seeds for contemporary notions that children need to be restrained, seen and not heard, and their behaviour monitored. For Phillipe Ariès, the results of 16th and 17th century moralistic thinking, and the emphasis on adult responsibility at the expense of childhood freedom, can still be felt in the early 1960s, when he was writing. He observes that modern thought is 'obsessed by the physical, moral, and sexual problems of childhood' precisely because of the emphasis in these earlier centuries on parents being children's 'spiritual guardians … responsible before God for the souls, and indeed bodies too, of their children' (Ariès 1962: 411–412). By attending to the historical regulation of children's bodies as well as their 'souls', Ariès helpfully pre-empts, I would argue, more contemporary anxieties surrounding children's bodies. An example of this panic can be found in recent comments by Pope Francis in which he draws a parallel between what he calls the 'ideological colonising' of gender theory and Hitler Youth (Butler 2023), which I come back to in more detail towards the end of the book. It is clear though, that over five decades since Ariès publication 'the physical, moral and sexual problems of childhood' are still occupying contemporary thought, which is why we see these anxieties being negotiated as thematic and material concerns within much of the performance practice discussed here.

As an embodied and body-based practice, performance that includes the people we call children cannot ignore the fact of their bodily materialities and this is, to some extent, acknowledged in the safeguarding of children through various laws and regulations relating to their employment, such as the limited hours that they are permitted to work and the employment of chaperones to care for their physical health amongst other aspects of their well-being. These formal policies surrounding the safeguarding and labour of child performers are undoubtedly vital for the safety and well-being of the people we call children. However, laws and regulations do not attend fully to all of the questions raised by their appearance in performance. Some of the performances that I focus on in this book foreground the materiality of the performer's body and in doing so either knowingly or unintentionally grapple with the innocent/evil child binary we inherit from thinkers such as Rousseau and Hobbes. In *The Hamilton Complex*, for example, 'innocent' images of teenage performers playing children singing sweetly in a choir are set against later images of them as red-hooded figures that reference the evil child of the horror film genre. These images are being negotiated in/through/on the material bodies of the people we call children and teenagers. The interplay between the inherited spectatorial expectation that we observe either an innocent child or an evil child and contemporary expressions of this expectation in the form of other binaries that are brought to bear on children appearing in performance, such as knowing/unknowing and trained/untrained, is one of the key concerns of this book. In these moments of interplay in *The Hamilton Complex,* it is not necessarily the image of either the evil or the innocent child that we are uncritically invited to accept, but we are arguably forced to confront the relationality of our own gaze and to witness the performers as *more* than embodied vessels for adult scripts.

In addition to shedding light on how we are being invited to read the materiality of the bodies of the people we call children in performance, the discourse of the evil child has the potential to draw our attention to how we might be elicited to situate the child as Other within our viewing habits. We see this othered figure of the evil child in contemporary culture from literature (*Lord of the Flies*, Golding 1954) to film (*The Exorcist*, 1973) to the demonisation of children more generally in contemporary news media. In the UK, the discourse of the evil child had a significant resurgence following the tragic killing of two-year-old Jamie Bulger in 1993 in the UK (Goldson 2001: 39, Scraton [1997] 2004: 167). The child who kills other children is often positioned as a potent signifier of evil (Jenks 2005a: 143) and they even become the symbolic placeholder for all children who have the propensity towards wrongdoing. This is strikingly evident in much of the news media response to the tragedy of Bulger's killing by two young boys, both of whom were aged ten years old. The sinister use of first person in a newspaper article by Gerald Warner in

The Sunday Times in 1994, published a year after the murder, echoes the evil child discourse in a way that others all children apart from the victim:

> What I did on my holidays the 1994 version. Put concrete block on railway line, am; abducted toddler from supermarket and beat him to death, pm. Who said that today's youngsters do not know how to make their own entertainment?
>
> (Cited in Scraton 2004: 166)

The people we call children are perceived here as lazy, bored, casual killers. As Phil Scraton in his edited book *Childhood in Crisis?* carefully argues, the author of this article condemns a whole generation of children for 'one of the most untypical crimes of the decade' (ibid.). For Scraton this representation typifies a larger societal problem of 'child-hate', which for him is as problematic as racial hatred and misogyny. By Warner's logic, extremely unusual examples of the people we call children committing murder are taken as representative of a widespread problem that frames young people more generally as morally corrupt and irresponsible. In short, evil.

Building on this tendency to essentialise the child, Chris Jenks identifies press commentaries and readers' letters in response to violent acts committed by children on other children, to argue that a 'composite creature' emerges in these public accounts: the 'adult-child' (2005a: 128). Adult-child is a category that marks children presumed evil as different, in order to maintain the image of childhood innocence by refusing the category of 'child' to the adult-child 'who commits acts of violence' (ibid.: 129). This in-between figure of the adult-child reveals a widespread ambiguity about the notion of the child in contemporary culture, which is still prominent in 21st century British media representations of children. A contemporary example of this in-between adult-child figure can be observed in UK news media coverage over the last few years concerning a young British female, Shamima Begum, who travelled from her home in Bethnal Green, London to Syria at the age of fifteen in 2015 to join Islamic State and since 2019 has been seeking to return to the UK.

I do not wish to focus here on the specifics of Begum's British citizenship being revoked and the appeals which followed that have culminated in the 2023 Special Immigration Appeals Commission ruling that the revocation of her citizenship was lawful (Siddique 2023). Instead, I want to attend briefly to the image of the adult-child figure that emerges in the news media most prominently in 2019 when Begum is in a Syrian refugee camp. At this moment in time, two of her children have died and she has just given birth. The conservative Home Secretary at the time, Sajid Javid stands firm against her return. Writing for *The Sunday Times* on 17 February 2019, Javid's opening paragraph references the attack at Ariana Grande's concert in Manchester, UK in 2017 where he makes a point of flagging up the presence of 'young girls' as victims of the bombing and then closing his article by recognising 'the children who have been killed in evil attacks like the one in Manchester' (Javid 2019). Conversely, Begum is mentioned only in reference to the 'case' of 'the Bethnal Green girls'. She is neither a teenager, nor a child, nor a mother in Javid's story. Her subjecthood is denied and her ability to occupy the category of child is prohibited. Javid names her only in the article's headline: 'If you run away to join Isis, like Shamima Begum, I will use all my power to stop you coming back'. He goes on to state:

> As a father I feel compassion for any child born or brought into a conflict zone. But in considering what actions need to be taken now, I have to think about the safety and security of children living in our country.
>
> (Javid 2019)

Begum's own baby similarly is afforded the status of 'innocence' in the form of a statement of compassion, but is not considered worthy of the same protection as British children, despite their mother's British passport. Begum's status as an adult-child is also evident in the wider news coverage (BBC 2019) despite the absence of evidence that she committed any crimes and irrespective of the arguably dominant public perception years earlier that she had been 'an innocent child who's been groomed online… the little girl who's been caught up in a death cult' (Segalov 2019). The media coverage of this case reveals a contradictory, conflicting, and highly politicised perception of children in the UK, who on the one hand need protection from the ever-present threat of being 'brain-washed' because of their own inexperience and immaturity and simultaneously have the (adult) capacity to be calculating and completely understand *their* decisions, in this case, to join Islamic State.

Whilst the 'adult-child' as a contemporary iteration of the evil child has been observed primarily in relation to children who commit or have been associated with crimes, this liminal figure nevertheless (re-)surfaces but in much more nuanced and arguably generative ways in some contemporary performances involving the people we call children in a way that has the potential to draw attention to its contradictions. The children of Mammalian Diving Reflex's *Nightwalks with Teenagers*, for example, exploit their position as 'untouchable' performers by climbing up the scaffolding of a building in front of an audience of nervous adults who do not have any power to intervene. These young performers at once demonstrate their potential for danger and elicit the protectionist gaze in a way that draws attention to their teenage status as occupying that 'adult-child' figure who is potentially denied the category of child.

Through playing with different iterations of the 'adult-child', performance can reflect back on adult audiences their potential to position young people as monstrous:

> We call children 'little devils', 'little monsters', 'little beasts' – with the full ambiguous force of their terms, all the complications of love, longing repulsion and fear … But the child has never been seen as such a menacing enemy as today. Never before have children been so saturated with all the power of projected monstrousness to excite repulsion and even terror.
>
> (Warner 1994: 43)

Marina Warner's observation nearly three decades ago during the Reith Lectures of 1994 still holds true for contemporary perceptions of children and captures the socio-cultural context within which the contemporary performances examined here are produced and received. Again, such perceptions of children can be observed in some public commentators' responses to the activism of young people in the 2019 climate strikes and protests. BBC broadcaster Jeremy Vine tweets: 'Wait. Are these schoolchildren, out marching against climate change, actually chanting "Fuck Teresa May"?' (15 February 2019). Such rhetoric by commentators who have cultural capital within the public arena arguably serves to generate fear of young people's activism and works to undermine their protests by capitalising on the ever-present discourse of innocence ('children don't swear') and their potential for evil ('children want to skip school and swear').

Indeed, the historical association of the evil child with anarchy is signalled by Hobbes for whom 'without parental constraint, the life of the child is anarchistic' (James *et al.* 1998: 11). Against the assumption that, left to their own devices, children will threaten or undermine 'the stability of [...] adult collectivity, the social order to which children in time will aspire' (James *et al.* 1998: 10), young people who act in the absence adult authority or who challenge adult authority are left open to the claims of evilness and the status of adult-child. Hobbes' perspective therefore still persists in a contemporary context that maintains both adult privilege as the status quo and the separation of children from the sphere of politics. Whilst in democratic contexts there are calls for children and young people's active participation in social and political life, as mentioned earlier, especially with the introduction of the UN Convention on the Rights of the Child (UNCRC), how effective the implications of the UN's convention are on a wider acceptance of children as political agents and citizens is questionable, given especially the backlash faced by many young activists on the global stage. Furthermore, many of the initiatives that have emerged out of the UNCRC have been addressed largely to adolescents despite growing evidence that children of primary school age 'already exhibit consistent, structured political orientations' (van Deth *et al.* 2011: 147). With its focus on examples of performance with people who are predominantly between 8 years of age and 13 years of age, the book identifies strategies through which contemporary performance is navigating different versions of this adult-child figure as well as interrogating ways of working with young people of the same age as a means of fostering spaces for activism and political engagement rather than upholding the myth of innocence to deny some people the category of child.

WHAT IS A CHILD?

> What a child 'is' is a darkening questioning. The question of the child makes us climb inside a cloud [...] leading us, in moments, to cloudiness and ghostliness surrounding children as figures in time.
>
> (Stockton 2009: 2)

Throughout Part I so far, I have spoken of the child and the people we call children. The spectrality and haziness that Stockton conjures up here resonate with my own anxiety when I use these terms since this study is similarly haunted by the question 'what is a child?' in its quest to examine how 'the child' is mobilised in contemporary performance practice *with* the people we call children *for* largely adult audiences. From the outset then, there is a contradiction in my focus towards performances that engage actual people we call children as performers, collaborators, and/or activists alongside the admission that the very category of the child is under scrutiny in these works and/or in my reading of them. Inevitably, I must invest in the ontological category of 'child' to some extent to identify children *as* children in performance and so it is important to clarify what meanings this book is invested in, in order to anticipate its scope and potential for future studies of the child and children in theatre, performance, and beyond. When I speak of the child, children, and childhood, then, what do I mean?

The question of the child is certainly not new but a substantial consideration of it within the fields of theatre and performance, and specifically in a contemporary context, has yet to be attempted. Within theatre history scholarship, research on child actors and performers is abundant, specifically in reference to the boy choirs of the 15th and 16th centuries and the all-child productions of the Victorian period.[11] However, very little attention has been paid to 'the child' and 'childhood' as ontological, discursive, and socially constructed categories. Some exceptions come close to questioning these categories *as* categories, including Carolyn Steedman's *Strange Dislocations: Childhood and the Idea of Human Interiority 1780-1930* (1995) which considers the way in which adult conceptions of the self at the end of the 18th century dictated a certain imagined idea of 'childhood' into the 19th century. Also, Marah Gubar (2012) critiques the widely held assumption that Victorian audiences liked to eroticise innocence by privileging as her evidence Victorians' own discursive attempts to categorise the child. Nevertheless, an explicit discussion of what constitutes 'the child' especially as a socially constructed category rather than a biologically given 'natural' phenomenon is still strikingly absent from theatre and performance literature.

In contrast to the lack of scholarly writing on what constitutes 'a child' in performance studies and its related disciplines, sociological perspectives offer well-established social theories on the child and childhood as analytical categories. In sociology and childhood studies, children have become research subjects in their own right, rather than being subsumed in other related themes of research such as families and schools as was the case with earlier research within these fields. There has been a concerted effort in sociological practice at least from the 1990s. onwards to recognise children as key players in producing their own cultures, and specifically to acknowledge them as 'social actors shaping as well as shaped by their circumstances' (James *et al.* 1998: 6). This move towards recognising individual children in research, as well as children's agency and autonomy more generally would not have been possible without the recognition of childhood as a social construction, and, more importantly, as a potentially limiting and reductive construction.

A key turning point in the academy's recognition of 'childhood' as a social construction was Philippe Ariès groundbreaking study *Centuries of Childhood: A Social History of Family* (1962), as mentioned earlier. Drawing evidence from the absence of children in medieval paintings, Ariès argued that childhood as a concept did not even exist prior to the 17th century. The lack of representation of children in medieval art, and mainly French paintings indicated, for him, that there was no shared perception of children as being essentially different from adults until after the middle ages:

> Medieval art until about the twelfth century did not know childhood or did not attempt to portray it. It is hard to believe that this neglect was due to incompetence or incapacity; it seems more probable that there was no place for childhood in the medieval world.
>
> (Ariès 1962: 31)

Criticisms of Ariès' theory, however, argue that his focus on artistic representation is largely limited to French culture and that there is in fact a wealth of evidence to demonstrate that children were given special consideration: from records and images following the 'children's plague' in the 1300s that suggest children were actually deeply appreciated, to the discovery of children's artifacts in Florentine homes in the 1400s, to children's clothes, furniture, and images revealed by archaeological digs (Averett 2015: 7–10).[12]

Despite its lack of substantial evidence, Ariès' thesis is a precursor to many historical and sociological studies that propose that the normalisation of the categories of childhood and the child mythically sustains these categories as natural phenomena. Recent critiques of disciplines in the social sciences, in particular psychology, take issue with the way in which 'childhood is apprehended largely in terms of biological and cognitive development through concepts such as maturation' (Jenks 2005a: 7). Challenges to the social sciences' normalisation of the child and childhood as natural, demonstrate that it is predicated on the assumption of 'growth' and often conflates anatomical changes in children with social development. Using these critiques as my theoretical grounding, I adopt the terms 'child' and 'childhood' critically and self-reflexively with the assumption that they are discursively and socially produced categories and that these categories are simultaneously inseparable from the actual experiences of living children. In doing so, I demonstrate how the appearance of children in contemporary performance not only parallels these social critiques of the natural child but also sets forth new understandings to unpack the dominant meanings of these categories in the 21st century UK contemporary performance scene in which the works were encountered.

When I speak of childhood, therefore, this should not be mistaken as referring to a natural phenomenon. Rather the term should be understood as a problematic 'totalizing concept, [which] describes a community that at some point has everybody as its member' (Jenks 2005a: 6). This appeal of 'childhood' as a concept is also its main drawback: everyone has experienced it in some form which feeds the assumption that it is a universal experience. In questioning the idea of childhood as *the* general and universal state of being a child, I do not seek to diminish the actual, material experiences of children who exist in the world. Indeed, following Margaret Mead and Martha Wolfenstein (1954), alongside many contemporary childhood studies scholars, I agree that there are multiple childhoods and I recognise what constitutes childhood is socially, politically, historically, and culturally contingent. However, since childhood necessarily exists in a binary relationship with dominant conceptualisations of adulthood, we simply cannot ignore the ways in which childhood, as a universalising concept, has been used to shape (perspectives on) children's lives. Prevailing ideas of childhood inevitably affect children's lived experiences and the material conditions of their actual childhoods, so I foreground in the book the idea that childhoods need to be understood in relation to the contexts in which they are discursively produced and experienced. That said, I am not interested in looking towards performance to uncover 'real' or 'authentic' childhoods, but rather to recognise different strategies that are adopted in contemporary practice to problematise prevailing notions of 'childhood' as a totalising concept in the global north.

Similarly, when I use the term 'the child', I am almost always foregrounding a concept, image, figure, notion, and idea of the child rather than an actual human being, living in the world. In contrast, when I speak of 'the people we call children' I am most often referring to actual human beings and bodies that have been identified as children in marketing materials, commentaries, interviews, reviews, or other forms of performance documentation as well as by their physical, anatomical appearance in performance. Specifically, I use the phrase 'people we call children' or 'people called children' as a reminder of the limitations of the category 'children' as a homogenising linguistic identifier that fails to capture the complex human beings who we name as such. I am also invested in the delineation of children as a group of people who share in common the fact that they are under the age of eighteen, and therefore I am deliberately echoing the definition of the child in the UN Convention on the Rights of the Child (UNCRC 1989). This reference to UNCRC is important because it is indicative of a dominant social order in which childhood and the category of the child are attributed to those under the age of 18 years old, whilst also promoting a radical relationship with children that is seldom realised in practice: 'States Parties shall assure to the child who is capable of forming his or her own views the right to express those views freely in all matters affecting the child' (Article 12, UNCRC 1989).

Artistic Director of Mammalian Diving Reflex, Darren O'Donnell refers directly to this statement in his book *Haircuts By Children and Other Evidence for a New Social Contract* (2018) to argue that '[c]hildren and young people should be folded much more into the decision-making processes that drive our society' and that artistic and performance practice has an important role to play in actually including children in 'all matters affecting [them]' (ibid.: 11). The framing of birth-to-17-year-old people in performance as 'children' and its relationship to this fraught context of the UN Convention, then, is as much a part of the analysis as any other aspect of the performances considered since the way in which they are given to visibility and/or audibility (or invisibility and inaudibility) inevitably determines the ways by which they are received and interpreted. Similarly, the billing of 'teenagers' rather than children or 'girls' instead of young females, sets up certain audience expectations in the same way that other discursive categories such as babies, infants, juniors, and adolescents promote taken-for-granted assumptions about what the spectator is about to witness. However, it is important to note that the category of babies and infants are beyond the scope of the book – and have been discussed elsewhere (Fletcher-Watson 2017, Garton and Rippel 2011, Senior 2016, Varty 2005) – as the performances I focus on mainly include people within an age range between 8 to 13 years old.

Whilst these observations around age categories may seem obvious, the tendency to subsume the different age groups suggested by these categories under the umbrella of 'children' or to uncritically reinstate these ways of classifying children has the effect of denying the people we call children in performance the same poststructural, feminist, and queer approaches to reading their bodies that are ordinarily afforded to adult bodies onstage. Furthermore, to accept these categorisations without question risks denying that the people we call children might not only be capable of making meaning in performance but that they may wish to challenge these limiting descriptors of their personhood through their meaning-making. I want to suggest a generalised use of the term children can often serve to reinforce an us/them logic inherent in dominant conceptualisations of the child (vs. the adult), children (vs. adults), and childhood (vs. adulthood), which in turn works to emphasise the supposed essential differences between these two groups: irrational/rational, immature/mature, unreasonable/reasonable. My claim, that there is a danger of reading the people we call children and their bodies differently because of this historic, binarised, and hierarchical logic, undoubtedly has implications for the methodological commitments I make in this book. Namely, my approach to reading 'children in performance' is careful to acknowledge and identify differences that exist between the people who fall into the categories of 'children' and 'adults' – not least issues relating to pressing contemporary concerns over children's power, agency, and autonomy – but in a way that avoids reductively essentialising these differences.

To do this, my overall methodological approach intentionally parallels the way I ordinarily read adult bodies in performance. That is, each performance analysed here demands a specific theoretical attitude that is consistent with what the work demands of me as a spectator (aesthetically, intellectually, experientially etc.) and the questions it poses. The disorientation I encountered, for example, when seeing Britt Hatzius' *Blind Cinema*, namely the intimacy of the spatial relationship between the young performers as whispering narrators and adults as blindfolded listeners, calls for a queer phenomenological reading of this work inspired by Sara Ahmed (2006), which may ordinarily be denied to young performers because of the predominance of the nostalgic, patriarchal, protectionist gaze that is often invited onto the bodies of the people we call children. Indeed, each chapter develops its own methodological approach in response to the practice being examined and, in turn, each performance poses questions back at the theoretical or methodological model to reveal both its possibilities and limitations when interpreting performances that include the child, childhood(s), and the people we call children.

CHILDREN ON STAGE

Rather than offering a broad overview of children's participation and representations of children in contemporary performance then, the book focuses on in-depth readings of key works of the last decade. These performances are selected not because of the gender or age of the children involved, but in terms of how they include young people to, irreverently at times, navigate the binarised categorisations of adult/child in relation to and in tension with dominant discourses of the child outlined here in Part I. The book proposes that these works develop strategies of age play beyond the all-encompassing idea of age transvestism that dominates how theatre and performance scholarship has historically characterised children playing adults onstage and vice versa. Instead, by reading these performances in a way that attends to the relational act of spectatorship and identifies the specific gazes that they elicit, I propose that we might instead consider age-related performance strategies under a more capacious term: trans*-age play. By reframing age transvestism as such and drawing attention to its limitations, I aim to identify a diversity of age-related play that intersects with other signifiers of identity and, therefore, take seriously the bodies and experiences of the people we call children when we encounter them in performance. In Part II, therefore, I draw attention to the political potential of what I am calling trans*-age play in performance, considering how it might be employed to facilitate equitable representations of the people we call children and inform ways of working with them in future contemporary performance and research, as I go on to explore in Part III.

Part II opens with a chapter which maps a brief history of age transvestism in British theatrical performance and locates the term within theatre history scholarship (Gubar 2012; Munro 2005). Entitled *From Age Transvestism to Trans*-age Performance: on children playing adults* Chapter 2 problematises the language of transvestism when applied to the many different ways that children might 'play' adults in theatre by attending to the original usage of transvestism within historically-situated queer practices, cultures, communities, and scholarship. Motivated by the necessity to take seriously Jay Prosser's (1998) and Jack Halberstam's (2005) shared (albeit differently nuanced) concern about the appropriation and misrepresentation of trans experiences in their critique of Judith Butler's work on gender performativity (1990, 1993), I propose that we move away from age transvestism to the more capacious idea of trans*-age strategies. By using the prefix trans* I hope to draw on the insights that this term opens up by offering a language for different types of age play in performance – fluidity, bending, crossing, reversal, non-binarising, non-conforming, disidentification – and precisely to acknowledge the diversity of bodies and experiences that enact and participate in these strategies, which vitally include trans* identifying people we also call children.

Chapter 3 *The Child as Adult in Five Easy Pieces* offers the book's first in-depth analysis of trans*-age play. It explores how age is negotiated in Milo Rau's play through the use of metatheatre; in the relationship between the live (children's) stage space and the virtual (adult's) screen space; and finally, in the young performers' interaction with the live feed that attempts to mark their performances as 'children playing adults' throughout. The play explores ethically difficult content related to the abduction, rape, and murder of girls by a man called Marc Dutroux in 1990s Belgium and so the analysis considers how age play is utilised to navigate sensitive material that already raises questions about children's participation in the work. The chapter considers the political potential and limitations of age-crossing as a performance strategy and concludes that *Five Easy Pieces'* age play is an example of adult-child crossing that depends largely on maintaining rather than challenging age-based norms (of the performers, personas, and characters). Whilst the use of age-crossing within *Five Easy Pieces* draws attention to the way in which age play should be read contextually in relation to aesthetic devices beyond costume and script, this particular version of trans*-age play is shown to be somewhat limited in opening up to critique how age intersects with race, gender, sexuality, and ability.

Recognising the limitations of age-crossing within *Five Easy Pieces*, Chapter 4 *The female-girl-child-teenager in The Hamilton Complex* explores how another Belgium-based company HETPALEIS, under the direction of Lies Pauwels, employs gender-based trans*-age strategies to perform heteronormative, patriarchal femininity to excess and to signal its relationship to the eroticisation of childhood/girlhood innocence. Unlike the mixed gender 8–13 years old in Rau's play, the thirteen female teenage performers who perform *The Hamilton Complex* invite a scopophilic male gaze that parallels a paedophilic gaze that the discourse of innocence would ordinarily appear to forget in the presence of the people we call children. Starting with Robin Bernstein's claim that childhood innocence has the ability to 'remember while appearing to forget' images and scripts of past abject and racist practices to preserve whiteness as an unmarked category (2011), the chapter argues that the young performers of *The Hamilton Complex* turn innocence on its head, instead *performing innocence* to intentionally mark 'adult' scripts such as paedophilia. This includes showing *the performance of* innocence to mark the shared emotional labour required by both the theatrical economy that the child performer participates in and the aesthetic economy of the cross-generational adult female roles that the performers play in order to highlight the operation of power, consumption, and potential for objectification, exploitation, and coercion within both aesthetic and theatrical economies. Through gender-specific trans*-age play I argue that the performance draws attention not just to an 'adult gaze' (Germano 2018: 45) but, more specifically, a patriarchal protectionist gaze that is shown to be dependent on the performance of innocence. Secondly, *The Hamilton Complex*'s trans*-age play gives rise to the 'female-girl-child-teenager' as its own complex and intersectional discursive and experiential position that destabilises the very patriarchal protectionist gaze it evokes. This subject position both resists being fixed, by containing multiple fluid and intersecting identities, and has the potential to draw the audience's attention to innocence as gendered and (to a lesser extent) raced white on the culturally and historically-located bodies that perform it.

Chapter 5. *From Gender to Age: a new approach to reading age in performance* brings Part II to a close by briefly identifying other trans*-age strategies such as age bending, age reversal, and age-related disidentification within contemporary performance. It goes on to ask how trans*-age strategies of children playing adults might further our understanding of reading and experiencing age play and 'age' in performance more generally. Building on the argument that trans*-age strategies contain within them the potential to destabilise socially accepted categories of age, the chapter proposes a new model for reading age in performance that draws on feminist, queer, and performance scholarship on gender and drag. Specifically, it reimagines what Judith Butler calls the 'contingent dimensions of corporeality' in their well-known discussion of drag as illustrative of gender performativity (1990) to propose that we might also consider the dimensions of age corporeality when reading age in performance: anatomical age, age identity, age performance, and the performance of age. As such, this new way of reading age through four dimensions of corporeality has the potential (1) to recognise the mechanisms through which trans*-age strategies have the means to call into question normative categories of adult and/or child and therefore reveal age as socially produced and iteratively naturalised; (2) to identify when age play might be reaffirming hegemonic age-based norms that are harmful to the people we call children.

Part III *Experiencing Children* moves beyond these more ocularcentric performances and aims to foreground the lived, relational, and embodied experiences of the people we call children who have been involved in professional contemporary performance. It opens with Chapter 6, *Queer(ing) Methodologies*, which proposes that we queer existing approaches to research *with* rather than on/about the people we call children and look towards queer theory to negotiate them both as makers/carriers of meaning and historically-situated subjects with their own embodied experiences in performance. This necessity to queer is also informed by the recognition that the 'social actor' in childhood studies of the global north is founded largely on the idea of an 'actor' as a unitary masculine and rational subject (Burman and Stacey 2010, Walkerdine 1988). To this end, Chapter 7, *The Embodied Child of Blind Cinema*, adopts Sara Ahmed's notion of queer phenomenology (2006) to develop an analysis of this work by Britt Hatzius that attends to the relational and intimate experience it generates with performers who do not conform to this reductive idea of the child as social actor. In *Blind Cinema*, a predominantly adult audience is blindfolded, whilst young performers of primary school age (between 8–11 years old) whisper into the audience's ears the descriptions of a film they are seeing for the very first time. As a pregnant person at the time of encountering this work, my shift to a queer, body-based critical framework is largely a direct response to the particularities of my embodied experience. However, as the performers are not framed through the visual-centric economy that so often dictates professional practice with the people we call children, this approach also felt necessary for capturing how the experience deviates from this normative orientation of 'seeing' children in performance. Drawing on research ordinarily reserved for adult research subjects and performers – that is research on the current and popular internet-based trend of Autonomous Sensory Meridian Response or ASMR (Bjelić

2016, Waldron 2017) in dialogue with scholarship on risk and intimacy in one-to-one performance (Chatzichristodoulou and Zerihan 2012, Wake 2017, Zerihan 2006) – the discussion sheds light on how the relational aspects of this performance challenge dominant modes of perceiving the people we call children. Instead, it highlights the performance's ability to create an 'intimate sonic space' that confronts the sometimes difficult territory of intimacy with children in performance.

The absence of the voices of people we call children from debates about their appearance and participation in contemporary performance is politically and ethically problematic and so Chapters 8 and 9, consider what it might mean to 'make space' for these voices as 'an act of decoloniality' (Mitra 2019). Making space for the people we call children within scholarly research builds on a symposium I hosted with a family of artists called the Institute for the Art and Practice of Dissent at Home in 2017 and an accompanying special issue of the journal *Performance Research* titled 'On Children' (2018). Chapter 8, *Growing Sideways Together: Zina Abaraonye and Sorrel Barnes on Men and Girls Dance and We Are Not Finished*, builds on these early iterations, by offering a more focused post-performance collaboration with two young people who participated in separate works by London-based company Fevered Sleep: Sorrel performed in *Men and Girls Dance* in Brighton at age 9 in 2016 and Zina was involved in research and development work for *We Are Not Finished* in 2019 at age 13. The dialogue between myself, Zina, and Sorrel queers a normative approach to researching children that is shaped by a developmental perspective that privileges 'growing up'. It does so by putting into practice Kathryn Bond Stockton's metaphor of 'growing sideways' as a methodological commitment to acknowledging 'the width of a person's experience or ideas, their motives or their motions' (Stockton 2009: 11), in a way that applies to each of us as collaborators in lateral contact with one another. The chapter proposes that it is through an ethical gesture of openness, vulnerability, and not-yet-knowing on the part of the adult, rather than simply an autoethnographic self-reflexive experience, that our shared past and present experiences as artists, researchers, children, teenagers, cisgender females (at the time of writing), and humans, can flourish and grow sideways together. The chapter charts what we can learn from young people about what it means to be a (pre) teenager making performance with a professional theatre company through a discussion of our shared anxieties and feelings surrounding affective relationships between adults and children and a range of attendant dualisms: in/equity, free/paid labour, non-/professionalism, power(lessness), and (lack of) authority.

Building on the previous chapter's commitment to doing research *with* the people we call children, Chapter 9, *The Child as Researcher and Archivist: documenting News News News*, seeks to capture, from their own perspectives, the experiences of the Manchester-based cast of *News News* News (2022). The chapter documents a workshop that I facilitated at the young people's school and also includes some parallel interview material that was gathered separately from the adult creators of the work, Andy Field and Beckie Darlington. Recognising the absence of child-led and child-informed documentation on the people we call children and their participation in contemporary performance within the academy - particularly young people of Black and global majority heritage which make up the majority of the *News News*

News cast - the chapter documents the workshop's re-positioning of the performers as researchers and archivists of professional performance. Mindful not to repeat historical classist and colonial attempts within the academy to 'give voice' to marginalised subjects and communities (Jackson and Mazzei 2009), the chapter instead makes space for material which is archived by the performers themselves in response to a game that was born out of an attempt to queer existing research methods that maintain adult privilege within northern childhood studies. I also provide a commentary around the documentation, presented in the margins, that acknowledges the messy implicated-ness of my interpretive work to draw out insights from the documentation and the inevitable power afforded to me as lead researcher and curator of these pages, despite attempts to seek a more equitable approach to research. The chapter closes with a child-authored manifesto, which sees the young performers of *News News News* taking up the invitation to re-appropriate the usually adult-driven genre of manifesto writing to dictate some future terms for 'making performance with children'.

The book draws to a close with the conclusion *The Glitch: child activism in performance*, which explores what potential 'glitching' might hold for performance makers and scholars who work with the people we call children to navigate their worlds using their existing knowledges of glitch. Drawing on Legacy Russell's glitch feminism (2020) and a teatime conversation about glitching with the children I gave birth to, the conclusion reaffirms the book's position that the bodies and experiences of the people we call children should be permitted the feminist and queer approaches to reading their bodies that are ordinarily afforded to adult bodies. In particular, the discussion considers the way in which the trans*-age and queering strategies identified throughout have created opportunities for the people we call children to 'glitch' dominant discourses that are harmful or limiting to them. By adopting glitch feminism here, I align with other feminist interrogations of the figure of the child and childhood (Berlant 1997, Bernstein 2011, Burman 2008, Castañeda 2002, Steedman 1995) in a context where (with the exception of these theorists) it is still the case that 'feminists have largely focused on challenging women's positions in relation to children, rather than on feminist approaches to children and childhood per se' (Burman and Stacey 2010: 229).

Instead, this final discussion proposes that contemporary performance and performance research turns patriarchal protectionism on its head and sets out to create spaces for glitching that 'protect' children and young people's capacity to be political agents and activists who advocate for change. Such spaces cannot, I suggest, operate through 'community' because of its 'constitutive exclusion' (Mouffe and Laclau 1986). Instead, I call for an assemblage that both welcomes 'bodies in their plurality' (Butler 2015) and is informed by a neuroqueer approach that shares with glitch an intention to dismantle and disidentify from reductive normative binaries associated with gender, sexuality, race, and other aspects of identity from neurodivergent perspectives and embodied experiences (Egnar 2019, Walker 2021). I suggest that such an assemblage could benefit from live, embodied performance whilst also exploiting (with appropriate safeguarding) the anonymity that the digital world permits to enable the people we call children to imagine new identities, new worlds and to create avatar bodies that ghost, refuse, remix, throw shade, and survive without fear of punishment or violence.

Why Children? Why Now?

Over two decades ago, Henry Giroux asked a question that bears repeating in today's climate of child-led political action: 'Where can children find narratives of hope, semiautonomous cultural spheres, discussions of meaningful differences, and non-market-based democratic identities?' (2000: 11) This book offers a response: in contemporary performance. Since the 1990s, we have witnessed a number of artists and theatre companies working with children in professional settings, often for adult-based audiences, from the iconic works of Italian theatre company Socìetas Raffaello Sanzio to the significant concentration of performance work with children in Belgium as a result of various collaborations with Ghent based art centre CAMPO (previously known as Victoria) including Gob Squad, Tim Etchells, and Milo Rau. Currently, there is an increased appetite for working with children and young people in live art, dance, and contemporary performance, especially in the UK. This is well-charted in the Live Art and Development Agency's publication of a 'Study Room Guide' on *Live Art and Kids* (2017) by Sibylle Peters. Indeed, over the past few years, there have been a number of examples of this appetite for working with children in more experimental contexts. In Sheffield, Forced Entertainment teamed up with Theatre Deli to establish 'Art Breakers', a performance group of young people between ages 11 and 16, facilitated by Hester Chillingworth. Meanwhile in London, The Famous Lauren Barri Holstein worked with The Queen's Yard Company on a piece called *Really Real Teenz* (2019) which is 'a show about bodies, pop culture, and what happens when you take young people seriously' (The Yard, 2019). The Yard's website for the show boasts 'this is not the work that usually gets made with young people. This might get uncomfortable'. Given the increased concentration of experimental work with children in the UK and Europe at the turn of the 21st century[13], a full-length study of children, outside of the wealth of literature on applied drama and drama in education, is long overdue within the fields of theatre and performance.

Undoubtedly, some of this work is often difficult and challenging for spectators and this book is certainly not claiming that all contemporary performance offers the semi-autonomous, non-profit, democratic spaces of hope for young people that Giroux seeks. Nevertheless, in a context where the child is 'defined as a kind of legal strangeness… a body said to need protections more than freedoms' (Stockton 2009: 16), performance as a bodily and embodied practice offers an important space to confront these peculiarities and their attendant anxieties and also to offer the people we call children opportunities to explore potential freedoms both individually and collectively. If we fail to recognise that the bodies of the people we call children can signify – perhaps because we prefer to think the child is playing not working onstage (unlike the adult) or we self-censor to avoid the challenges and sensitivities of talking about children's bodies – then we limit our reading of the people we call children to the eternal, innocent child who is in need of adult protection, thereby ignoring their potential as political agents, subjects, performance makers, and artists. If we fail to acknowledge the hierarchical structures and discourses that manage and sustain the categories of 'adult' and 'child', then young people will forever be infantilised or demonised in an attempt to maintain the status quo, at the expense of the freedoms of which Stockton speaks. Lastly, if we fail to recognise children beyond innocence and developmentalism narratives, then we also deny the lives and specific disadvantages of particular children such as trans children as 'politically disenfranchised [people who are] subject to a regime of racially and gender normative governance by medicine and other social institutions, including the family' (Gill-Peterson 2018: 10).

These (adult) failures are problematic for the lives of actual children since, as Jenks argues, 'the ways in which children relate and are related to in everyday life are, inevitably, in terms of the conceptual structures through which they are previously envisaged' (Jenks 2005a: 124). This book goes some way to redressing the current imbalance between the way we read and encounter the bodies of the people we call children on the one hand and the bodies of the people we call adults on the other with in performance, as well as recognising the way in which performance currently negotiates and might take seriously young people's cultures and experiences in the future. But more than this, with the increasing global presence of young people mobilising political protests and action, the role that performance plays in supporting, and potentially undermining, the political status of the figure of the child and the activist practices of the people we call children demands urgent attention. At the UN Climate Change Conference in 2018, Greta Thunberg turned the discourse of futurity back on the political adult leaders of the world to tell them 'you are stealing [children's] future in front of their very eyes' (2018). The child Thunberg represents is neither the innocent child of Romanticism nor the evil child of Puritanism. She rejects the implication of the blank slate discourse that adults are fully developed through her activism when she says 'you are not mature enough to tell it like it is. Even that burden, you leave to us children' (ibid.). The wider field of performance has a role to play in this global political context, but we cannot begin to understand what that role is or might be until we pay serious and careful attention to both 'the child' and the people we call children in performance now. That is, in the words of Thunberg, until we tell it like it is.

Notes

1 Words and Music by Antony Copus (c) 2012 Out of the Ark Ltd, Middlesex TW12 2HD. Used with kind permission of Out of the Ark Ltd.

2 On the contrary, the nativity provides a fruitful example for Alan Read to think through the child's face as offering an 'ethics of hospitality' (2000: 62). Following Emmanuel Lévinas' discussion of the ethical relationship as one of asymmetry (1969), Read points towards the child performer's recognition that by welcoming the spectator as the guest to their host, they become hostage in this theatrical exchange.

3 Historic examples of children's participation in protest action include the 'Children's Crusade' of 1963 in Birmingham, AL, against racial segregation during the Civil Rights Movement, the protests and student demonstrations of 1968, and the UK-wide school strikes concerning the Conservative government's Youth Training Scheme (YTS) in 1985.

4 For more information, there is a wealth of scholarly literature on the work of Theatre of Research, including writing by the founder and director Sibylle Peters (2018, 2019). A useful introduction to the work of Mammalian Diving Reflex includes the artistic director Darren O'Donnell's book, Haircuts by Children, and Other Evidence for a New Social Contract (2018).

5 Children's literature scholar Marah Gubar has noted that we can also observe the figure of the innocent child prior to the Romantic period in the work of 'Pelagius (d. circa 418),

Julian of Eclanum (d. circa 455), Henry Vaughan (1621–1674) and Thomas Traherne (1637–1674)' (2011: 124).

6 For a detailed discussion and further examples relating to the sexualisation of innocence by corporations, see Henry Giroux's *Stealing Innocence: Youth, Corporate Power and the Politics of Culture* (2000). Giroux convincingly argues that popular culture rather than corporations themselves have been systematically blamed by media critics for erotically charged imagery of childhood innocence.

7 Rousseau's thinking around the innocent child, and its persistence into the 19th century, has profoundly influenced the current emphasis on child-centred learning in the contemporary Western world (James *et al.* 1998: 14–15) and brings with it questions around adult responsibility and children's freedom.

8 Current licensing requirements for children from birth to the end of compulsory school age in entertainment industries, such as theatre, are guided by legislation including the Children & Young Persons Act 1933 & 1963, the Children (Performances) Regulations 1968, the Children (Performance) (Miscellaneous Amendments) Regulations 1998(1), The Children (Performance) Amendment Regulations 2000, The Children (Performance) (Amendment) (No.2) Regulations 2000, and more recently The Children (Performances and Activities) (England) Regulations 2014. Licensed children are generally required to have licensed chaperones and theatre organisations that work regularly with children usually have their own safeguarding policy and procedure with respect to issues such as recruitment of staff, DBS (Disclosure and Barring Service) checks, data collection, communication with children, children's working hours, and payment etc.

9 For an in-depth discussion of the multiple roles children were cast in and child prodigies on the 19th century stage, see Marah Gubar's chapter 'The Drama of Precocity: Child Performers on the Victorian Stage' in Denisoff (2008).

10 See Peter's Coveney's (1957) *Poor Monkey* for more examples of the 'evil' child in 19th century literature.

11 See, for example, Richard Dutton's 'The Revels Office and the Boy Companies, 1600-1613: New Perspectives' (2002) and Lucy Munro's book *Children of the Queen's Revels: A Jacobean Theatre Repertory* (2005). In addition to Gubar (2008, 2012), scholarship on 19th century children's troupes includes Shauna Vey's work on the Marsh Troupe of juvenile actors in the U.S. (2015) and Peter Downes' (2002) writing on children's operettas in Australia and New Zealand.

12 For an in-depth discussion of the portrayal of the child in art history and criticisms leveled against Ariès see Matthew Knox Avarett's introduction to *The Early Modern Child in Art and History* (2015: 1–20).

13 Among these individual examples of mainly theatre-based performance practice, it is worth noting that the live art festival context in the UK has also seen a rise in events with children making, participating, curating, and performing in professional practice such as at the Transform Festival in Leeds which created its own young people's collective of creative artists called Future Radicals alongside the programming of a performance about the student occupations of 2015-16 by students from São Paulo who form the Brazillian-based coletivA ocupação. More recently, as part of the same festival in 2023, Icelandic artist Ásrún Magnúsdóttir worked with a collective of young Leeds-based performers and artists on a piece called *Secrets*. Other examples include Manchester's bi-annual Haphazard Festival by Word of Warning and Z-Arts billed as 'Live art for all ages', which is now in its seventh year, and the Liverpool Biennial that has included works such as Marvin Gaye Chetwynd's *Dogsy Ma Bone* (2016).

References

Ahmed, Sara (2006) *Queer Phenomenology: Orientations, Objects, Others*, Durham, NC and London: Duke University Press.

Amar, Paul (2016) 'The Street, the Sponge, and the Ultra: Queer Logics of Children's Rebellion and Political Infantilization', *GLQ: A Journal of Lesbian and Gay Studies*, 22 (4): 569–604.

Archard, David (1993) *Children: Rights and Childhood*, London: Routledge.
Ariès, Philippe (1962) *Centuries of Childhood: A Social History of Family*, New York: Vintage.
Averett, Matthew Knox (2015) *The Early Modern Child in Art and History*, London and New York: Routledge.
Barlee, Ellen (1884) *Pantomime Waifs, Or, A Plea for Our City Children*, London: Partridge.
BBC (2018) Eagles of Death Metal Shooting Survivor: Parkland Campaigners 'vile', BBC News US and Canada, 27 March: https://www.bbc.co.uk/news/world-us-canada-43549912 (accessed 13 March 2019).
BBC (2019) 'Shamima Begum: Ex-Bethnal Green Schoolgirl who Joined IS "Wants to Come Home"', BBC News UK, 14 February: https://www.bbc.co.uk/news/uk-47229181 (accessed 13 March 2019).
Bergman, Herbert, Douglas A. Noverr, and Edward J. Recchia (eds.), (2003). *The Collected Writings of Walt Whitman* vol. 2. New York: Peter Lang.
Berlant, Lauren (1997) *The Queen of America Goes to Washington City: Essays on Sex and Citizenship*, Durham and London: Duke University Press.
Bernstein, Robin (2011) *Racial Innocence: Performing American Childhood from Slavery to Civil Rights*, New York and London: New York University.
Bjelić, Tasha (2016) 'Digital Care', *Women and Performance: A Journal of Feminist Theory*, 26 (1): 101–104.
Brill, Abraham (1921) *Basic Principles of Psychoanalysis*, New York: University Press of America.
Burman, Erica (1994) 'Innocents Abroad: Western Fantasies of Children and the Iconography of Emergencies', *Disasters*, 18 (3), 238–253.
Burman, Erica (2008) *Developments: Child, Image, Nation*, Hove and New York: Brunner-Routledge.
Burman, Erica and Stacey, Jackie (2010) 'The Child and Childhood in Feminist Theory', *Feminist Theory 11*(3): 227–240.
Butler, Judith (1989) 'Foucault and the Paradox of Bodily Inscriptions', *The Journal of Philosophy*, 86 (11): 601–607.
Butler, Judith (1993) *Bodies That Matter: On the Discursive Limits of 'Sex'*, London and New York: Routledge.
Butler, Judith ([1990] 1999) *Gender Trouble*, New York: Routledge.
Butler, Judith (2015) *Notes Towards a Performative Theory of Assembly*, Havard University Press.
Butler, Judith (2023) 'Who is Afraid of Gender?', Public Lecture, University of Cambridge, Wednesday 26 April 2023: https://www.youtube.com/watch?v=yD6UukSbAMs (accessed 18 January 2024).
Castañeda, Claudia (2002) *Figurations: Child, Bodies, Worlds*, Durham and London: Duke University Press.
Chatzichristodoulou, Maria and Rachel Zerihan (2012) 'A Discussion on the Subject of Intimacy of Performance, and an Afterword' in Maria Chatzichristodoulou and Rachel Zerihan (eds.) *Intimacy Across Visceral and Digital Performance*, Basingstoke: Palgrave Macmillan, pp. 213–34.
Coclough, Dyan (2016) *Child Labor in the British Victorian Entertainment Industry 1875-1914*, Basingstoke: Palgrave Macmillan.
Corsaro, William (2005) *The Sociology of Childhood*, 2nd edn., Bloomington: Indiana University Press.
Coveney, Peter (1957) *Poor Monkey: The Child in Literature*, London: Rockcliff.
Cunningham, Hugh (1991) *The Children of the Poor: Representations of Childhood Since the Seventeenth Century*, Oxford: Blackwell.
Davis, Tracy C. (1986) 'The Employment of Children in the Victorian Theatre', *New Theatre Quarterly* 2 (6): 117–35.
Denisoff, Dennis (2008) *The Nineteenth Century Child and Consumer Culture*, Aldershot: Ashgate.

Department for Education (2012) 'Biggest Overhaul to Child Performance Regulations in Over 40 Years', Press Release, 24 May: https://www.gov.uk/government/news/biggest-overhaul-to-child-performance-regulations-in-over-40-years (accessed 14 March 2019).

Donaldson, Sue and Will Kymlicka (2018) 'Children and Animals', *The Routledge Handbook of the Philosophy of Childhood and Children*, Routledge

Downes, Peter (2002) *The Pollards: A Family and its Child and Adult Opera Companies in New Zealand and Australia 1880–1910*, Aotearoa: Steele Roberts.

Duschinsky, Robbie (2012) 'Tabula Rasa and Human Nature', *Philosophy*, 87 (04): 509–529.

Dutton, Richard (2002) 'The Revels Office and the Boy Companies, 1600-1613: New Perspectives', *English Literary Renaissance*, 32 (2): 324–251.

Edelman, Lee (2004) *No Future: Queer Theory and the Death Drive*, London: Duke University Press.

Egnar, Justine (2019) '"The Disability Rights Community Was Never Mine": Neuroqueer Disidentification,' *Gender & Society* 33 (1): 141.

Elkind, David (1998) *Reinventing Childhood*, Rosemont: Modern Learning Press.

Ellis, Justin R. (2022) 'A Fairy Tale Gone Wrong: Social Media, Recursive Hate and the Politicisation of Drag Queen Storytime', *The Journal of Criminal Law*, *86*(2), 94–108.

Escolme, Bridget (2006) 'Authority, Empowerment and Fairy Tales: Theatre for Young People', in Joe Kelleher and Nicholas Ridout (eds.) *Contemporary Theatres in Europe: A Critical Companion*, New York: Routledge, pp. 163–74.

Fawcett, Millicent Garrett (1889) 'The Employment of Children in Theatres', *Contemporary Review, Vol. 56*, pp. 822–29.

Fletcher-Watson, Ben (2017) 'Acting Up: Baby Performers on the Contemporary Stage' *With Children: The Child as Collaborator and Performer*, symposium, Leeds Beckett University, Saturday 28 January 2017.

Forrester, John (1990) *The Seductions of Psychoanalysis: Freud, Lacan and Derrida*, London: Routledge.

Foucault, Michel (1976) *The History of Sexuality: Volume 1*, trans. R. Hurley, Harmondsworth: Penguin.

Foucault, Michel (1977) *Discipline and Punish*, London: Allen Lane.

Foucault, Michel ([1971] 1998) 'Nietzsche, History, Genealogy' in *Aesthetics: Essential Works Volume 2*, James D. Faubion (ed.), London: Penguin.

Freshwater, Helen (2017) 'Agency, Power and the Inner Child: The 'Revolting Children' of Matilda the Musical', *With Children: The Child as Collaborator and Performer*, Leeds Beckett University, 28 January.

Frykberg, Mel (2015) 'Children of the Palestinian Revolution', *DW Online*, 22 July 2015: www.dw.com/en/children-of-the-palestinian-revolution/a-18596912 (accessed 05 February 2024).

Gardner, Lyn (2008) 'Theatre for Adults is Child's Play', *The Guardian*, 27 October: https://www.theguardian.com/stage/theatreblog/2008/oct/27/children-teenagers-theatre (accessed 21 February 2019).

Gardner, Lyn (2011) 'Matilda – Review', *The Guardian*, 25 November: https://www.theguardian.com/stage/2011/nov/25/matilda-review (accessed 21 February 2019).

Garton, Rosie and Ildiko Rippel (2011) 'Virtual Infants in Zoo Indigo's *Under the Covers*', *Body, Space & Technology*, 10 (1). http://doi.org/10.16995/bst.88

Germano, Isis (2018) 'So Cute, So Creepy: Children Undoing the Human in Het Hamiltoncomplex', *Performance Research*, 23 (1): 44–51.

Gill-Peterson, Julian (2018) *Histories of the Transgender Child*, Minneapolis: University of Minnesota Press.

Giroux, Henry A. (2000) *Stealing Innocence: Youth, Corporate Power and the Politics of Culture*, New York and Basingstoke: Palgrave.

Goldson, Barry (2001) 'The Demonisation of Children: from the symbolic to the institutional' in P. Foley, J. Roche, & S. Tucker (eds.) *Children in Society: contemporary theory, policy and practice*, Basingstoke: Palgrave, pp. 34–41.

Gubar, Marah (2008) 'The Drama of Precocity: Child Performers on the Victorian Stage', in Denis Denisoff (ed.) *The Nineteenth-Century Child and Consumer Culture*, Aldershot: Ashgate, pp. 63–78.
Gubar, Marah (2011) 'Innocence' in Philip Nel and Lissa Paul (eds.) *Keywords for Children's Literature*, New York and London: New York University Press.
Gubar, Marah (2012) 'Who Watched *The Children's Pinafore*? Age Transvestism on the Nineteenth-Century Stage', *Victorian Studies*, 54 (3): 410–426.
Halberstam, Jack (2005) *In a Queer Time and Place: Transgender Bodies, Subcultural Lives*, New York and London: New York University Press.
Hegel, Georg ([1826] 2006) *Lectures on the History of Philosophy, II*, Robert Brown (ed.), Oxford: Oxford University Press.
Hendrick, Harry (1990) 'Constructions and Reconstructions of British childhood: An Interpretive Survey, 1800 to the Present' in Allison James and Alan Prout (eds.) *Constructing and Reconstructing Childhood*, Basingstoke: Falmer, pp. 34–62.
Heywood, Colin (2001) *A History of Childhood: Children and Childhood in the West from Medieval to Modern Times*, Cambridge: Polity Press.
Hobbes, Thomas (1839-45) *The English Works of Thomas Hobbes*, Sir William Molesworth (ed.), Vols. 1–11. London: Bohn.
Holehouse, Matthew (2014) 'West End Musicals May Benefit From Reform to Child Labour Rules', *The Telegraph*, 24 August: https://www.telegraph.co.uk/culture/theatre/theatre-news/11054206/West-End-musicals-may-benefit-from-reform-to-child-labour-rules.html (accessed 14 March).
Horn, Pamela (1996) 'English Theatre Children, 1880-1914: A Study in Ambivalence', *History of Education*, 25 (1): 37–54.
Jackson, Alecia Y. and Lisa A. Mazzei (2009) *Voice in Qualitative Inquiry*, London: Routledge.
James, Allison, Chris, Jenks and Alan, Prout (1998) *Theorizing Childhood*, Allison James, Chris Jenks, and Alan Prout (eds.), Cambridge: Polity Press.
Javid, Savid (2019) 'If You Run Away to Join Isis, Like Shamima Begum, I Will Use All My Power to Stop You Coming Back', *The Sunday Times*, 17 February. https://www.thetimes.co.uk/article/if-you-run-away-to-join-isis-like-shamima-begum-i-will-use-all-my-power-to-stop-you-coming-back-8r2lpkfnn (accessed 18 February 2019)
Jenkins, Henry (1998) 'Introduction: Childhood Innocence and Other Myths' in *Children's Culture Reader*, New York and London: New York University Press.
Jenks, Chris (2005a) *Childhood*, 2nd edn, Oxon: Routledge.
Jenks, Chris (2005b) 'Childhood and Transgression' in Jens Qvortrup (ed.) *Studies in Modern Childhood: Society, Agency, Culture*, pp. 115–27.
Katz, Cindy (2008) 'Childhood as Spectacle: Relays of Anxiety and the Reconfiguration of the Child', *Cultural Geographies* 15 (1): 15–17.
Kehily, Mary (2004) *An Introduction to Childhood Studies*, Maidenhead: Open University Press.
Kehily, Mary and Heather Montgomery (2004) 'Innocence and Experience: A historical Approach to Childhood and Sexuality' in Mary Kehily (ed.) *An Introduction to Childhood Studies*, Maidenhead: Open University Press, pp. 70–92.
Kincaid, James (1998) *Erotic Innocence: The Culture of Child Molesting*, Durham, NC: Duke University Press.
Kincaid, James (2000) 'Dickens and the Construction of the Child', in Wendy S. Jacobson (ed.) *Dickens and the Children of Empire*, New York: Palgrave, pp. 29–42.
Kincaid, James (2004) 'Producing Erotic Children' in Stephen Bruhm and Natasha Hurley (eds.) *Curiouser: On the Queerness of Children*, Minneapolis: University of Minnesota Press, pp. 3–16.
King, Peter (1998) 'Thomas Hobbes's Children' in Susan M. Turner and Gareth B. Matthews (eds.) *The Philosopher's Child: Critical Essays in the Western Tradition*, University of Rochester Press, pp. 65–83.

Lévinas, Emmanuel (1969) *Totality and Infinity: An Essay on Exteriority*, trans. Alfonso Lingis, Pittsburgh: Duquesne University Press.
Locke, John (1693) *Some Thoughts Concerning Education*, London: A. and J. Churchill.
Locke, John (1689] 1836) *An Essay Concerning Human Understanding*, 27th edn., London: T. Tegg and Son.
Mead, Margaret and Martha Wolfenstein (1954) *Childhood in Contemporary Cultures*, Chicago: Chicago University Press.
Mitra, Royona (2019) 'Making Space in Dance Theatre and Performance Studies: An Act of Decoloniality', Decolonizing Theatre, Dance and Performance Studies panel, Theatre and Performance Research Association, University of Exeter, 5 September 2019.
Munro, Lucy (2005) *Children of the Queen's Revels: A Jacobean Theatre Repertory*, Cambridge: Cambridge University Press.
Mouffe, Chantal and Ernesto Laclau (1986) *Hegemony and Socialist Strategy*, London: Verso.
O'Donnell, Darren (2018) *Haircuts by Children and Other Evidence for a New Social Contract*, Toronto: Coach House Books.
Park, Haeyoun (2014) 'Children at the Border', *New York Times*, 21st October 2014. https://www.nytimes.com/interactive/2014/07/15/us/questions-about-the-border-kids.html (accessed 05 February 2024).
Parsons, Talcot and Bales, Robert F. (1955) *Family, Socialization and Interaction Process*, New York: Free Press.
Peters, Sibylle (2018) 'A Plea for Transgenerational Research in Live Art,' *Performance Research*, 23 (1): 98–101.
Peters, Sibylle (2019) '"The Ghosts Insurance": Participatory research in haunted schools by the Theatre of Research', *Ephemera*, 19 (1): 153–162,157A–157D.
Postman, Neil (1994) *The Disappearance of Childhood*, New York: Vintage Books.
Prosser, Jay (1998) *Second Skins: The Body Narratives of Transsexuality*, New York: Columbia University Press.
Read, Alan (2000) 'Acknowledging the Imperative of Performance in the Infancy of Theatre', *Performance Research*, 5 (2): 61–69.
Read, Alan (2018) 'Child & Co': In The Company of Your Own Making, *Performance Research*, 23 (1): 5–23.
Robertson, Priscilla ([1974] 2006) 'Home as Nest: Middle Class Childhood in Nineteenth Century Europe' in Lloyd de Mause (ed.) *The History of Childhood*, Oxford: Rowman and Littlefield, pp. 407–431.
Roms, Heike (2022) The avant-garde is child's play: The appearance of children in 1960s Happenings and Fluxus, Kids on Stage - Andere Spielweisen in der Performancekunst transgenerational. transkulturell. transdisziplinär, Athena bei wbv, 185–206.
Rose, Jacqueline (1992) *The Case of Peter Pan: Or, The Impossibility of Children's Fiction*, Philadelphia: University of Pennsylvania.
Rousseau, Jean-Jacques ([1762] 1947) *The Social Contract*, New York: Hafner Press.
Rousseau, Jean-Jacques ([1762] 1955) *Emile, or On Education*, trans. B. Foxley, London: Dent/Everyman.
Russell, Legacy (2020) *Glitch Feminism: A Manifesto*, London and Brooklyn, New York: Verso.
Scraton, Phil ([1997] 2004) 'Whose "Childhood"? What "Crisis"?' in Phil Scraton (ed.) *Childhood in Crisis?*, London and New York: Routledge.
Segalov, Micheal (2019) 'Shamima Begum was Groomed. She Deserves the Chance of Rehabilitation', *The Guardian,* 14 February: https://www.theguardian.com/commentisfree/2019/feb/14/shamima-begum-grooming-islamic-state-pregnant-uk (accessed 18 February 2019).
Senior, Adele (2016) 'Beginners On Stage: Arendt, Natality and the Appearance of Children in Contemporary Performance', *Theatre Research International*, 41 (1): 70–84.
Senior, Adele (2018) 'Florida School Shooting: Urgency of Gun Reform Calls for Dramatic Action from Young Survivors', *The Conversation*, 2 March: https://theconversation.com/florida-school-shooting-urgency-of-gun-reform-calls-for-dramatic-action-from-young-survivors-92692 (accessed 18 February 2019).

Senior, Adele and The Institute for the Art and Practice of Dissent at Home (2018) 'On Children (Editorial)', *Performance Research*, 23 (1): 1–4.

Sharman, Jon (2018) 'Florida Shooting Survivors Taunted by Right-Wing Commentators and Conspiracy Theorists', *The Independent*, 21 February: https://www.independent.co.uk/news/world/americas/florida-shooting-survivors-dinesh-dsouza-mock-cpac-conspiracy-theory-crisis-actors-social-media-a8220716.html (accessed 13 March 2019).

Siddique, Haroon (2023) 'Shamima Begum Ruling Deals Bitter Blow to Chances of UK Return', *The Guardian*, Wednesday 22 February 2023: https://www.theguardian.com/uk-news/2023/feb/22/shamima-begum-case-lawyers-can-appeal-but-only-on-point-of-law (accessed 28 January 2024).

Skinner, B.F. ([1957] 2014) *Verbal Behavior*, Vermont: Echo Point.

Spencer, Charles (2009) 'Billy Elliot, Victoria Palace Theatre, Review: "triumphant"', *The Telegraph*, 15 January: https://www.telegraph.co.uk/theatre/what-to-see/billy-elliot-at-the-victoria-palace-theatre-review/ (accessed 21 February 2019).

Spencer, Charles (2011) 'Matilda, Cambridge Theatre Review', *The Telegraph*, 25 November: https://www.telegraph.co.uk/theatre/what-to-see/matilda-cambridge-theatre-review/ (accessed 21 February 2019).

Stanglin, Doug and Christal Hayes (2018) 'Conspiracy Theorists Find Florida Student Activists Too Good to be True', *USA Today*, 21 February: https://eu.usatoday.com/story/news/2018/02/21/conspiracy-theorists-find-florida-student-activists-too-good-true/358148002/ (accessed 13 March).

Steedman, Carolyn (1995) *Strange Dislocations: Childhood and the Idea of Human Interiority, 1780–1930*, Cambridge, MA: Harvard University Press.

Stockton, Kathryn Bond (2009) *The Queer Child or Growing Sideways in the Twentieth Century*, Durham and London: Duke University Press.

The Stage (1888) 'Children and the Theatre', *The Stage*, 16 November, p.8.

The Yard (2019) 'Really Real Teenz': https://theyardtheatre.co.uk/theatre/events/really-real-teenz/?spektrix_bounce=true (accessed 6 March 2019).

Thunberg, Greta (2018) 'Greta Thunberg Full Speech at UN Climate Change COP24 Conference': https://www.youtube.com/watch?v=VFkQSGyeCWg (accessed 13 March 2019).

UNCRC (1989) United Nations Convention on the Rights of the Child: https://downloads.unicef.org.uk/wp-content/uploads/2010/05/UNCRC_PRESS200910web.pdf?_ga=2.236163779.333501690.1552479510-1520726232.1552479510 (accessed 13 March 2019)

van Deth, Jan, Simone Abendschön and Meike Vollmar (2011) 'Children and Politics: An Empirical Reassessment of Early Political Socialization', *Political Psychology*, 32 (1): 147–173.

Varty, Ann (2005) 'The Rise and Fall of the Victorian Stage Baby', *New Theatre Quarterly* 21(3): 218–229.

Vey, Shauna (n.d.) 'Roundtable Discussion with Marah Gubar and Shauna Vey', Interviewed by Martin Woodside: http://www.shcy.org/features/commentaries/revisited-chc-season-2-episode-4-roundtable-discussion-with-marah-gubar-and-shauna-vey/ (accessed 6 March 2019).

Vey, Shauna (2015) *Childhood and Nineteenth Century American Theatre: The Work of the Marsh Troupe of Juvenile Actors*, Carbondale, Illinois: Southern Illinois University Press.

Wake, Caroline (2017) 'The Ambivalent Politics of One-to-One Performance', *Performance Paradigm*, 13: 163–173.

Waldron, Emma Leigh (2017) '"This FEELS SO REAL!": Sense and Sexuality in ASMR', *First Monday*, 22 (1-2). https://firstmonday.org/ojs/index.php/fm/article/view/7282 (accessed 6 March 2019).

Walker, Nick (2021) *Neuroqueer Heresies: Notes on the Neurodiversity Paradigm, Autistic Empowerment, and Postnormal Possibilities*, Fort Worth, TX: Autonomous Press.

Walkerdine, Valerie (1988) *The Mastery of Reason*, London: Routledge.

Warner, Marina (1994) *Managing Monsters: The Reith Lectures*, London: Vintage.

Warner, Marina (1995) *Six Myths of Our Time*, New York: Vintage

Zerihan, Rachel (2006) 'Intimate Inter-actions: Returning to the Body in One to One Performance', *Body, Space and Technology*, 6 (1). http://doi.org/10.16995/bst.174

Part II

Reading Children

2 From Age Transvestism to Trans*-age Performance

On Children Playing Adults

There is a long history of children playing adults onstage, from the boy companies of the Jacobean and Elizabethan eras to the all-child productions of the 19th century, which saw children playing adult roles in Lilliputian operettas. Indeed, the Victorian fascination with childhood as a separate category from adulthood is a key concern for Marah Gubar who uses the term 'age transvestism' in her analysis of miniature Gilbert and Sullivan operettas to interrogate why Victorian audiences 'loved to see children acting like adults' (2012: 410). Age transvestism, however, was first used by Lucy Munro in *Children of the Queen's Revels: A Jacobean Theatre Repertory* to describe how the boy actors of the children's companies within early modern theatre were not just playing roles that crossed gender or a different social status to their own but also that they 'engaged in age play' too (2005: 2). In particular, she discusses the repertoire of the Children of the Chapel, which often featured old male and female characters played by pre-pubescent or pubescent boy actors (ibid.: 42).

Munro's discussion of age transvestism is particularly useful as a means of developing our understanding of how age play operates within contemporary performance. Firstly, Munro's conceptualisation of age transvestism foregrounds the way in which some of the content of the Chapel plays was conscious of and drew attention to the incongruence between a child playing an adult. Secondly, she identifies the anatomy of the performer as being a significant component of this incongruence. For example, when discussing the relationship between costume, dialogue, and a boy actor's physicality in John Marston's *The Dutch Courtesan* she states:

> Attention to facial hair is part of Marston's physically precise bawdy in his depictions of relations between the sexes, reminding the audience that these are sexually liminal adolescent performers.
>
> (Munro 2005: 47)

More recently, Julie Ackroyd (2017) extends our understanding of how age transvestism functioned within early modern theatre, again with particular reference to the use of the artificial beard as a 'theatrical shorthand for agedness' by pre-pubescent boys playing adult males. Alongside specific gestures and a style of theatrical presentation that did not rely on 'faithful mimicry', Ackroyd notes that

DOI: 10.4324/9781003043072-4

beards were not just a key adult signifier for these child companies but also served as a metatheatrical device when employed by a child performer in a male adult role (2017: 95). One example she cites includes the use of the beard to comment on the lack of difference in the quality of performances by the child actors within the boys' companies in comparison with adult actors of the time who had instead come through the apprentice system of theatrical education (ibid.). Ackroyd also attends closely to the way in which early modern audiences would have read 'male development' which again suggests audiences were making readings based on their perceptions of the anatomies of the performers and their relationship to social categories of age at the time:

> The "child", a male younger than fourteen, is categorized as being 'smooth' faced [...] "Youth" is characterized as having "hair on his head, but none on the face" and finally a "Man" is defined as "having a beard" [...]
>
> (2017: 97)

My approach to reading children playing adults within *Five Easy Pieces* and *The Hamilton Complex* in the chapters that follow, resonates with both Ackroyd's attention to metatheatricality as a key part of age transvestism and Munro's acknowledgement of the incongruence between boy player and the adult character they impersonate. The authors' shared nod to the way in which age transvestism in an early modern context referenced the performers' anatomies is a common aspect of age play that I want to propose we can still observe in contemporary performance. A significant point of departure when examining children playing adults in the contemporary UK and European context, however, is that we cannot assume that children are often seen and experienced – as it is assumed they were seen in this historical context – as only partially developed humans who are unable to self-regulate like adults (Fudge 2006, Munro 2018, Witmore 2007). Neither, however, can we assume that the performers we call children are perceived by an audience as fully formed subjects. What is interesting is how 'age transvestism' or what I am calling 'trans*-age' performance strategies in this context navigate potential perceptions of the performer's subjecthood.

It is precisely this uncertainty around how young performers in a contemporary context might be perceived that draws me to a closer examination of, and revision to my earlier use of the term 'age transvestism' (Senior 2018) to instead propose the idea of 'trans*-age' strategies, whilst still retaining an attitude of 'transvestism' as 'a space of possibility' (Garber 1992: 17). For Garber, whose focus on the 'transvestite' is historically situated at the time they are writing in the early 1990s, a space of possibility emerges through the figure of the transvestite who becomes the container for a 'category crisis elsewhere [...] that destabilizes comfortable binarity', even whilst gender may not serve as the primary thematic content within an artistic context. If we approach *age* transvestism similarly, as a space of possibility, it is not only in the act of children playing adults where the comfortable binarity of adult/child is challenged, but also the age-crossing child has the potential to signal a 'category crisis' that is happening elsewhere. Part II suggests, that we can think of this crisis as located in the relational act of audience perception. As we will see, the binarised categories related to performer/audience and performer/character relationships are put under strain in *Five Easy Pieces* through its age-crossing. It is through age play that the performance both mobilises and, at times, undermines the fixity suggested by binaries that operate between the fictional world and the theatrical environment in which the work is staged, such as real/representational, intention/effect, control/freedom, and rehearsed/improvised. Also, the space of possibility that this age-crossing creates in order to reveal and destabilise the child/adult binary, is only made available because other dualities, on which contemporary adult/child distinctions rely to be legible, are identifiable as such in the performance and are called into question. Therefore, as I have argued previously, to think about children playing adults as a space of possibility is to retain Garber's sense of the term transvestism as a challenge to the very notion of category itself.

However, the language of age transvestism feels increasingly limited in its ability to discuss the complexities of children playing adults in performance. Beyond theatre scholarship, 'transvestism' is rooted in historically-situated queer practices, cultures, communities and scholarship, and as a term it has been problematised over the years. 'Transvestism' was first coined by sexologist Magnus Hirschfeld in the early 20th century in a way that aligned it with sexuality and erotic practice (Flanagan 2008: 3). Hirschfeld describes transvestism as a condition whereby a person has an 'irresistible tendency to dress in the clothing of the opposite sex' (Dekker and van de Pol 1989: 54). Whilst the term itself has evolved, this historical connection with a 'behavioural fetish' (Flanagan 2008: 3) is arguably still retained within its contemporary usage, and is also challenging in the sense that this early definition potentially pathologises the act described. When transvestism is appropriated in relation to children playing adults and adults playing children as 'age transvestism' then, there is the potential of imbuing what is an age-based performance strategy with eroticism and sexuality. To do so is reductive and does not account for aesthetic choices in performance that are *not* aligned with sexuality and eroticism. Describing an age-based performance strategy as 'transvestism' may inadvertently invoke a sexualised or eroticised intentionality over these choices that does not exist in the practice. The issue of choice is further complicated by both live performance and questions about child-adult power relations because, unless the performance itself or its surrounding materials offer a framing for its reception which confirms the intentions of a particular agent in the moment of being 'read' (whether that is a performer, artist, director, writer etc.), there is no way of accurately aligning a particular intention with a young performer or anyone else for that matter.

Whilst I wish to retain Marjorie Garber's nuanced reading of transvestism as a space of possibility then, I am also conscious, in addition to these complications around intention, that adopting the language of 'transvestism' to describe a performance strategy might be interpreted more widely as a reductive and homogenising representation of trans identities and lived realities. In other words, aligning performance practice with transvestism, may be read as violently limiting wider trans' experiences to the realm of self-presentation, theatrical artifice, and the mythological scene that is implied by its use in the context of performance practice. Similar criticisms have been levelled at Garber and also Judith Butler in relation to their use of the figure of the transsexual. Although Marjorie Garber has acknowledged that cross-dressing is 'bound up with the story of homosexuality and gay identity' (1992: 4) her work, alongside Butler's work in *Gender Trouble* (1990) and *Bodies that Matter* (1993), has been challenged for using the figure of the transsexual in a way that privileges the theoretical concept of border-play, rather than foregrounding the 'real' lives of transsexuals and transvestites (Namaste 1996 and Prosser 1998).

It is helpful to further understand the scholarly context for these claims. Jay Prosser's main criticism is that Butler's theory of gender performativity assumes that the transgender subject is always already subversive. In his book *Second Skins: The Body Narratives of Transsexuality* Prosser suggests that Butler's theory is problematic because 'there are transsexuals who seek very pointedly to be non-performative, to be constative, quite simply to be' (1998: 32). Jack Halberstam summarises Prosser's argument helpfully as follows:

> [M]any transsexuals do not want to represent gender artifice; they actually aspire to the real, the natural, indeed the very condition that has been rejected by the queer theory of gender performance.
>
> (Halberstam 2005: 30)

One could argue that Butler's position still holds some weight in the sense that existing as a trans person in a deeply oppressive, transphobic world is always already a political and subversive act even if not intended as such. However, this is a differently nuanced concern to that of Prosser who suggests that Butler's theory positions transsexual experiences as inherently transgressive and therefore undermines 'transsexual claims to legitimacy' (Halberstam 2005: 31) by positioning gender within the realm of artifice. Does using 'transvestism' to describe age play within the context of contemporary performance risk the same theoretical border-play Prosser accuses Butler of participating in?

In order to fully attend to this question, it is worth revisiting Halberstam's critique of Prosser's argument, namely that Halberstam finds Prosser's positioning problematic because it relies on the assumption that there is both 'transsexual desire for realness' and that 'gender realness is achievable' (ibid.). In other words, Halberstam identifies the homogenising and essentialist thinking that grounds Prosser's argument and reveals the fragility of these claims to 'realness' by poignantly asking: 'what actually constitutes the real for Prosser in relation to the transsexual body? The penis or the vagina? Facial hair or shaved legs? Everyday life as a man or a woman?'. The term transsexual can sometimes place great significance on anatomy, external genitalia, and an expectation of 'full transition' and therefore the term is not representative of a multiplicity and diversity of trans' experiences. Whilst 'transsexual' is an affirmative term for some, because it is sometimes adopted to emphasise external anatomical signifiers, it can be employed to reinforce binarised sex and gender categories, particularly in medical discourse. In 2017, for example, sexologist Raymond Blanchard compared 'transsexual' identity during an interview on BBC Newsnight to 'normal gender identity' (Blanchard 2017). By this, he reinscribed binarised sex as that which is determined by external genitalia.

Instead, to describe the way in which self-authorised and biographical narratives play a role in archiving trans lives, Halberstam employs the term 'transgender' as 'a marker for all kinds of people who challenge, deliberately or accidentally, gender normativity' (Halberstam 2005: 32). In doing so, however, Halberstam also makes a distinction that could be seen as similarly problematic in a contemporary context between 'transgender biography' and 'transsexual autobiography'. So, whilst he recognises the value in Prosser's argument that the 'transsexual has been used in queer theory as a symbol for the formulation of a subjectivity that actually threatens transsexual claims to legitimacy' (ibid.: 30), in creating a distinction between transgender biography and transsexual autobiography, Halberstam's formulation also arguably rests on the very hegemonic distinction between gender and sex that Judith Butler sought to unpack in *Gender Trouble*. That is, Halberstam in this text is at risk of reifying the still prevalent sex/gender distinction, which assumes the fixity of sex even whilst he considers both gender and sex to be open to change.

Although the arguments levelled at Butler by Prosser and, in turn, at Prosser by Halberstam are not without their problems, my shift away from 'transvestism' to describe a continuum of age play within performance is motivated by the need to take seriously the authors' shared concern about the appropriation and misrepresentation of trans experiences. I turn to the term trans* then precisely in order to acknowledge that trans* experiences *and* bodies can also play with age in performance, whilst taking care not to repeat the essentialist underpinnings that position transsexual experiences within the realm of the real and transgender experiences in the realm of the representational. Just as trans* seeks to encompass different expressions of non-normative gender presentation *and* or *as* lived experiences in a contemporary context, I wish to adopt the term trans* to describe a multitude of different iterations of age presentation *and/as* lived age-based experiences. In doing so, I hope to draw on the insights that the term trans* opens up – which are related to fluidity, bending, crossing, reversal, non-binarising, non-conforming, disidentification – under the umbrella of trans*-age strategies precisely not to erase or dilute histories to either the realm of 'theory' or to the mythical scene. Instead, to refer to trans*-age strategies is to acknowledge the diversity of bodies and experiences – which vitally include trans* people we call children etc. – that participate in age-related strategies in contemporary performance with the capacity to challenge essentialist understandings of the real/representational in terms of both form and content.

This shift towards a more capacious concept of trans*-age strategies, beyond age transvestism, feels urgent because contemporary performance is both an embodied and bodily practice and the examples I focus on here sit within theatrical worlds that deliberately undermine an essentialising, hierarchical distinction between real and representational whilst foregrounding (to a greater or lesser extent) the materiality and lived experiences of the performers on stage. This move to recognise a diversity of trans*-age strategies also reflects a similar dissatisfaction with the historically-inflected version of transvestism in other disciplinary contexts. In her 2008 book *Into the Closet: Cross-Dressing and the Gendered Body in Children's Film and Literature,* Victoria Flanagan situates transvestism (and transsexualism) in relation to the broader cultural history of cross-dressing. However, she also takes issue with the 'adult-oriented concepts of transvestism and transsexualism', where 'adult-oriented' relates to sex and sexuality, because, for her, they are not compatible with the gender-crossing characters she observes in the children's literature, preferring instead to use the terminology of cross-dressing. However, the idea of cross-dressing as 'behavioural and cultural practices that involve wearing clothes considered socially appropriate for the opposite sex' (Flanagan 2008: 2) I would argue is similarly reductive when appropriated for describing age play in performance because it rests on the assumption of a binarised gender or, in our case, binarised age identity (adult/child). Of course, where literature (for Flanagan) is making direct reference to binarised gender norms then age-crossing like cross-dressing could be employed as a useful descriptor in performance to make reference to expectations of and the crossing of age-based norms. However, in a contemporary context in which some practice of age play refuses to fit neatly into binarised age-related boundaries (adult/child, young/old), the idea of 'crossing' fails to account for a plurality of ages as much as 'cross-dressing' fails to account for genders outside of the hegemonic gender binary.

Just as there are more than two genders (Stockton 2021), the bodies we encounter in performance do not always fit neatly with age-based norms to the extent that we could accurately describe all forms of age-based performance strategies as age-crossing. As audience members, we may hazard a guess at a performer's anatomical age, for example, but unless the performance operates to confirm or challenge our estimation then we are always assuming age, based on our interpretation of whatever is available or legible to us. We know from early modern scholars that anatomy – and here I would specify that these scholarly claims are *perceptions of anatomy* mediated through interpretations that are historically, geographically, and socially situated – are fundamental to meaning-making when it comes to theatrical age transvestism. Regardless of the wider problematics and issues associated with 'reading' children's bodies, how we read any body in performance undeniably involves assumptions about age, based on perceptions of anatomy alongside any other information that is made available to us regarding categories of age identity. This includes how perceptions of age are affected by the framing of the theatrical world and/or other aspects of the performance, which may or may not afford children the ability to describe their own age or age in their own terms. Readings of age also have to consider that perceived anatomical age might not align with the diversity of ways in which a performer (regardless of how young or old they are) might perceive, live, present, and/or identify with their own age both within or outside of the context of performance.

In particular, I turn to this language of trans*-age strategies and the embodied knowledges and histories it signals, precisely because of its relationship to body-based practice and diverse lived experiences. For me, the term trans* recognises the complexities of body-based practice specific to performance and my approach to investigating them here is founded on the assumption that age, whilst socially produced, is also lived, and in performance is an embodied experience from the performer's perspective. By attending to trans*-age strategies in performance, I hope to foreground that like gender, age – as a socially produced phenomenon and lived social reality – also invites discrimination, even *on* the bodies of children. As I begin to unpack in the next few chapters, how we read age in performance inevitably intersects with other areas of identity politics and inequities including class, race, gender, sexuality, and ability. To apply terms such as fluid, crossing, bending, reversal, non-conformity, non-binarised, and disidentification under the umbrella of trans* age with the hope of developing our understanding of how age play is negotiated onto/with/by children and children's bodies is undoubtedly a politically-inflected move. It is, however, a necessary move given that the bodies of the people we call children have largely been marginalised from non-scientific academic discussions until the last two decades or so (Burman and Stacey 2010, Castañeda 2002, Flanagan 2008, Kincaid 1998, Prout 2000).

Similarly, in the context of the 'gender critical' movement in Europe (see Kuhar and Paternotte 2017) and increasing transphobic rhetoric, particularly within the UK where the performances discussed in this book were staged, trans children's very existence is questioned and treated as up for debate. To consider trans*-age strategies in performance therefore is an intellectually motivated attempt to reinstate the importance of challenging reductive, binarised thinking around the adult/child that has the potential to exclude trans* people we also call children. In this respect, my employment of the term trans* takes its lead from Marquis Bey's conceptualisation of transness as that which:

> [u]nfixes gender from essentialist moorings and posits itself precisely as that unfixation, as a departure-from without the presumption of a stable destination, or indeed a departure that itself destabilizes destinational desires.
> (2022: 3)

To consider the way in which transness might inform an understanding of trans*-age strategies in performance is to acknowledge the possibility that age might also be unfixed from its essentialist moorings. To recognise transness within trans*-age practices is an attempt to draw attention to the way in which essentialised norms around age fail to account for: a plurality of lived and embodied experiences of age; authorship through self-identification or disidentification; the regulatory discursive regimes that frame historically and culturally-situated perceptions on age; identities that intersect with age; and the relational work of interpretation when it comes to 'reading' age within the context of performance practice.

It is important to note, however, that attending to trans*-age strategies does not guarantee and, indeed, does not set out here to generate insight and evidence of the material realities of collaborating with children: the terms of their contract, whether they are paid/unpaid, issues around consent, inequities, and exploitation etc. However, I want to suggest that trans*-age strategies have the potential to create a space of possibility for non-hegemonic re/presentations of 'the child' to emerge and also for the people we call children, including trans* children, to occupy the position of subject, co-subject, body, and human in performance. Such re/presentations as negotiated through the bodies we witness on stage or in performance more widely may raise questions about the material realities of collaborating with the people we call children and the ethics of children's participation in performance practice. However, the following chapters will not focus on gathering data on those realities and experiences directly from the people we call children. Those will be attended to in Part III. Instead, by identifying and unpacking the specific kind of age play *Five Easy Pieces* participates in within the next chapter, I hope to shed light on the particular political and ethical issues the work itself generates through the way in which the performance adopts trans*-age strategies. This includes analysing how age is negotiated through the use of metatheatre; in the relationship between the live (children's) stage space and the virtual (adult's) screen space; and finally, in the children's interaction with the live feed that attempts to mark their performances as 'children playing adults' throughout. In response to the piece itself, an intersectional attitude to reading age in performance is employed in direct response to Lies Pauwels' work in Chapter 4, *The female-girl-child-teenager in The Hamilton Complex,* where I consider how age and gender intersect to negotiate and disrupt performances of childhood innocence. In particular, I examine the way in which a gender-specific trans*-age strategy is employed to perform heteronormative, patriarchal femininity to excess and to signal its relationship to the eroticisation of childhood, and specifically girlhood, innocence.

References

Ackroyd, Julie (2017) *Child Actors on the London Stage, Circa 1600: Their Education, Recruitment and Theatrical Success*, Brighton: Sussex Academic Press.

Bey, Marquis (2022) *Black Trans Feminism*, Duham and London: Duke University Press.

Blanchard, Raymond (2017) BBC Newsnight, 11 January: https://www.youtube.com/watch?v=AcRs703k5mA

Burman, Erica and Jackie Stacey (2010) 'The Child and Childhood in Feminist Theory', *Feminist Theory,* 11 (3): 227–240.

Butler, Judith (1993) *Bodies That Matter: On the Discursive Limits of 'Sex'*, London and New York: Routledge.

Butler, Judith ([1990] 1999) *Gender Trouble*, New York: Routledge.

Castañeda, Claudia (2002) *Figurations: Child, Bodies, World*, Durham and London: Duke University Press.

Dekker, Rudolf M. and Lotte C. van de Pol (1989) *The Tradition of Female Transvestism in Early Modern Europe*, New York: St Martin's Press.

Flanagan, Victoria (2008) *Into the Closet: Cross-Dressing and the Gendered Body in Children's Literature and Film*, New York and London: Routledge.

Fudge, Erica (2006) 'Learning to Laugh: Children and Being Human in Early Modern Thought' in Andrea Immel and Michael Witmore (eds.) *Childhood and Children's Books in Early Modern Europe, 1550–1800*, New York and London: Routledge, pp. 19–39.

Garber, Marjorie (1992) *Vested Interests: Cross-Dressing and Cultural Anxiety*, New York and London: Routledge.

Gubar, Marah (2012) 'Who Watched The Children's Pinafore? Age Transvestism on the Nineteenth Century Stage', *Victorian Studies*, 54 (3): 410–426.

Halberstam, Jack (2005) *In a Queer Time and Place: Transgender Bodies, Subcultural Lives*, New York and London: New York University Press.
Kincaid, James (1998) *Erotic Innocence: The Culture of Child Molesting*, Durham N.C: Duke University Press.
Kuhar, Roman, and David Paternotte (2017) *Anti-Gender Campaigns in Europe: Mobilizing Against Equality*, London: Rowman and Littlefield.
Munro, Lucy (2005) *Children of the Queen's Revels: A Jacobean Theatre Repertory*, Cambridge: Cambridge University Press.
Munro, Lucy (2018) 'Queering Gender, Age, and Status in Early Modern Childrens' Drama' in Jennifer Higginbotham and Mark Johnston (eds.) *Queering Childhood in Early Modern English Drama and Culture*, Cham: Palgrave Macmillan, pp. 215–37.
Namaste, Ki (1996) 'Genderbashing: Sexuality, Gender, and the Regulation of Public Space', *Environment and Planning D: Society and Space*, 14 (2): 221–240.
Prosser, Jay (1998) *Second Skins: The Body Narratives of Transsexuality*, New York: Columbia University Press.
Prout, Alan (2000) 'Childhood Bodies: Construction, Agency and Hybridity' in Alan Prout and Jo Campling (eds.) *The Body, Childhood and Society*, London: Palgrave Macmillan, pp. 1–18.
Senior, Adele (2018) 'Age Transvestism' in Contemporary Performance and Live Art with Children', *Performance Research: A Journal of the Performing Arts*, 23 (1): 26–36.
Stockton, Kathryn Bond (2021) *Gender(s)*, Cambridge, MA: MIT Press.
Witmore, Michael (2007) *Pretty Creatures: Children and Fiction in the English Renaissance*, Ithaca: Cornell University Press.

3 The Child as Adult in *Five Easy Pieces*

During the mid-1990s a horrific crime shook the nation of Belgium. A man called Marc Dutroux abducted and raped six girls, murdering four of them. Dutroux was later convicted and imprisoned for his crimes, but shortly after his arrest a large demonstration known as the 'White March' took place on 20 October 1996 in Brussels to protest the handling of the case by the judicial system and government of the time (Walgrave and Manssens 2000: 217). A high court decision to remove the examining magistrate (Jean-Marc Connerotte) from the investigation, because he had allegedly shown too much sympathy for the victims, sparked a series of riots, sit-ins, and strikes across Belgium. The public unrest eventually led to a silent demonstration organised by the parents of the victims, which became known as the White March. The demonstration involved around 300,000 people, largely families, holding white balloons and flowers in memory of the children affected (ibid.). The Dutroux case, and the protest action it mobilised, is still widely known across contemporary Belgium, bolstered by extensive news media coverage of the case between August and October 1996, unlike any other in Belgium's media history (ibid.: 221).

This socio-political context led Swiss theatre and film director, Milo Rau, to focus on what he believed 'most concerned' children in Belgium, after he was approached by the Ghent-based arts centre CAMPO to work with a group of young actors (Gardner 2017). For Rau, whose background is sociology, the Dutroux case both generated and provided an outlet for a more general sense of public unease and dissatisfaction with the government of the time, which coincided with the loss of the country's mining industry (ibid.). Rau suggests that the public anger concerning how the authorities dealt with the Dutroux case fed into a general sense of disquiet and 'paranoia' over the role of the establishment and governmental authorities, which he notes can still be observed in contemporary Belgium society following other events of national trauma, such as the more recent terrorist attacks in Paris and Brussels (Gardner 2017). In their study, 'The Making of the White March: The Mass Media as a Mobilizing Alternative to Movement Organizations', Stefaan Walgrave and Jan Manssens (2000) cite polarising media discourse on the Dutroux case. This discourse might account for the disquiet Rau observes and specifically the perception that there was a widening 'gap' between the Belgium population and the judicial apparatus. Walgrave and Manssens note that unrelated political

DOI: 10.4324/9781003043072-5

affairs began to be linked with reporting on the Dutroux case. Unsolved child disappearances were retrieved from the archives and republished, alongside historic high-level political scandals that were re-told in this new context to conclude that '[t]he people are good, but the system is corrupt' (cited in Walgrave and Manssens 2000: 226). Notably, over the course of months in 1996, the media coverage of the case had shifted from a human-interest story to a political story (ibid.: 227).

Two decades later, Rau's play, entitled *Five Easy Pieces* (2016) echoes this shift, locating specific characters involved in the case – from police officers to Dutroux's family to the victims themselves – in relation to a different but related historical political context, beginning with the Democratic Republic of Congo's independence from Belgium colonial rule:

> It's about the big issues which lurk behind this very specific and utterly wretched Dutroux affair: the decline of a country, the national paranoia, the mourning, and the anger which followed the crimes. The production begins with Congo's declaration of independence and ends with the funerals of Dutroux's victims; in the background you perceive the disappearance of just about all the illusions which you might have lived under as a Belgian in recent decades: the illusion of safety, trust, freedom, and a future.
>
> (Rau in Press Kit 2016: 9)

Whilst there is no discernible evidence that the Dutroux case is of particular concern to children in Belgium, *Five Easy Pieces* – which was created by Rau and his company the International Institute for Political Murder (IIPM) – certainly mobilises a conversation about the significance of children performing a piece about paedophilia, rape, and child murder. In addition to the significance of using young performers to tell a theatrical version of this story, it is children playing adults which is at the centre of Rau's artistic interest:

> I had Belgium, I had children, so certainly we had to do a play about Dutroux. But in fact, this Dutroux story is really just an allegory to think about emotions, to think about mimicry, to think about what happens to us when we see children playing adults.
>
> (Rau 2017)

Rau is capitalising, I would argue, on the incongruence between child performer and adult character to explore an anti-illusion based theatricalisation of the Dutroux case, which echoes the loss of societal 'illusions' he notes above. Michael Shapiro's observation of child performers in satire and comedy applies to Rau's play despite the latter not drawing explicitly on comedic form: '[t]he point is not so much that they are children but they are conspicuously *not* identical with their characters. As a consequence, the medium becomes the message. The form winks at the content' (cited in States 1985 32). In *Five Easy Pieces*, Rau is similarly exploring an approach to incorporating children that 'by its very nature innoculates [sic] the audience *against* belief' (Shapiro cited in States 1985: 32), in an attempt to resist creating a single, faithful, hegemonic, illusory story. Whilst the fact that the performers are people we call children is highly significant in this work, it is partly this mismatch in iconicity between child performers and the adult characters they play, which protects the audience from falling for the illusions put forth in the work.

In this chapter I discuss three key ways trans*-age strategies are negotiated in *Five Easy Pieces*: through the use of metatheatre and how it intersects with readings of the performers' bodies; in the relationship between the live (children's) stage space and the virtual (adult's) screen space; and finally, in the young performers' interactions with the live feed that marks their performances as 'children playing adults' throughout. By drawing on this performance specifically, I intend to develop a complex understanding of trans*-age play as it operates in contemporary performance, beyond the assumption that the more dominant idea of age transvestism is inherently politically subversive as discussed in the previous chapter. This is contrary to what meanings have been previously asserted about 'transvestism'. For Marjorie Garber (1992), for example, gender transvestism is fundamentally subversive. As she outlines in her book *Vested Interests: Cross-Dressing and Cultural Anxiety* (1992), gender transvestism 'offers a critique of binary sex and gender distinctions' precisely because as a practice it 'denaturalizes, destabilizes and defamiliarizes sex and gender signs' (ibid.: 185). Whilst I would argue that age transvestism has the potential to reveal age-based norms and categories as socially constructed, this is not always guaranteed in performance. A close analysis of *Five Easy Pieces*, offers a particular approach to age-crossing that will later help to inform a new model for reading age, which accounts for the complexity of trans*-age strategies in performance by drawing on the insights of feminist and gender scholarship. The chapter asks: What is the political potential of age play as a performance strategy and what are the implications for thinking through adult-child crossing in a performance, particularly where the content is considered ethically difficult, as in Milo Rau's *Five Easy Pieces*?

Age-Crossing and Metatheatre in *Five Easy Pieces*

Referencing the title of Stravinsky's *Cinq pieces faciles* (1917) or *Five Easy Pieces*, a series of piano duets that Stravinsky composed for his children, Rau's play has a five-part structure that involves a series of pre-scripted 'lessons' for seven 8 to 13 years old performers.[1] When asked in an interview 'what are the children learning in your play?' Rau outlines the structure of the performance according to its five pieces/lessons, which suggests there is an intentional parallel between what the performers and what the characters learn:

> The first lesson is mimicry, how to play old and sick. The second is about biographical design: you are playing a policeman who is finding the murdered children, how do you construct his character on stage? The third is called 'essay on submission', and is about the relationship between actor and director. The fourth is about emotion: the children have to play parents

> who have lost their children, they have to cry on stage. Then comes the last lesson, rebellion: how to revolt against everything they have just been asked to do.
>
> (2017)

Before sharing these five lessons with the audience, *Five Easy Pieces* establishes itself as a metatheatrical work – a comment on theatre – from the outset. The opening scene involves the child performers *playing* performers participating in an audition process guided by the adult 'Director' (Peter Seynaeve). Seynaeve is also the actual assistant director for Rau's play outside of this fictional world. In addition to playing the Director onstage, the audience comes to know him as 'Marc Dutroux' through the narrative's subtext and at moments when the same performer plays Dutroux alongside other adult performers who only ever appear on a pre-recorded screen, intermittently, at the back of the stage. The metatheatrical framing is not only significant because the play draws an uncomfortable parallel connection between Dutroux's crimes and the unequal power dynamics of theatrical direction, as we shall see, but it is vital to how we understand the operation of age play in *Five Easy Pieces*. Indeed, children playing adults in the performance both facilitates and is implicated in the very questions of power and inequity that are generated by the thematic content.

The play's metatheatrical device creates the conditions for the children to shift between performing a version of 'themselves' as performers and playing (mainly) adult characters throughout the performance. In doing so, the children's demonstration and illustration of character, which follows the audition scene, draws the spectator's attention directly to age-crossing within the work. During the audition, Maurice, for example, is seen applying wrinkles and lines using exaggerated makeup in the opening scene whilst the Director asks him 'what do you think is the hardest thing for an actor to play?' to which he responds 'Something that is unlike yourself [...] playing someone old when you're young. Or acting that you're ill when you're healthy'.[2] Later, Maurice's desire to play 'old and ill' is realised when he takes on the role of Marc Dutroux's elderly father, Victor Dutroux. Polly is likewise asked a theatre-related question, which is immediately followed up by a question that moves into a much darker conversation about death and being asked to imagine the death of a child:

Director:	Aren't you scared of being onstage?
Polly:	No … a bit … I don't know
Director:	What are you scared of?
Polly:	I'm afraid of dying. I don't know why. And if I imagine what it would be like if my parents were dead <pause> No, I can't imagine it.
Director:	Ah you can't imagine it. Imagine you were a mother and your child was dead. What do you feel? … What do you feel? … Polly? What do you feel? …
Polly:	<silence>

The potentially violent dynamics of theatre direction are already beginning to be felt in this scene as an overly-familiar adult male director asks a very young female actress to imagine and then describe the feeling of losing someone close to her – a feeling she has just admitted scares her. Like Maurice, Polly in a later scene goes on to perform one of the parents of the Dutroux's victims, allowing the audience to call back to this earlier metatheatrical scene and consider what it means for Polly to play this role given the fear of loss she shares to the contrary. For the audience, Polly's age-crossing in the later scene, when she plays the victim's parent is therefore always haunted by her earlier admission of what scares her as an 'actor'. With this metatheatrical quality, age play functions here to heighten a double reading of Polly's later performance, inviting the spectator to constantly and consciously shift between the script of the adult character she is playing and the version of herself she presents as a performer, which she played in the audition scene. I use the term 'heighten' here with the assumption that children in performance are ordinarily read in relation to an adult-centric perception of them operating on a sliding scale of intention that has the effect of generating questions for the spectator such as: Did s/he intend to do that? Does s/he know what she's doing? A child performer's very presence in a theatrical environment is always haunted by questions of their consent and their capability to 'fully' understand their participation (see States 1985: 31) and Rau's work is no exception. So, whilst the presence of children in the theatrical space always already gestures towards this double reading between character and performer, albeit nuanced differently depending on the context, the metatheatrical framing of age-crossing here works to exacerbate what Bert O States might call the 'double vision' that children as performers invite (ibid.). This dual perspective of seeing both performer and character is then situated in relation to theatre as a form of directorial manipulation and control over the performer. In the same scene Winne's script, for example, captures both this dual perspective and directorial control when he is asked by the Director 'What does theatre mean to you?' to which he replies 'That's simple. Theatre is like puppetry but with real people instead of puppets'.

The result of this exchange is that the spectator is left guessing whether the words that Polly speaks are her own or those of a 'puppet' controlled by a hidden adult puppet master. This question concerning their capacity for intention and agency, hangs over every one of the young performers in *Five Easy Pieces* particularly when they speak as 'themselves' in their personas and especially as the play further blurs the boundaries of performer/persona by using their own names in these out of character moments. In these instances where the performers play themselves *as performers*, it is important to note that the text sounds scripted – or at least cleaned up and edited – in its delivery, which seems to intentionally suggest more involvement of an adult hand. We also know from the later 'reveals' of the performer and character connection that the script is not improvised here, for example, Maurice goes on to play Dutroux's father after announcing the challenges of 'playing old' in an earlier scene. However, the content assumes a verbatim quality and at times the dialogue is self-referential, for example, when Winne shares with the audience the story of an operation he had and then reveals an actual scar on his abdomen. Evidently, some of the script has been created from actual rehearsal conversations, which suggests a certain level of authorship on the part of the child performers, but its scripted quality nevertheless harks back to the question of directorial control that we are encouraged to ponder via the script's content. The form does more than wink at the content here.

Before the audition scene concludes with an invitation from the Director to all of the performers to identify a photograph of Marc Dutroux (which they do), the other performers are similarly questioned by the Director on issues relating to their age, talents, and skills as well as their thoughts on acting and theatre. If we take these words verbatim, I would agree with Debra Levine when she suggests that the metatheatrical form of *Five Easy Pieces* allows for the child performers to demonstrate their understanding of how information can be manipulated via theatrical and narrative convention whilst simultaneously illustrating that they are capable of absorbing 'sensitive' information about violence and death:

> By showing the audience the child actors' capacity to assimilate [...] knowledge through experiences of making, showing, and telling, Rau destabilizes arguments for patriarchal protectionism based on claims that all exposure to knowledge of human violence automatically traumatizes.
>
> (2017: 150)

When experiencing the work as a spectator, one is still concerned that the content is potentially harmful for the children and this inevitably creates some tension, but the young performers' skilful approach to characterisation and their direct address undermines and disrupts the 'innocent, in need of protection' gaze which an audience might be tempted to bestow upon these 'child actors'. Whilst Levine reads the responses of the performers as 'show[ing] each child's capacity for philosophical and emotional reflection, and how well they absorb, respond to, or deflect the question' (150) another significant but related function of the metatheatrical content is to foreground the bodies of the performers and, in some cases, *in relation to* the adult characters they then go on to play. Maurice, for example, tells the audience how he was born with pneumonia and would often be felt by his mother coughing *in utero*. When asked 'Can you show us how?' by the Director, Maurice coughs vigorously and then stops immediately when the Director calls 'thank you'. This same cough is heard intermittently during the scene when Maurice plays Dutroux's elderly father. The coughing is convincing and the spectator is now aware that Maurice can perform it *on cue*. Age-crossing functions here, therefore, as a demonstration of the performer's skill in portraying this adult character.

If the audience is tempted towards patriarchal protectionism, they are quickly jolted out of this mode of relation by Maurice's persistent interrupting cough as Victor Dutroux that calls back to the young performer himself who plays the scene as a matter of fact and without a whiff of trauma to himself. In another scene, our attention is drawn to Maurice's body when he spits onto the stage after a long coughing episode as Victor. Indeed, the audience is never allowed to settle, as any attempt to psychologise how Maurice 'the child' is feeling is undermined by his visible and audible ability to physically imitate. If he can imitate well, the audience is reminded that the performer they saw during the earlier audition scene could also be a performance: a deliberate and conscious performed version of himself too: a persona. Here, age-crossing with the support of metatheatre becomes a vehicle through which the audience is arguably denied the capacity to suspend their disbelief in relation to either the character of Victor Dutroux or the *persona of* the child performer that Maurice plays when seemingly out of character.

Another significant moment where a visible connection is made between the body of the child performer and that of their adult character is when Elle Liza, who is mixed-race, is asked by the Director 'do you consider yourself more as an African or a European?'. Taking issue with the question and thus foregrounding its reductive quality, Elle Liza concludes that 'In Africa I am white and in Belgium I am black'. In doing so she anticipates a racialising gaze that draws attention to perceptions of her skin colour and how her body is raced differently in particular geographical contexts. Her reluctance to answer the question on the Director's terms becomes significant when we witness her playing the only character of colour, Patrice Lumumba the first Prime Minister of the former Republic of Congo (now, the Democratic Republic of the Congo), during a scene that stages the ceremony that took place on 30 June 1960 to mark Congo's independence from Belgian colonial rule. In this scene, she delivers an edited version of Lumumba's original speech:

> *Lumumba (played by Elle Liza)*: Today we have won our struggle for independence. We have been taunted with irony and insults. We have been beaten in the morning in the afternoon and at night. Because we were negroes. We, whose bodies have suffered through colonial oppression we say to you: today it is all over! Now will come a time of freedom and mutual understanding.

Here, the connection between character and performer is largely based on her anatomy, what her skin colour might suggest about her 'race', and what Piet Defraeye refers to as 'an obvious nudge to Lumumba's ethnicity' (2020: 219). I would argue it is precisely through age-crossing that 'Elle Liza's material presence, and the roles in which she is cast, both signify "race" and postcolonial subjectivity' (Levine 2017: 152). For example, in the scenes where she reenacts Lumumba's speech and later his assassination, Elle Liza's body is framed to signify the historic racism of Belgium's colonial rule of the Congo, where Marc Dutroux spent his early years before moving to Belgium. These scenes of Elle Liza playing Lumumba – delivering his speech, experiencing torture, and then being murdered – are juxtaposed with moments when she plays a version of herself that voices an explicit postcolonial critique, taking issue with the Director's attempt to fix her as either African or European. Furthermore, when she sings John Lennon's iconic song 'Imagine' shortly after, its call for a border-free peaceful world is positioned firmly in relation to the adult character that ghosts her performance, Lumumba, and a wider political struggle for independence in the context of race-based oppression.

In this latter metatheatrical context, it is worth noting that Elle Liza is treated differently by the Director in comparison to the other young performers when playing her child performer persona. The Director impatiently asks for 'the first child please?' when summoning Elle Liza whilst referring to the other children by their names. He also appears to deliberately mishear her pronunciation on more than one occasion. In addition, he asks her directly and with a slightly interrogative tone 'do you know this man?' whilst showing her a photograph of Patrice Lumumba – a test of knowledge that is not inflicted on the other child performers during their 'audition' – and then he acts impressed when she identifies Lumumba. Most significantly, he abruptly interrupts Elle Liza's solo at the precise moment when she sings the first line of the second verse of Lennon's lyric: 'Imagine there's no countries'. Although there is a slight air of impatience in his interactions with all the young cast members at times, the racist overtones of the Director's interaction with Elle Liza frame his theatrical role as Director in terms of an unequal power relationship that is inclusive of race-based prejudice as well as ageism. The audience is therefore solicited to adopt a dual perspective that highlights both the proximity and distance between the character (Lumumba) and the performer (Elle Liza's persona); between a male adult 'African hero and freedom fighter' (as the narrator tells us) and a female, young mixed-race subject whose experiences of racism and discrimination – as suggested through these interactions with the Director – are both intimately bound up with and distinctly different from Lumumba's experiences at one and the same time. This dual perspective is exacerbated by the fact that 'there is no effort in finding a Lumumba simulacrum, neither in voice, nor in appearance' (Defraeye 2020: 219). The spectator can therefore shift effectively and perhaps more critically between meanings that are created through Elle's Liza's persona and those meanings available through her characterisation of Lumumba, precisely because there is very little physical likeness between them.

Another instance where the audience's attention is drawn to the performer's body brings us back to Winne's personal story of having an operation that left him with an abdominal scar. However, the connection of Winne's persona's story with his adult character (the Belgian King) is not dramaturgically exploited in his case. In his own words as 'Winne' and in a rather neutral delivery, he tells us he was given a 'dead child's liver', drawing another loose but noticeable parallel between his own anatomy and referencing the abuse and violence done to the deceased children and specifically their bodies at the hands of Dutroux. Alongside Maurice's story of childhood pneumonia, Winne's experience makes visible the physical and emotional traumas that he, as a child, has already suffered. These life experiences serve to undermine or at least challenge any uneasiness a spectator might feel about the children experiencing trauma as a direct result of narrativising the Dutroux case. The metatheatrical framing thus makes available and foregrounds a reading that the bodies of the child performers actually carry a history of their past experiences and, in some cases, near-death experiences, which, in turn, problematises any simplistic reading of these young people as blank slate subjects who are neutral until 'contaminated' by 'adult' themes that are deemed beyond their age.

Beside the Adult Double

Although most of the action in *Five Easy Pieces* is live, a screen at the back of the stage plays intermittently and features pre-recorded footage of adult performers playing the same characters that are performed by the children in the live space. For example, there is both an adult performer and a child performer playing the Belgian King, Patrice Lumumba, police officers, crime scene investigators, and the parents of one of Dutroux's victims. This dual space of 'live children' and 'pre-recorded adults' highlights age-crossing in the work as a performance strategy that *Five Easy Pieces* is consciously invested in, not just in terms of a relationship between child performer and adult character but also in the relationship between child performer and adult performer. In simple terms, we are invited as an audience to shift between and compare the 'adult' we see on screen and the 'child' we see in the live space. What is most significant to note is that the adult performers bear a strong resemblance to the child performers, which is established in the very first scene during a close-up of all the adults on the screen. Rather than emphasising a potential familial connection or pointing towards their adult future selves, the physical resemblances help to position the filmic performance of the adults as a 'copy' of the children's performances, as I will explain.

This synchronous performance between the live child performer and the mediated adult performer occurs in all but one of the five pieces that structure the play. In *Piece 1: Father and Son*, the backstage screen shows adult performers enacting a moment from the declaration of independence ceremony, whilst the children play out the same scene in the live space. This is followed by a street scene with Victor Dutroux's character walking into what we presume is his apartment and passing a busker playing the accordion, which is performed both live by the young performers and onscreen by adults. In *Piece II What is Acting* Willem along with other cast members performs a live version of the crime scene re-enactment that took place during Dutroux's trial, against the backdrop of the same pre-recorded scene being played out with adult performers in an outside wooded area. Later, two of the performers play the parents of one of Dutroux's victims alongside their virtual adult counterparts in *Piece IV Alone in the Night* and, finally, the funeral of one of the child victims of Dutroux is similarly enacted on both the live stage and in the mediated space in *Piece V: What are Clouds*. In all of these examples, there is some attempt to sync up the gestures, movement, and action of the child performers in the live space with the adult performers on the screen but there is no attempt at simulacra or to hide any differences that emerge in their simultaneous performances. Indeed, the differences between the live and the screen action are marked, precisely because there is no obvious desire to achieve perfect synchronicity.

For spectators familiar with CAMPO's previous work, the convention of 'live children' and 'virtual adults' in *Five Easy Pieces* strongly resembles a performance that CAMPO (formerly known as Victoria Theatre) collaborated on some years earlier entitled *Übung* (2001) by Josse De Pauw. In this work, live child performers between 9 and 15 years old play adults whom they see on a film screen behind them. Unlike the children in Rau's play, however, the young performers in *Übung* are aiming for synchronicity with their upstage virtual adult counterparts, visibly copying them from television screens placed downstage. Indeed, the child performers in De Pauw's work lip-sync, wear identical costumes, and speak the dialogue of the adult performers, which renders the children's performance a derivative ghosting of the 'original' adults' onscreen performance. The staging of *Five Easy Pieces,* on the other hand, does not imply a hierarchy in favour of the adult-led filmed performance as the primary source of action. Whilst the adult performers and young performers in *Five Easy Pieces* wear similar costumes, the dialogue is instead nearly always delivered by the performers we call children in these moments of shared live and virtual action, putting auditory and visual emphasis on the young performers in the live space. As a spectator of *Five Easy Pieces*, I am not expected to arrive at the conclusion that 'the children are copying the adults' but rather, in a counterintuitive move, I experience the adults as uncannily copying the performers called children even though the adults are obviously pre-recorded. This feeling that the adults are doing the copying is supported by a metatheatrical framework which foregrounds the young performers and is not afforded to the onscreen adult performers, therefore, drawing closer focus and attention to the younger live performers. Within this framework, we are actively encouraged to invest in the people called children onstage as *both* performers *and* characters. Furthermore, the visual focus placed on the young performers via live feed camera close-ups, and the slightly off-sync moments where the adults' gestures are slightly delayed, positions the virtual adults as secondary, almost parasitic figures as the narrative unfolds. Lumumba's speech, for example, begins with a pre-recorded voice that is out of sync with the female adult actor it appears to be originating from onscreen, until Elle Liza swiftly takes over the audio with a live delivery of the speech. The effect of this asynchronous vocal moment is that her adult counterpart appears to be lip-syncing Elle Liza's live text.

Another deviation from *Übung* that sheds further light on the operation of age-crossing in *Five Easy Pieces,* is that the child performers in the former work are not participating in any psychological investment in their characters. For *Übung* the child performers are simply seen imitating the adult performers in the moment of performance in stark contrast to their adult counterparts who are entirely invested in a process of psychological realism (Quick 2006: 155). For Andrew Quick, the difference in the children's and the adult's approach to characterisation in *Übung* has the effect of bringing attention to the children's improvisation and the unscripted exchange of glances that they share with one another as they try to work out and mimic the gestures they see on film. Whilst there are moments of improvisation, unscripted exchanges, and unexpected gestures in *Five Easy Pieces*, each performer's approach illustrates fidelity to an imagined or archived reality of the characters they play when the live feed camera begins to roll. For example, Maurice's delivery as Victor Dutroux is slow, considered, concentrated, and his dialogue is psychologically driven, even as the Director (Syenaeve) notes Maurice's self-applied makeup is 'a bit over the top'. Maurice's approach to characterisation suggests that he might have spent some time watching video footage of Victor Dutroux himself in preparation for the part, rather than imitating the adult performer who plays the same character on the backscreen (as in *Übung)*. In his monologue as Victor Dutroux – when Maurice is not accompanied by his adult screen-based doppelganger – there is audible vocal fry present in Maurice's delivery and his gestures and speech are largely congruent, which is suggestive of a representational rather than demonstrative approach to performing his character. Nevertheless, the performance is always ghosted by the child performer doing the work of performing and the metatheatrical form always ensures that there is no danger of suspending disbelief. Although Maurice's makeup suggests a highly stylised aesthetic will follow, his performance is actually measured and indicative of speech and movement one might ordinarily find in such a domestic setting. His characterisation is also consistent with the realist set he performs in. A leather armchair, an antique lamp, and a blanket draped over the chair imply a 'typical old person's flat' as Winne comments during the scene's setup. Maurice's actions as Victor Dutroux are also underscored by a realist soundtrack of birds and traffic which Polly confirms is a faithful representation of where the man himself lives: 'Dutroux's father's flat is in a very busy street with lots of cars and buses' she says before the scene begins. This lack of dependence on their recorded adult doppelgangers and the child performers' ability to portray complex, three-dimensional characters, elevates the child performers' storytelling, positioning the (onscreen) adult performers *beside them*, rather than in a hierarchical relationship to them. The adult performers, it appears, are simply there to tell another version of the story alongside the young performers.

Unlike *Übung*, the way in which the adult performers are filmed and the limited time we see them onscreen renders their characters somewhat two dimensional; a less developed copy of the rich and complex performances given by their counterparts, the live, young performers. This limited screen time for the adults reads as a conscious dramaturgical decision and one which is shored up by the fact that the young performers do not overtly acknowledge the screen itself, therefore, reducing its potential signifying power. Similarly, the children are not negotiating the film in the moment of performance, as they do in *Übung*, a title which aptly translates as 'exercise' and 'practice'. Indeed, we do not see an exercise or practice in *Five Easy Pieces* when it comes to the child performers' relationship to the screen. That work has already been done in rehearsals. Neither are the child performers seen 'processing the information that the film presents to them' (Quick 2006: 155). Rather, the film seems to be processing them, I would argue, with the effect being that the spectator is not encouraged to see them as negotiating a pre-existing 'adult world' on screen (Quick 2006: 157). Again, since 'imitation' is not taking place in a 'moment by moment response to the screen', it is almost as if the adults onscreen are instead negotiating the young performers' world. Age-crossing is not simply 'adults playing children' here, it is the adults' performances that are approximated through the children's performances in a way that flips the adult-centric perspective observed in *Übung*. In this regard, I read the filmic performances of the adults in *Five Easy Pieces* as failing to repeat and imitate the children's staging of a live version of this story. The adults' performance, instead, sits beside the people called children's performance as it defamiliarising other; disrupting linear time and reminding us not to become too psychologically invested, especially when – as the persistent discontinuity between the screen and stage action reminds us – there are multiple ways to tell this story.

The only 'piece' that neither adheres to the live and onscreen convention nor the child-playing-adult device is 'Piece III: Essay on Submission', a scene for which *Five Easy Pieces* is often known because of its controversial content. In this scene the onstage Director asks the visibly youngest female performer Rachel, who is about to play one of Dutroux's imprisoned victims, to take off her top 'like in rehearsals'. With its paedophilic overtones, it is unsurprising that this moment and the playing of one of the victims by 8 years old performer Rachel Dedain has often been mentioned in news media reviews of Rau's play (Al-Othman 2017, Green 2019). It certainly makes for difficult viewing. Not only does this scene break the convention of the pre-recorded screen featuring adults ghosting the children's actions, but it is also the only piece in the whole play that does not involve a child playing the role of an adult character. Herein lies the issue. The audience is solicited to test out their earlier assumption: that all these child performers (including Rachel) are 'performing', even whilst they present a version of themselves. However, to acknowledge that the child performers are performing even in those moments when they play themselves is perhaps only possible because of the legibility of age-crossing, by which I mean not just children playing adults but young performers *showing* playing adults.

When the distinction between 'child' and 'adult' is already fairly clear – for example when the other performers play a Belgian King, a police officer, an old man, and a prime minister – the spectator can shift between performer and character with relative ease. However, here the audience is being asked to consider whether Rachel is capable of performing a version of herself that is non-consenting, which she signifies through her silence and reluctance to comply with the Director's initial instruction. I imagine this also brings into doubt for some spectators her ability to play a character that is based on a sexual abuse and rape victim. The difficulty of reading her initial non-consent as an intended 'performance' is compounded by her anatomically young age, her closeness in age to the child victim she goes on to play, and the (performance of the) adult/child inequitable power dynamics in operation between her and the onstage Director. In the absence of the adult 'other' character on which age-crossing depends, the distinction between performer and character is blurred so much so that where the real/representational and real/fictional begin and end is undoubtedly at its most ambiguous.

As a result of this break with convention, the audience is asked to become more aware of a child playing a child (Rachel) and an adult playing an adult onstage (Peter):

> I always thought it was strange that, when you see children's theatre, you can feel there is an adult director. But he's [sic] not on stage. That is why we have my assistant director, Peter [Syenaeve], on stage as my alter ego, the performance coach. You can see him leading the children more and more into a dark space of paedophilic play. For example, he asks one of the young girl actors to get naked to play a scene. He says, 'but you did it in the rehearsal,

> why don't you do it now? You have to do it, that's how Dutroux did it'. This is the reality of theatre, this is what theatre directors do. But when you do it with children, you understand the violence of direction. I wanted the play to reflect this: that the strategies of a director are the strategies of a criminal.
> (Rau 2017)

In this moment, the usually invisible adult director behind the children's theatre that Rau speaks of here, becomes the absent presence of Rau himself, Marc Dutroux, and a symbol of *any* (adult) director through Peter Syenaeve's character. The potential violence of theatrical direction is palpable. The audience is reminded that even as the child performers seem to be exercising some agency in their creative decisions, the improvised, scripted, and directed aspects of the work take place in a 'rule-bound space' (Quick 2006: 153) that is, I would add, a visibly *adult-driven* rule-bound space. Furthermore, the adult that commands this space is available to be experienced by the audience not only through this on-going physical presence of an adult director but in at least two other ways: via an adult male narrator's voiceover that governs the overarching narrative as well as through the live feed camera. Let us now turn to the live feed as it plays an important role in exercising control over meaning-making by archiving, recording, and attempting to fix a single perspective despite the layers of meaning being generated on stage. In doing so, the live feed adds some further complexity to the operation of age play as we experience it through the adult character/child persona relationship.

The Live Feed

The play's driving narrative, which also organises stage space and time, is that the young performers and the Director are making a black and white documentary-style film of these 'five easy pieces' via a live feed that is streamed to a backstage screen. This structure allows for a number of preparatory 'setting up' and transition scenes to be established before and after the camera starts and stops rolling. As already discussed in relation to the audition scene that opens the play, such scenes offer space for the performers to adopt their personas and share experiences that, again, remind us that they are complex humans who have witnessed more than a patriarchal protectionist gaze would like to admit with its rendering of children as 'innocent, in need of protection'. During the setup for 'Essay on Submission', for example, Rachel asks the Director how to play dead and after he offers her some advice, she follows up with 'when I was small I once saw a dead person [...] it was really creepy'. This then gives the Director permission to ask the rest of the cast 'what's the creepiest thing you've ever seen?' to which Winne says 'I once saw a film where a man kissed a corpse'. Another example of the performers' challenge to the patriarchal protectionist gaze by communicating their complex human thoughts and feelings is when Elle Liza shares the ambiguity she feels when the physical boundaries of a familial relationship are unintentionally breached: 'I find it creepy when my mother kisses me on the cheek but accidently kisses me on the mouth'. These admissions are sometimes delivered by the direct address which, at times, awkwardly emphasises their scripted quality but, on the whole, intensifies the assumption that the young performers are referring to encounters they have actually experienced. Again, the dialogue sounds like verbatim material, albeit edited, which is taken from the creative process. However, as this material is not filmed by the live feed camera, it holds a supplementary status to the character-based work that is foregrounded by the camera's live feed. The lack of filmic framing of the performers' personal admissions when in their personas has the effect of giving weight to these moments where they resist being reduced to two-dimensional images of the innocent child in need of protection.

These moments of setting up for their own performance-to-camera character-based scenes again give space for the audience to become familiar with each young performer's persona in a way that impacts how we then go on to perceive their character. For example, Willem appears to be making choices in the moment of performance (or perhaps the other cast members are more accustomed to hiding these choices) and he starts playing for laughs when delivering some of his lines. The improvisatory quality of these off-camera moments only emphasises how well-rehearsed Willem's performance is during the live feed content when he plays a police officer investigating the Dutroux case. Following a couple of false starts where he corpses, for instance, Willem shifts into character with an intentional and deliberate physicality. He assumes a direct gaze to the camera and his delivery is focused and specific. His performance to the camera, along with some evidence of performer training, has the effect of fictionalising the character of the police officer. Even whilst the black and white screen and dialogue suggest a documentary-in-the-making, the live feed performances read as though they are actors' *reconstructions* of documentary-based interviews because they are shown to be mediated through a camera that roles in front of the performers. It is not surprising then that, according to Rau, the performers also perceive the actual adult figures they are playing as fictional characters:

> Every child knows more or less what [Dutroux] did. But it's more like in a fairytale, and they also played it like this. It's like if I'm asking you to play Richard III. You will not think, Oh fuck, I will be traumatised, he's such a monster. When the children understood that we could meet the father of Dutroux – who lives more or less in front of the theatre where we rehearsed – it was quite funny and strange for them.
>
> (Rau 2017)

The live feed itself becomes a mechanism through which some psychological distance from the characters seems to be maintained *by* and perhaps *for* the performers, which resonates with Rau's assertion that the performers already relate to the figures in the Dutroux story as fictional characters.

The live feed is introduced throughout the play by a performer who holds a film clapper and shouts '*Five Easy Pieces*, Scene [X] take one' followed by the universally recognisable prompt 'action' by the Director. Marking the *demonstration* of character via the live feed draws on a well-established tradition within epic theatre; the use of Brechtian verfremdungseffekt to reveal the fictional lens through which, in this case, *Five Easy Pieces* is constructed (Brecht 1964). Verfremdung – a process of theatrical defamiliarisation that encourages the spectator to see something supposedly natural anew and thus to exercise a critical eye upon it – is being played out here in a number of ways: the hyper-visible use of the camera onstage highlights a particular perspective on the events to draw attention to their constructedness; both the social attitudes encoded in the play and the approaches to acting and directing that attempt to maintain illusion become available for critique via the off-camera and metatheatrical content already discussed; and the historical positioning of each adult character is situated in contrast to the child performer's own self-referential presence within the real time of the performance to deny the audience an illusory identification with the characters. The Director, for example, interrupts the live feed to express his frustration, albeit in a light-hearted tone, with Willem's (or perhaps Rau's) move towards an arguably more psychologically invested portrayal, denying in turn the spectator any attempt to psychologise and therefore empathise with the character of the police officer:

Director: Willem? Keep to the point please.
Willem: (enjoying the Director's discomfort) But the audience needs precise background information about the character
Director: Yes, but it's a play about the Dutroux affair, not a play about the problems of a policeman and his hippy father.

Indeed, one could argue that age-crossing always already contains within it the same distancing capacity as Brechtian defamiliarisation. This is because the mimetic quality of the young performer who plays an adult is always unstable, since the performer's body can never faithfully resemble the adult character to which it refers and always marks its difference from it. A child playing a police officer leading a murder investigation that had already been widely criticised in the Belgium-based context in which the performance first premiered, certainly denaturalises a simple reading of the police officer as either part of a corrupt law enforcement agency or as an individual officer simply doing his duty (for better or worse). However, it is a combination of factors that guarantee Verfremdung's denaturalisation of the status quo and not just a mismatch in iconicity between performer and character that draws attention to the representational work of the theatrical sign system *as* a sign system here. In Willem's case, for example, the prompt for the spectator to look anew is possible not just because of the clear anatomical mismatch with the adult police officer he plays but for a number of reasons: the live feed that marks the break from a corpsing performer to a serious and authoritative character foregrounds the character as part of a representational economy where both performer and character are historically contingent. We see Willem's character is subject to socio-historical circumstances that have the potential to change particularly when in his role as a police officer he says: 'Belgian police don't have a very good name, to put it mildly. They call us incompetent, at the very least'. Moments of his dialogue, for example 'as a child I often played burglar and policeman' draw attention to the duality of a child playing a police officer and dismantle a linear progression of time in a way that is jarring and interrupts any investment with the character that may reinforce the hegemonic and/or monolithic representation of the establishment he represents within this specific context. Willem's playful, non-serious delivery as the police officer is also somewhat unexpected and allows from some critical distance as a spectator, especially given the seriousness of his role (the lead on a murder investigation) and, at times, the difficult content of his dialogue.

So, whilst age-crossing or what is often described as 'age transvestism' lends itself to the technique of defamiliarisation, it does not inherently participate in denaturalising that which 'ideology makes seem normal, acceptable, inescapable' (Diamond 1988: 85). One need only think about the way in which beauty pageants participate in age transvestism – people we call children playing adults or adult roles – to know that the visibility of age-crossing does not always guarantee critique. Rather, different theatrical elements – including but not limited to the distancing effect of the live feed, the metatheatrical reference to the performers' anatomies, the lip-syncing adults onscreen, and the children's shifting performance modes – are working together to encourage the spectator to look afresh at what is taken for granted. Looking afresh is invited even if the spectator's first encounter with the Dutroux case is via this play, as might have been the case for some audience members during the tour run beyond Belgium. The incongruent nature of the child performer/adult character relationship does, however, create the conditions of possibility for the spectator to 'see' the character here as a demonstration of their behaviour rather than losing oneself in the illusion, as it were. In particular, placing Brechtian theatrical theory in dialogue with *Five Easy Pieces* illuminates how the young performer is made available to be read as a historically-situated subject. In her intertextual reading of Brecht's much discussed theory in terms of its feminist potential in performance, Elin Diamond helpfully points out that 'the Brechtian Gestus: a gesture, a word, an action, a tableau by which [...] the social attitudes encoded in the playtext become visible to the spectator [...] is effected by a historical subject who supplements (rather than disappears into) the production of meaning' (1988: 90). This begs the question: can the child in performance ever be this historical 'subject' who is seen and heard as authoring and interpreting meaning whilst they create it? *Beyond Innocence* suggests that they can, but only via specific strategies that intentionally disturb and disrupt a patriarchal protectionist gaze.

That some spectators were unable to separate Rachel's role as a performer from the character she plays suggests that the critical, passionate detachment that Brecht sought is not always possible, and perhaps particularly difficult to achieve when young performers play children. That moment, when the Director asks her to remove her top 'like in rehearsals', is deliberately ambiguous, blurring the distinction between performer and character, and subsequently for some spectators could raise ethical concerns for the performer's well-being and consent in a way that arguably overrides the spectator's capacity to recognise Rachel's own ability to understand, interpret, and create meaning *as a subject*. This means that the Gestus of the scene is rendered elusive, potentially lost in this moment of slippage between 'the real' and 'the representational', even whilst the social attitude encoded in the text (i.e. that theatrical direction shares in the violence of manipulation and abuse we see in the Dutroux case) is embodied in the scene itself. The Gestus is perhaps only ever realised if the spectator recognises Rachel as a subject who, like the spectator 'becomes historicized – in motion and at risk, but also free to compare the actor/character's signs to 'what is close and proper to [herself] – her material conditions, her politics, her skin, her desires' (Diamond 1988: 90). For me, Rachel is given some space within the play to show awareness of her material conditions particularly in the moments leading up to that scene when, as her persona, she responds to the Director's question 'Rachel, would you kiss another actor onstage?' with a very deliberate and funny retort 'Kissing, me and you? Now? No way!' Whilst Rachel's material situatedness does not make the scene feel any less uncomfortable, my particular reading here is a person called a child who is capable of playing not only a character but also performing a version of herself. It is the performer's capacity to play a persona that creates resistance against the hegemonic temptation to get emotionally invested in the 'idea' of her as a child who is not capable of understanding the complex layers of this scene. In short, I think we are invited to recognise her subjecthood.

Diamond goes on to argue that '[i]f feminist theory sees the body as culturally mapped and gendered, Brechtian historicisation insists that this body is not a fixed essence but a site of struggle and change' (Diamond 1988: 89). What focusing on age-crossing in *Five Easy Pieces* reveals is the way in which 1. the body of the person we call a child needs to work hard (and perhaps harder than most adult bodies) to be *seen* as culturally mapped and gendered and 2. the body of the person we call a child is not often *visible* or made legible as a site for struggle and change, beyond the obvious physical transformations that are suggested by, for example, an explicitly 'pre-pubescent' or 'teenage' anatomy in performance. There are moments in *Five Easy Pieces* that emphasise the young performers' bodies as being culturally mapped, Elle Liza's racialised body for example, as well as sites for change when we hear about Winne's operation. However, the play only takes us so far because the young performers are largely scripted or edited from an adult perspective. Even in the play's final moment of 'revolt' – which I will come back to in the closing of this chapter – the action is continually ghosted by adult direction, which is keenly felt throughout the performance and far exceeds the 'adult' control and presence of the character of the Director that intentionally plays on the spectator's knowledge that there is an absent director (Rau). Following the complex analytical work that feminist theory and Brechtian historicisation might bring to our understanding of age-crossing in *Five Easy Pieces*, but which has been afforded largely to the adult body in performance until now, let us move to the question of how we navigate this terrain of age play and children's bodies in contemporary performance. As we do so, it is important to bear in mind the particular challenges of visibility for the people we call children and their bodies to be read in performance as culturally mapped, gendered, and fluid subjects.

From Gender to Age: The Politics of Age Play

In my analysis of *Five Easy Pieces*, I have mainly been focusing on age-crossing as a strategy for exploring performer/character and adult/child relationships both in terms of form and content. In *Five Easy Pieces,* we have seen the double signification between the perceived age of the performer and age-related identities being played out in the theatrical exploitation of the distinction between the anatomy of the performers as children and the adult characters they perform. This distinction is most clearly reinforced where the age of the performer is notably different from the adult they are playing. For example, when Maurice plays the role of Marc Dutroux's elderly father, the age distinction is emphasised by his youthful body in opposition to his grey wig, a slow-moving gait, walking stick, lowered and cracked voice, and the exaggerated makeup he is seen applying to his face in the opening scene to suggest wrinkles. Similarly, when Willem plays the role of a policeman the audience is not only invited to read back and forth between child performer and adult character but also between child performer and police officer, a law enforcement role that is, of course, never available for a child to socially inhabit outside the realms of fictional 'dress up' type play. On a fundamental level, when Rau suggests that '[w]hen a child puts on a policeman's uniform they do it in a way that makes you understand the absurdity of all uniforms' (Rau in Gardner 2017) we can assume he is acknowledging that the identification of the performer as 'a child' is available to the spectator as an indicator of their rough anatomical age. To nuance Rau's claim with the recognition that these are 'adult' uniforms is important, however, since the act of seeing a child in a school uniform within the boundaries of theatrical performance does not have this same absurdist resonance.

However, the perceived anatomical age of the performers, especially as suggested by their bodies, the metatheatrical framing even as it is offered in marketing or press material, is important because it gives the performers, or perhaps Rau, permission to create further ambiguity in relation to performer/character relationships, especially as the play progresses. Polly, for example, questions 'If I kiss someone, is it Polly or is it her character that's kissing?' We later see Polly as the mother of a child victim briefly kissing the father, who is played by Pepjin, in a moment where they perform comforting each other and sharing grief. Here, we are encouraged to recall the earlier question that Polly posed, about the distinction between the real and the fictional, the performer and the character, in a way that is complicated by the age that is suggested by the very materiality of both Polly and Pepjin's bodies before and during the act of kissing. In other words, it is significant to the reading of this moment that she and Pepjin are visibly older than many of the other cast members. The audience's assumptions about their anatomical age cannot be taken for granted, even whilst the performance does not thematically exploit the anatomical age of these performers in the way it does with Rachel's visibly 'younger' body. Polly and Pepjin's anatomical ages are nevertheless a component of meaning-making here because, against the backdrop of onscreen adult actors kissing one another, the spectator's perceptions of what it might feel like to be directed to kiss another performer whilst approaching or during one's teenage years comes to the fore. Furthermore, the spectator might become self-aware of their own gaze as they empathise with a young person's feelings of being watched and seen by an audience during an intimate moment, and what this could imply about one's sexuality at an age where questions of sexuality are deemed socially appropriate to articulate in a way they are not for 'children' of Rachel's age. Indeed, the fact that Polly and Pepjin's scene follows on from Rachel's scene raises questions about our assumptions concerning what age we deem appropriate for the people we call children to be directed in these more intimate actions. The spectator is encouraged to reflect: is asking teenagers to kiss on stage more socially acceptable than asking a younger, pre-pubescent female child to remove her top in front of an audience? In short, how the spectator perceives the anatomical age of the performer is extremely important to their reading of and experiential engagement with the work.

Age-crossing can problematise one's assumption of the anatomical age of a performer we call a child because it necessarily involves the performance of age, which may reinscribe or challenge the age-based norms associated with the presumed or known age of the performer. The quotation marks that signal that age is being performed in *Five Easy Pieces* range from the theatrical walls surrounding the play that literally tell us 'this is a performance'; to the references to dressing up that signal an infant's world of imaginative play; to the parallels with puppetry that are drawn throughout and mark a distinction between adult as puppet master and child as a puppet; as well as to the theatrical devices of Brechtian epic theatre (metatheatre, direct address, demonstrative albeit complex characterisation) that permit the development of the young performers' personas in parallel with the characters they play. The bodies of the young performers (as well as those of the adults) onstage are interpellated by these theatrical and performance references and devices in a way that constitutes a performance of age that offers some consistency with or deviation from age-based norms. On the whole, however, I would argue that *Five Easy Pieces* maintains the status quo where age is concerned. The casting of each of the performers in certain kinds of (mainly) adult roles on the basis of their anatomical age reinforces normative age representation and reaffirms age-based norms that are constructed around assumed differences between 'adult' and 'child'. Willem and Winne, for example, are visibly young boys who appear to be around 8 to 10 years old and play a king and a police officer, which is consistent with the type of play and roles that one might engage with at their age. Maurice who reads as roughly 10 to 12 years old plays a more specific character as Dutroux's father, although Maurice's motivation for playing him is framed for the audience as his fascination with playing 'old', as a type, rather than playing a more developed character. Again, this is consistent with societal expectations for his age, that he can 'handle' a more complex role.

Similarly, the older performers are given the arguably more nuanced roles of the parents of the victim and the layered figure of Lumumba as freedom fighter/activist/prime minister. For older performers, these roles are in keeping with expectations regarding the level of skill and experience they bring to the role that is (supposedly) not available to the younger performers. Notably, the youngest child is the only performer given the role of a child, although the type of role she plays (a child victim) challenges expectations around the appropriateness of that role for a child of her age. Furthermore, the unequitable relationship of power between the adult director and child performers parallels the thematic thread the play explores of puppet master and puppets to suggest a familiar hierarchy of power and authority based on young/old, child/adult age norms: lacking autonomy/autonomous, submissive/dominant, follower/leader, and controlled/controller. However, because the play has very visible theatrical quotation marks placed around it through the metatheatrical framing, this binarised hierarchical relationship is marked, and therefore more available for critique as a relationship that is not to be taken at face value by the spectator. Although it is worth pointing out that this potential critique does not, in turn, affect the performance of age-based norms, which remain consistent with the perceived anatomical age of the performers and are maintained throughout the play.

Whether the normative hierarchical relationship of adult/child is reversed and/or challenged during the course of the performance, therefore, is questionable. Even in Piece V *What Are Clouds?*, which Rau frames as 'rebellion: how to revolt against everything they have just been asked to do', the young performers are still confined to the adult rule-bound world of both the offstage director and the on-stage Director. Following the funeral, Piece V sees the performers return to their personas and begin to engage in an argument about the Belgium police where they express a range of perspectives about the authorities being slow to respond, corrupt, 'idiotic', or just not as well equipped to deal with 'clever and international' gangsters. We also hear more about the creative process from Willem 'I found it difficult. A huge number of lines. But I like wearing a uniform' and from Rachel: 'I would like to have changed a few things. But because it all happened in real life, that wasn't possible'. The performers' personal thoughts and preferences continue with Winne being given permission by the Director to fulfil his wish to be shot dead in his role as the King, whilst Elle Liza has her request to sing *Stay* by Rhianna granted whilst the shooting of the King happens. The play ends with a monologue by Polly who talks about the narrative of a film she saw in which an adult puppet teaches a young puppet how to play a range of emotions and actions (sorrow, joy, listening, giving speeches, playing dead). When the young puppet, who has never seen the outside of the theatre asks the older puppet 'what are clouds?', Polly's dialogue makes a clear comparison between Dutroux's plans and the enclosed theatrical institution within which the children are performing:

> *Polly*: [The news media] said that in his cell, Marc Dutroux was making plans for an underground city in the passages of the old coal mines. A city only for children. I think that's the most terrible thing that can happen to you. Never seeing the sky again.

Whilst, again, a sense of authorship is communicated through these personal stories, the scripted delivery somewhat undermines the performers' ownership of the words and so the capacity for the performers to work against normative expectations of their age is limited to the playscript and the bounds of the theatrical world Rau has established as well as the assumptions of anatomical age brought to bear by the spectator.

Overall, the use of age-crossing within *Five Easy Pieces* does not open up critique of how age intersects with race, gender, sexuality, and ability, and yet it still depends on these intersections for its meaning-making, especially where these meanings are received as relationships of power between adult and child. To this extent, *Five Easy Pieces* draws attention to the limited practice of age transvestism, or what I nuance here as age-crossing, more generally in that it depends on the maintenance of age-based norms of performers and/or personas and/or characters. The play's version of age transvestism as crossing only takes us so far in this regard, even whilst its metaphorical references to the bodies of the performers, use of out of sync adult onscreen doppelgangers, distancing live feed, and young performers whose shifting performance modes do shed light on the usefulness of defamiliarisation to invite some critique. There is only one example of gender-crossing within the age play we see in *Five Easy Pieces* through the figure of Elle Liza a female performer playing the male adult Patrice Lumumba. Whilst the political potential of age-crossing as a performance strategy is signalled in *Five Easy Pieces*, especially when it is marked in a way that makes visible a child's complex historically situated subjecthood and dismantles a patriarchal protectionist gaze, it is limited because it fails to fully attend to how the intersecting identities of the people we call children might be made legible and can play an important role in how we read 'age' in its complexity within performance.

In the following chapter, I analyse Belgium-based HETPALEIS' *The Hamilton Complex* in order to develop a more capacious approach to reading children and to recognise the breadth of trans*-age play in performance by attending to the overlooked relationship between children's bodies and intersectional identity politics. An intersectional methodology that unpacks how the production and reception of performance operates to ideologically police the bodies of young performers – ensuring that they align with the social norms associated with a particular age, race, gender, and ability – feels urgent as a means of considering how we performatively resist norms that are oppressive and work to maintain the marginalisation of the people we call children.

Note

1 The child performers are Elle Liza Tayou, Polly Persyn, Rachel Dedain, Willem Loobuyck, Pepjin Loobuyck, Winne Vanacker, Maurice Leerman, herein referred to by their first names.
2 Script by Milo Rau/IIPM accessed via English surtitles on the video documentation of the performance at Kunstenfestivaldesartes Brussels supplied by kind permission of CAMPO (Rau, Milo and CAMPO, 2016).

References

Al-Othman, Hannah (2017) 'Director Behind Marquis De Sade Play Featuring Down's Syndrome Youths Brings New Show to Paris About Infamous Belgian Child Killer Which he Admits "Could be Seen as Paedophilia"', *Daily Mail*, 15 March: https://www.dailymail.co.uk/news/article-4317178/Director-stages-infamous-Belgian-child-killer.html

Brecht, Bertolt (1964) *Brecht on Theatre: The Development of an Aesthetic*, ed. and trans. John Willett. New York: Hill & Wang.
Defraeye, Piet (2020) 'Lumumba on Stage: X Times a Murder' in Matthias de Groof (ed.) *Lumumba in the Arts*, Belgium: Leuven University Press.
Diamond, Elin (1988) 'Brechtian Theory/Feminist Theory: Toward a Gestic Feminist Criticism', *TDR: The Drama Review*, 32 (1): 82–94.
Garber, Marjorie (1992) *Vested Interests: Cross-Dressing and Cultural Anxiety*, New York and London: Routledge.
Gardner, Lyn (2017) 'It's Supposed to be Funny': Young Actors Perform Play About Child Killer Marc Dutroux, *The Guardian*, 22 March: https://www.theguardian.com/stage/2017/mar/22/young-actors-play-child-killer-marc-dutroux-five-easy-pieces-milo-rau (accessed 18 June 2019).
Green, Jesse (2019). "An Unnerving Alliance of Children and Art." *New York Times*, 9 March: https://go.gale.com/ps/i.do?p=ITOF&u=lmu_web&id=GALE|A577633561&v=2.1&it=r&sid=bookmark-ITOF&asid=f131a017 (accessed 21 June 2021).
Levine, Debra (2017) 'Not Just Adult Entertainment: Milo Rau and CAMPO's Collaborative Five Easy Pieces', *The Drama Review*, 61 (4): 147–155.
Press Kit (2016) '*Five Easy Pieces. Milo Rau/IIPM – International Institute of Political Murder*', Press Kit: http://international-institute.de/wp-content/uploads/20160414_Press-kit_Five-Easy-Pieces.pdf (accessed 19 June 2019).
Quick, Andrew (2006) 'The Gift of Play: *Übung* and the Secret Signal of Gesture' in Joe Kelleher and Nicholas Ridout (eds.) *Contemporary Theatres in Europe: A critical companion*, Oxon and New York: Routledge, pp. 149–162.
Rau, Milo and CAMPO (2016) *Five Easy Pieces*, video documentation of performance at Kunstenfestivaldesartes Brussels, private link provided by CAMPO.
Rau, Milo (2017) 'Milo Rau: "I'm Actually Not Trying to Break Any Taboos"', Interview with Bella Todd, WhatsOnStage, 28 February: https://www.whatsonstage.com/brighton-theatre/news/milo-rau-interview-sick-festival-five-easy-pieces_43001.html (accessed 18 June 2019).
States, Bert O. (1985) *Great Reckonings in Little Rooms: On the Phenomenology of Theater*, Berkeley and Los Angeles, California: University of California Press.
Walgrave, Stefaan and Jan Manssens (2000) 'The Making of the White March: The Mass Media as a Mobilizing Alternative to Movement Organizations', *Mobilization: An International Journal*, 5 (2): 217–239.

4 The Female-Girl-Child-Teenager in *The Hamilton Complex*

During the UEFA Euro 2020 football championship, which took place in 2021 due to the COVID-19 pandemic, a Lancashire Primary School in the United Kingdom posted a video to their social media account of teachers and pupils performing to the soundtrack of the 1998 football anthem *Vindaloo* by British band Fat Les. The school later suspended its Twitter account after allegedly receiving complaints about the content of the video. The footage soon became part of the 'culture wars' narrative that has enjoyed significant coverage in UK newspapers during the past few years, where the language of the culture wars can be understood as 'journalistic vernacular to describe a wide range of cultural divides in the UK' (Duffy *et al.* 2021). Following the suspension of the school's Twitter account, which was later reinstated, the right-wing newspaper *The Daily Mail* published a headline that read 'Primary school suspends Twitter account after woke complaints that Vindaloo video of children cheering on England's footballers showed "a sea of aggressive white faces" and promoted "mindless hooliganism"' (Daily Mail 2021). Foxhole news website, which was created by a Brexit campaign group called Leave.EU, similarly framed the content in positive terms as '[a] heart-warming video' (The Foxhole 2021).

One of the main Twitter respondents who was quoted in both these newspaper articles and whose comments were then recycled by other news media outlets was, in fact, reacting not to the school's Twitter account but to an inflammatory tweet that had misappropriated an earlier 2018 version of the video with the accompanying text: 'Nice job @Flakefleet & not a Woke in sight [eye-rolling emoji]'. On social media there were actually at least two videos in circulation at the time that were being posted interchangeably: an earlier version of 'Vindaloo' that the school had recorded in support of the 2018 World Cup, and the later 2021 version, *The Daily Mail* and *The Foxhole* had linked to in their articles. The respondent had challenged the video with a tweet that read:

> Very depressing. What does it even mean? Poor kids, already brainwashed. A sea of aggressive white faces … Is that global Britain? Just check the amazing English team and learn from it.

This responding tweet was accompanied by an image of England's male football team at the time that read 'England without immigration' with all but three

DOI: 10.4324/9781003043072-6

of the players' faces crossed out. Both of these tweets, the woke-related comment and the white faces comment, were posted prior to and separate from the abhorrent racist abuse that was both publicly and privately directed at three of England's football team's Black players after their defeat in the UEFA final. What becomes apparent on viewing these cultural artefacts and the ensuing social and news media narratives around them is how the relationship between children's images, bodies, and presumed 'innocence' are intertwined with nationalist discourse and ideology in a way that one could argue is echoed in the primary school's 2018 Youtube video itself. As a departing point for considering the material and symbolic figurations of the child in contemporary performance as a specific cultural discursive location, this video is indicative of a contemporary representation of children and nation that is highly dependent on intersections of gender, race, and age and that I would argue, following Robin Bernstein (2011), illustrates the role of innocence as a means of both cultural forgetting and maintaining whiteness as an unmarked category.

The opening scene of the Youtube video shows a male-presenting teacher performing aggressive barging through a line of female-presenting teachers, all of whom have their faces painted white with a red-centred cross that references the national flag of England. Anyone familiar with the original video to the soundtrack will recognise this barging action as a callback to the original *Vindaloo* video, which, in turn, parodies the music video *Bitter Sweet Symphony* by the 90s British band The Verve. However, this connection is so loose and also specific as to render it meaningless to many viewers of the primary school's version, unless they are familiar with this niche reference. Alongside teachers donning white facial makeup who are divided along binarised gender lines with an active white male aggressor role pushing through passively-positioned female teachers, the opening moments of the video offer only an image of banal nationalism, emphasised by the reference to white face that is intimately tied up with white, male, colonial privilege. Largely white, seemingly able-bodied primary-aged boys and girls march to the lyrics 'Where on earth are you from, we're from England? Where you come from, do you put the kettle on?'. The lyrics' terrestrial reference here establishes a clear us/them binary that is founded on the racist assumptions of human/alien, same/other, which places England and English fans in the privileged, primary position of the coloniser. The schadenfreude chants of 'nah nah naaah… we're gonna score one more than you' within the chorus are reminiscent of playground competitive talk and the young people's participation in the video serves only to minimise the more disturbing colonising discourse that underscores the children's militarised action of marching, waving flags, and soundless cheering.

Red and white striped headbands worn by staff and students read as preparation for a physical fight, referencing hyper-masculinised physical aggression. However, on the heads of the young children who wear them, the militarised, conformist, nationalist scripts that their bodies inhabit are simultaneously downplayed. The video invites the assumption that the people we call children in this video are oblivious to these 'adult' scripts, yet at the same time, these scripts are repeated and materialised on and through the bodies of children. The white face referenced by the use of white facial makeup, worn by both adults and children is, for example, softened by the familiar association of face painting with young children's roleplay and birthday parties. Similarly, the claims of 'innocent children' (*Daily Mail*) 'harmlessly marching' (*The Foxhole*) are used by the right-wing news media as a way of minimising legitimate concerns about the video and rendering alternative readings of it as 'woke' – itself a term that has been re-appropriated from Black culture and 'weaponized to sneer at the values of many young, Black liberals' (McGrady 2021: np).

Whilst the white facial makeup undoubtedly harks back to the use of white face and Black face in theatre and film history as a means of reifying racial stereotypes, even if not consciously intended by the wearers, it also taps into similar social anxieties surrounding 'masculinity and interracial dependence' that have been discussed with regard to the historic use of white face in mainstream entertainment, for example, in Buster Keaton's performances (Linville 2007). In this way, the school's video announces an image of white masculinised dominance, as the single male teacher also in white makeup waves a large flag whilst jumping on a desk against the backdrop of various scenes of the school children, who are choreographed to march in groups on the ground below. The image of nationalism being evoked here thus reinstates normative gender roles and reifies whiteness as a racial opposite to its supposed absent other, whilst simultaneously masking these gendered and raced assumptions in plain sight on the bodies of 'innocent', mainly white, children.

In *Racial Innocence: Performing American Childhood from Slavery to Civil Rights* Robin Bernstein observes that '[h]istorians have shown that the materials and practices that surround living children, as well as historically-located representations of children, have unique abilities to recapitulate adult culture whilst seeming to deflect it' (2011: 7). Bernstein offers the re-appropriation of jokes from 19th century minstrel shows in both contemporary and 20th century north American children's culture as an example of how adult culture is repeated, albeit with difference, in the popular 'why did the chicken cross the road?' joke. Whilst reciting the joke does not, in itself, suggest a conscious and intentional reference to minstrelsy, the reference is nevertheless retained even whilst hidden by its articulation out of the 'innocent' mouths of babes who are assumed to be oblivious to its racial resonances. If minstrelsy was no longer acceptable for 19th century adults, the strong association of childhood with innocence and, in turn, the conflation of children's innocence with obliviousness meant that children's culture could, and still can, as we have seen above, retain images and scripts of past abject and racist practices like minstrelsy whilst simultaneously *appearing* to forget the histories from which they emerge. Indeed, Bernstein points out that the repurposing of material taken from a racist theatrical form means that '[a]nyone who can correctly answer these riddles has memorized a part of a minstrel script' (ibid.). For Bernstein, this ability of childhood innocence to 'remember whilst appearing to forget' is politically significant because it is beneficial for the on-going preservation of whiteness as an unmarked category.

In this section, I consider the way in which the young performers in HETPALEIS and Lies Pauwels' *The Hamilton Complex* (2016) recapitulate an 'adult' culture of suspicion, liability, and patriarchal protectionism, particularly as this culture emerges in response to a contemporary conceptualisation of paedophilia as an 'abject practice', to borrow from Bernstein. However, rather than deflecting these scripts of adult culture, as in Bernstein's example of the repurposed minstrel joke, the performers, I suggest, give visibility and voice to adult images and scripts related to paedophilia that ordinarily go 'unmarked' when in the presence of the people we call children themselves. This marking of the unmarked, specifically through their bodies which are gendered female within the performance, occurs in a number of different ways over the course of the piece and, I argue, ultimately leads to a repurposing of the *performance of* childhood innocence as a strategy: a strategy not for performed cultural forgetting, but instead for remembering and marking these scripts of 'adult' culture.

In what follows, I consider how age and gender in particular intersect to negotiate this performance of childhood innocence as a way of recalling 'adult' scripts by focusing on how *The Hamilton Complex*, first, employs gender-specific trans*-age strategies to perform heteronormative, patriarchal femininity to excess and to signal its relationship to the eroticisation of childhood and specifically girlhood innocence. Second, I argue that *The Hamilton Complex* overtly and consciously invites a scopophilic male gaze to draw parallels with the perceived threat of the paedophilic gaze that the discourse of innocence would ordinarily *appear* to forget. Third, I propose that the performance marks the shared emotional labour required by both the theatrical economy that the child performers are participating in whilst they *perform* innocence and the aesthetic economy of the cross-generational female roles they play in order to recall and remember the operation of power, consumption as well as the potential for objectification, exploitation, and coercion within both aesthetic and theatrical economies. By performing innocence to memorialise and mark adult scripts, I want to nuance Isis Germano's proposal that *The Hamilton Complex* invites an 'adult gaze' (2018: 45) by considering that the work specifically elicits a patriarchal protectionist gaze. It is this gaze which is shown throughout the work to be entirely dependent on the *performed* innocence of these 'female–girl–child–teenage' performers as a more specific identification than that of simply 'children'. This multiple, differential, and yet shared identification that the performers inhabit is undoubtedly framed in the performance in relation to the binarised human-adult/inhuman-child of Enlightenment logic whereby 'the adult [is] white, male and rational' as Isis Germano has carefully argued (ibid.). However, I want to explore the significance of the performance of innocence on bodies that show the female–girl–child–teenager to be its own complex and intersectional discursive and experiential position, which has the potential to draw the audience's attention to innocence as gendered and potentially raced white on the culturally and historically-located bodies that perform it.

The Feminine Future

The intersection of age and gender is key to the way in which the performance of innocence is negotiated as a strategy in *The Hamilton Complex*.[1] In particular, the kind of gender-specific trans*-age strategies that the performance engages in plays a significant role in its ability to deliberately remember, rather than appearing to forget, societal anxieties around the eroticisation of children's bodies and the threat of adults who desire them. These anxieties are marked rather than hidden in the performance as one might initially expect given the participation of young people in the work itself. In the opening scene, this cultural remembering is achieved through the young performers playing the role of 'air hostess' against the backdrop of performed childhood innocence. Donning flight attendant uniforms, complete with skirts, jackets, hats worn off-to-the-side, neckerchiefs, and high heels, thirteen young female performers enter the stage, they stand in a line and begin to sing a French choral piece *Vois Sur Ton Chemin* (*Look to Your Path*) by Bruno Coulais, which was featured in the 2004 film *Les Choristes* directed by Christophe Barratier. The song draws on images of childhood innocence, calling for the listener to 'show a better future' to the 'lost and forgotten' children.

The performers' serious yet energetic delivery of sentimental lyrics that solicit an adult spectator to not only 'do better' but also to *feel* hope, passion, and glory, jars with the visual spectacle of an ensemble of air hostesses which the spectator sees before them. The performers' very presence as a unified choir, complete with beautiful harmonies, blatantly nods to romantic cultural associations of children's choirs with 'angelic voices', especially when underscored by the imagined 'innocent, in need of protection' children conjured by the lyrics. However, this scene of childhood purity is interrupted by the performers wearing an adult costume that is synonymous with the performance of heteronormative, patriarchal femininity and an invitation to look. These young female performers are immediately situated in relation to the potential for an objectifying, scopophilic male gaze that is marked by the costume's relationship to compulsory heteronormative femininity. The audience is encouraged to notice the invitation to occupy this gaze in the juxtaposition of the air hostess with the imagery of the innocent child being painted by the marriage of form (the children's 'heavenly' voices) with content (the innocent children imagined by the lyrics). A scopophilic gaze is largely solicited and marked here, at the beginning of the performance, by means of what I argue is a gender-based trans*-age strategy. This strategy encourages the spectator to recognise the play between the performer's young anatomical age and the imagined age identity of the air hostess as a young adult whose profession is commonly aligned with gender-conforming femininity.

The play between the 'child girl' performer and 'adult female' hostess takes place in the context of a theatrical production that situates itself as an ocular-centric economic contract, with the performer firmly situated as a producer and spectator as a consumer. The economics of this exchange are suggested through *The Hamilton Complex*'s own visual-economic conditions as a theatrical performance in its opening scene precisely via the figure of the female air hostess who still pervades popular culture as an example of sexualised work. As Katherine Duffy *et al.* argue:

> The sexualization of the female flight attendant and the enduring myth of the glamorous 'hostess' remain ubiquitous in media and popular culture more

> generally; from Barbie's Virgin Atlantic incarnation to the best-selling Ann Summers flight attendant costume, the sexualization of women's work in the airline industry remains firmly encoded in the popular consciousness.
> (2017: 266)

In an occupational context, the role of flight attendant demands the regulation of her outward appearance as part of her paid work to such an extent that the implied comparison in *The Hamilton Complex* is that the young performers are also to be seen as workers onstage who 'maintain' their emotions for us in exchange for our ticket fee. Furthermore, the performance's title situates the work in relation to the ocular-centric controversial practice of British photographer David Hamilton who, working during the latter half of the 20th century until his death in 2016, is known for photographing naked teenage girls. Hamilton's photography has faced allegations of child pornography (Carvajal 1998), and two owners of his photographs have been convicted for possession of indecent images, with one conviction later overturned (Samuel 2016, Warmoll 2005). Before his death, Hamilton also faced a number of sexual assault and rape allegations from adults that he had photographed as children (Samuel 2016). The performance, not least through the reference within the title, is keenly aware of the controversy surrounding Hamilton's work with young girls. To spectators familiar with his photography and the public discourses and allegations surrounding it, the objectifying gaze suggested by the female air hostess imagery in the performance runs parallel to the voyeurism and sexualised gaze arguably invited by Hamilton's photographs. The performers are shown to be trapped in the visual economy of a heteronormative, gender-conforming feminine future: desirable as innocent girls and desired as to-be-looked-at adult females.

Emotional Labour

The performance's employment of the figure of the female air hostess not only capitalises on the 'to-be-looked-at-ness' spectacle of this profession within a visual consumer economy, but the audience is called to negotiate the parallels that emerge in this opening scene between the child theatrical performer and the hostess as a figure that participates in what Gernot Böhme refers to as the aesthetic economy (2003). I want to suggest that these parallels between theatrical work and the aesthetic economy perform a cultural remembering of the operation of power, consumption, objectification, exploitation, and coercion in relation to the paedophilic gaze that is overtly referenced by the performance, and, furthermore, that the discourse of innocence would ordinarily appear to forget. In particular, the fact that performers called children play air hostesses in this theatrical context – while their age identity as children is already somewhat ambiguous being identified as teenage girls in pre-show publicity material – only serves to draw attention to this role as indicative of a worker who has to appear corporeally and emotionally engaged in 'the presentation, maintenance and performance of a mode of embodiment that is specified or compelled by [her] employing organization' (Duffy *et al.* 2017: 263). Whilst theatrical performers also partake in a form of employment where their mode/modes of embodiment are often (although not always of course) determined by someone or something else (director, choreographer, disciplinary traditions, institution etc.), the question of whether a performer is 'compelled' or not to maintain and perform a specific mode of embodiment is more pronounced when it comes to the child onstage. Questions of whether child performers have agency over the modes of embodiment that they occupy and/or whether they have been exploited are not hidden in *The Hamilton Complex*. Instead, these questions are very much brought to the fore in the relationship between this adult costume, the presumably pre-pubescent and pubescent bodies that wear it, and the imagined innocent child in need of protection that is summoned by the lyrics and voiced by a choir of harmonising children.

What is most striking about this visually excessive opening of the show is paradoxically what cannot be seen. The absent referent of the young performers' performances as adult air hostesses is the obligatory smile with which the latter are often synonymous. None of these people we call children on stage are smiling, which gives the impression that they are not fully 'in role'. The absence of this gesture reads as a refusal to fully participate in the aesthetic economy of the airline service industry that is referenced through the costumes. As passengers, we know that flight attendants are engaged in a performance of managing their own emotions in order to manage ours. We are aware that their performed smiles are not (always) an outward expression of an authentic inward feeling or emotion. Yet, regardless of whether the attendant's actual feelings are congruent with this organisational expectation to smile, the smile still needs to be performed. In a profit-driven context where care is marketised, flight attendants are even 'taught' how to feel, manage their emotions, and 'smile like you really mean it' (Hochschild [1983] 2012: 4). In scholarly research, the flight attendant's smile has been frequently cited as an indicator of 'emotional labour', which is defined by Arlie Hochschild as 'the management of feeling to create a publicly observable facial and bodily display' (Hochschild [1983] 2012: 7). Hochschild further observes that this emotional labour has 'exchange value' because it is sold as part of the product or service that the customer is consuming. It is the shared emotional labour of the air hostess and the child performer that is being hailed in this moment of the performance. The child performer's 'innocence' is not offered to the audience as an inherent quality that they possess but instead, it is framed through the figure of the air hostess as a labour that is *performed*, much like the performed authenticity enacted by the smile gesture. Whilst the child performers hold up their end of the economic contract by providing the sweet voices of an angelic choir that the adult gaze might expect, the absence of the smile on their faces nevertheless punctures the consuming gaze that would read these performers merely as 'products' that readily align with either the innocent (smiling) child or the 'service with a smile' hostess.

If emotional labour 'requires [the worker] to induce or suppress feeling in order to sustain the outward countenance that produces the proper state of mind in others' (Hochschild 2012: 7) the child performers are shown to be subject to the theatrical and spectatorial structures of power that determine how they ought to appear and are therefore shown during this scene to be emotional labourers just as much as their adult character counterparts. Importantly, however, these young performers illustrate their non-compliance with these spectatorial expectations through the absence of the compulsory smile. In the midst of this ambiguity around how one should read these somewhat reluctant emotional labourers, the ability of emotional labour to 'produce the proper state of mind in others' is highlighted by the performers' non-compliance. In *The Hamilton Complex,* the 'others' of Hochschild's formation are the spectators and it is their gaze and what this gaze suggests about their expectations from the child performer that is under scrutiny not only in this opening scene but throughout the performance. In particular, during *Vois Sur Ton Chemin* the fetishising gaze hailed by the figure of the airline hostess is uncomfortably aligned with the so-called asexual, protectionist gaze that demands an 'innocent' child performer. The layering of signification that invites at one and the same time objectification and protectionism is the theatrical realisation of James Kincaid's observation that innocence has been eroticised in contemporary culture for the viewing pleasures of adults in ways that fetishise, idealise and ultimately objectify children's bodies (Kincaid 1998). Only, in *The Hamilton Complex*, we are reminded of, and encouraged to acknowledge and potentially critique, these gazes in operation simultaneously rather than being seduced by uncritically enacting them. The reference to childhood innocence (or lack thereof) – specifically through gender-based trans*-age play as a performance strategy – therefore encourages an audience to recall and remember the abject paedophilic gaze, in a way that is uncomfortably close to, if not imbricated within, the gaze that fetishises innocence.

Fetishising Innocence

Both the paedophilic and the protectionist gaze are further marked and made visible by the performers themselves in the scene that follows this opening choral number. Still in character as air hostesses, the performers deliver a series of physical gestures, as if they are standing in the aisles of a plane. These gestures echo the verbal instructions offered by a performer who steps up to a microphone and introduces herself as 'Gift'. She begins: '[T]oday we are here to assist you and to guarantee your safety', again situating and reinforcing their roles as hostesses who are in the service of the audience, keeping them calm, happy, and above all 'safe'. The role reversal she enacts, with children looking after adults, is humorous. As Gift takes us through all the safety measures, including designated exits, fire safety, and recording prohibitions, the content of her speech gradually becomes more uncomfortable, deliberately provoking an air of suspicion in the auditorium:

> Gift: *We also wish to notify you that a fully equipped medical team is on standby should you take ill. After the event you can also have yourself tested*

> *for bacterial or viral infections. However, we cannot be held liable for any conditions that are of a sexually transmittable nature. Nor are diseases transmitted by saliva or blood our responsibility.*

In this pre-COVID-19 context, references to viral infections at the opening of a performance are highly unusual and unexpected. By appropriating and re-purposing familiar 'adult' discourses of liability, responsibility, and health and safety, the script echoes the invisible but ever-present patriarchal protectionist logic that would seek to keep these young female-presenting performers safe from paedophilic threat by drawing attention to the audience as potentially leaky, abject bodies:

> Gift: *Standard safety procedures dictate that we will dim the lights as soon as we start. We advise you to sit still and keep your hormones in check! So we kindly ask that girls and boys undergoing puberty, menstruating women, menopausal women and men – all men – endeavour to practice self-control.*

In particular, Gift's words mark a potential risk posed by audience members' bodies, specifically 'all men', which explicitly generalises and essentialises their potential for bringing a paedophilic gaze to the performers' bodies. The specificity of this risk is named and addressed directly as the speech continues:

> Gift: *Oh yes, there's just one other thing. We don't wish to humiliate or offend anyone, but given our young age, it seems a good idea to know whether there are paedophiles here today. We don't want to condemn anybody or anything, but I do hope that you can understand our point of view – you never know if there is someone here who loves a bit of 'not quite grown-up and not-quite-a-child'. Those of you who are betwixt and between, as the saying goes.*

Hearing a young female-identifying performer articulate a risk that patriarchal protectionism cannot ordinarily utter in the presence of children, but which nevertheless has to be imagined by this position of patriarchal protectionism in order to 'assess' the level of threat, seems to tip the balance of power in favour of the performers. They appear to be setting the terms. The performers' refusal to take responsibility for audience responses, should they become 'sexual' or 'infectious', further asserts the authority of the ensemble who in the choral number have already unapologetically scanned the audience with their eyes. As Germano has argued '[r]ather than being passive objects vulnerable to our gazes, these girls look back and speak' (2018: 44). The theatrical device of an ensemble of air hostesses coupled with their performed innocence (as part of a girls' choir) enable the performers not only to invite and then refuse their own objectification but also to anticipate, name, and indeed problematise the gaze that, by seeking to protect their so-called innocence, also participates in their ultimate objectification.

Gift's naming of the ensemble's discursive age as *'not quite grown-up and not-quite-a-child'* in the script, creates further and deliberate ambiguity in terms of how we are invited to encounter the performers' bodies and subjecthood as well as their performed personas. With regard to anatomical age, some of the performers appear significantly younger than the advertised 'thirteen-year-olds' which has the effect of reducing them to the discursive category of 'girls' at moments in the work where this category aligns with their fictionalised framing in the work. In the opening scene, for example, I largely interpret the performers as children and girls, rather than teenagers, because of the resonances with the innocent children they sing about and the distinction between their youthful bodies and the adult role of hostess they play. However, there is a deliberate shift in this moment where Gift takes ownership of an anticipated perception of the teenager as '*betwixt and between*', and the invitation to see the performers as teenagers is reinforced shortly after by an outbreak of stereotypical fan 'hysteria', that includes the performers screaming, running, changing clothes, jumping, and dancing to the Beatles track *Love Me Do*. Gift leads the other performers into this highly energetic scene by loudly announcing: 'We want to become safe, be safe and stay safe. Safety First. We want Matteo Simoni…', a famous Belgian actor from the TV Series *Safety First* (2013–15), who the performers scream for in scenes reminiscent of 1960s teenagers at the height of the so-called Beatlemania moment.

Taking place after a measured and controlled display of innocence, albeit queered innocence through its deliberate markedness *as performance*, the performers' illustration of hysteria is not only drawing on a cultural stereotype of teenage libidinousness, but importantly it references the historically gendered understanding of hysteria as a specifically female trait or malady precisely because it arrives to us via *the bodies of female-identifying and female-presenting performers*. The performers' exaggerated gesticulation of gender-conforming behaviours associated with patriarchal femininity, such as raising their hands to their mouth in a state of feigned shock or seeming overcome with emotion, reinforce this connection to the societally accepted version of femininity of the air hostess role they play. Nevertheless, this display of heteronormative, patriarchal femininity is carefully undermined by references to multiple versions of the non-conforming hysteric female figure that we see onstage played by the people we call teenagers, girls, and children, who stand in defiant opposition to their behaviour being corrected and policed by a single male performer who paces frantically below them, in front of the stage, in an effort to institute some control with his quieting gestures and accompanying whistle.

The alignment of the performers with hysteria thus positions their female teenage bodies as a perceived threat to the social order. This perception is further enhanced by the sight of this male performer who appears to shadow male doctors, like Jean-Martin Charcot, who historically sought to contain so-called female hysteria. Donning a suit and carrying a whistle, this male figure more overtly references the patriarchal disciplinarian character, Captain Vontrapp, who uses a whistle to establish military-style control amongst his seven children in the musical *The Sound of Music*. The bodies of the people who author and own these screams in *The*

Hamilton Complex, however, refuse to be silenced and contained by this man who symbolically stands in for patriarchal order, and as a consequence, we are invited to look differently at these young, female performers.

If the discourse of idealised innocence would prefer us to see young female performers as asexual, these performers defiantly refuse to conform through their illustration of the 'emotional excess' of the hysteric teenage female fan. Their performed sexuality and sexual energy are not exhibited *for* us, to be consumed by the audience, as Charcot's patients' 'hysteria' was exhibited in his 19th-century clinic in France. Instead, the scene seems to enact the rebelliousness of the figure of the hysteric (Russo 1994), which has since been reclaimed by feminist thinkers (Furse 2020) in an act of resistance to the backdrop of hysteria as a so-called illness that has perpetuated pervasive and negative historical connections between women and mental ill health. The performers' relentless and loud screaming, in particular, is not only pointing towards the excessive emotion associated with the figure of the hysteric, but it is being celebrated in its delivery, largely in the performers' commitment to the act of screaming and in the obvious distinction of the screams from Gift's previously calming words in her more restrained role as an air hostess. This distinction is even more pronounced as the performers remove the restrictive pencil skirts and neckerchiefs to do an onstage costume change into luminescent green skirts and pink short-sleeved shirts in an act that reads as a symbolic rejection of the idealised 'adult' femininity contained within the stereotypical representation of the air hostess.

There also appears to be a conscious awareness within the performers' commitment to this collective act of the affective potential of their screaming on the bodies of the audience, which, as a spectator, I experienced as a powerful call on the limbic system's response to activate a fight, flight, or freeze reaction. The audience is – as Gift anticipated – invited to be physiologically invested albeit not via an unquestioning or desiring gaze. The performers' command of this moment I would argue ensures that the spectator is prevented from adopting a problematic gendered understanding of hysteria or taking at face value the performers' apparent loss of control as an indication of their actual arousal onstage. Instead, the performers seem to be saying 'no' to the 'compulsory citationality' (Butler 1993: 232) of the social order that enacts 'the forcible citation' (ibid.) of gender norms and, I would add here, intersecting age norms. These are neither the screams of 'innocent' children's play, children in need of protection, nor the teenage screams of sexual arousal in the presence of a celebrity, even whilst the scene might draw on these references. Instead, by paralleling the figure of the hysteric that resists being ordered and managed by the patriarchal gaze that is embodied in the male performer's character, these young, female performers' screams challenge both gender norms associated with normative femininity and the way these interact with age norms related to the innocent child, the child in need of protection and the stereotype of the sexually-driven teenager. The decision to stop the screaming, which is collectively arrived at by the performers rather than forced on them by the actions of the male character, further highlights the performed nature of the screams and therefore the performers who author(ise) them. The young performers are shown to be very much in charge here.

The Patriarchal Protectionist Gaze

James Kincaid has previously argued that '[b]y insisting so loudly on the innocence, purity, and asexuality of the child, we have created a subversive echo: experience, corruption, eroticism' (1992: 4–5). I would argue that this echo is tackled head-on and embodied by the young female performers in *The Hamilton Complex* as they run around the stage playfully flashing their underwear to the male performer and the audience. The flashing of their underwear takes place after a movement routine which is performed reluctantly – as the performers' shared expressions of boredom suggest – *for* the gaze of the male performer who looks on in his formal suit and tie. The movement, which is performed in unison by the female performers, sounds scripted and invites us to see them as conforming to adult will, whereas the scene that follows reads as more improvisational and driven by the performers' own decision to lift their skirts at a time and in a position on the stage of their own choosing. The female performers and specifically (what the performance copy describes as) 'girls' mockingly and knowingly raising their skirts whilst laughing, screaming, and performing can-can kicks is a powerful direct acknowledgement of and confrontation to the absent but ever-present threat of the paedophilic gaze. This moment is both unsettling and humorous. The humour is created by the performers' own mischievous demeanours and their unwavering ownership of the material within their irreverent action, whilst the male performer tries and fails to scrabble around stopping them from lifting their skirts and hoping to re-establish the same kind of order that is implied by his formal attire. As the performers disperse and leave the stage, just one performer remains and, stepping up to the microphone, begins to sing a breathless and tired version of *Edelweiss* returning us again to another innocent child reference from *The Sound of Music*.

The well-timed placing of this exhausted exhibition of performed innocence immediately following the unruliness of the skirt-raising scene is crucial. There is a direct attempt in the dramaturgical placement of these activities together to emphasise a connection between the societal expectation of childhood innocence and its co-dependence on that which it defers: the assumption that children might be 'guilty', knowledgeable, and experienced as Kincaid suggests. Only, in this case, the laughter of the young soloist as the male performer runs on, interrupts her song, and carries her away from the microphone kicking and giggling, suggests that she is knowledgeable of childhood innocence as something that can be *performed* rather than as an inherent quality of the child. By attempting to prevent her from singing the *Edelweiss* solo, the male performer demonstrates that he is also aware that she is consciously, self-referentially, and irreverently marking her own performance of innocence *as performance* in this moment. After all, if his bodybuilder persona believed her delivery to be sincere, he would have permitted her song to continue and undoubtedly encouraged such a display.

The song itself calls back to the image of Christopher Plumber's Captain Von Trapp at a pivotal instance in his narrative arc when he softens his previously established patriarchal, disciplinary edge to sing to and with his children in the film version of *The Sound of Music*. With echoes of a different kind of masculinity that is available in this iconic moment in film and musical theatre history, the suited performer's attempt to prevent the young performer from finishing the song in *The Hamilton Complex* can instead be interpreted as an attempt at restoring his own heteronormative masculinity as organised, unsentimental, and rational. As he tells us in the following scene 'I am mentally alert, morally straight... I am disciplined... I am brave... I am pure in thought and deed'. Billed simply as a 'bodybuilder' in the marketing material, his mental strength is aligned with his physical strength in the fictional world of the performance, which he exhibits for us in a series of static poses designed to emphasise his defined musculature.

What is steadily revealed, however, is the co-dependence of the idea of his masculinity on the idea of the young female performer's innocence and inexperience. When she refuses to stop singing, returns to the microphone, relentlessly laughs at him, and climbs on him, his attempts to stop her become more physically aggressive and uncomfortable to witness. When she does not comply with the version of the well-behaved child his patriarchal protectionist logic expects – i.e. the child who is inherently innocent rather than one the audience actually sees who performs and pokes fun at the constructedness of both the innocent child figure and the heteronormative masculinity it upholds – the bodybuilder's hyper-masculinised ability to control the situation as the responsible adult is brought into question. This scene is a stark reminder of the 'force' that often meets gender and age-based nonconformity when citationality within the social order is not achieved: the potential for male violence and misogyny. This is signalled in the way he roughly throws her into various spins, holds her by the wrists, and drops her to the floor without care. The movement is undoubtedly choreographed and does not put the young performer in any actual danger, but in its execution, it possesses a raw quality which creates some nervousness during its reception.

Female–Girl–Child–Teenager

Throughout the remainder of the performance we see images of horror and fairy-tale-inspired tropes that sit uncomfortably in-between the good girl-child and evil girl-child moulds that these genres ordinarily perpetuate. When the female performers don red hooded coats and disguise their faces, for example, they occupy an ambiguous space between the innocent Red Riding Hood victim and the threatening red-hooded child-like figure that can be found in Nicholas Roeg's 1973 film adaptation of Daphne Du Maurier's short story *Don't Look Now*. The performers' faceless, disembodied voices – the originators of which are hidden beneath their hoods – become distorted via a microphone sound effect that deepens their voices and bolsters the visual imagery of the binarised innocent/evil child. Beneath their hoods they ask questions of the male performer that sound more 'adult' in content than their playful costume would suggest:

Q: Are you a prostitute?

Q: Are you here legally?

Q: Do you feel guilty?

Q: What is your sexual orientation?

Q: What is your political conviction?

In this moment, I am reminded that the performers are both teenagers and female: the technologically-induced deepening of the voice recalls the physical change that happens to young people's voices during their teenage years, and their gender presentation as female is perhaps highlighted by deferral because the deepening quality is more often made legible for boys, that is, people assigned male at birth, when their voices 'break' in adolescence (even though cisgender females also experience a lowering of the voice). Trans*-age play operates as a kind of ventriloquism here, which others the performers through the technological manipulation of their voices to sound both older and to imbue them with a non-human quality. This is later contrasted with the hyperfeminised image of the performers playing doll-like characters, lip biting, and twisting their hair around their fingers whilst looking coyly at the audience. With satin dresses and excessive, full-length wigs in white, pink, blonde, purple, and blue, the performers sway and perform shyness to the soundtrack of Shelley Duvall's version of Harry Nilsson's 'He Needs Me' from the 1980 film version of *Popeye,* in which Duvall played Olive Oyl. Witnessing female presenting teenagers intentionally playing eroticised infantile innocence, and echoing the muted sexuality of Olive Oyl, whose lyric is entirely concerned with Popeye's desire rather than her own, emphasises the on-going absence of a discourse around the self-described and self-authored sexualities of both young and teenage girls:

> Within mainstream media and public discourses, acknowledging girls as positively desiring sexual subjects is controversial. Adult acknowledgement of girls' desire as an expected and positive part of adolescence is rare … female sexuality is constituted in opposition to the virility of male sexual desire, as muted and receptive (Holland *et al.*, 1994).
>
> (Allen and Ingram 2015: 143)

Similarly, the presence of hypermasculinised, virile figures such as the bodybuilder onstage and the competitive, physically strong animated character Popeye that is conjured by the soundtrack highlights that the options through which girls' and teenagers' diverse sexualities and sexual experiences as a maginalised gender can be expressed are often limited only to the heteronormative male desire that often shapes their public appearance and reception. In this case, however, the teenagers stare back at us, performing their role to excess and refusing to allow the viewer to slip uncritically into eroticising the innocence they put on display.

Watching female teenagers perform living dolls not only references girl stars like Shirley Temple whose 'body was…constructed as an intensely erotic spectacle in her films from the 1930s' (Osterweil 2009: 1) but I would suggest their references also echo filmic representations of age-crossing, where older female characters play young girls. Performing gestures of childlike shyness to excess, this scene in *The Hamilton Complex* echoes Bette Davis's character, Baby Jane Hudson who as an older and forgotten performer tries and fails to reenact her childhood stardom and charm as part of the narrative for the horror film *Whatever Happened to Baby Jane* (1962). With excessive makeup, tight curls in her hair, and donning an adult version of the costume she wore as a child onstage, Baby Jane Hudson croons and dances to one of her old vaudeville songs 'I've Written A Letter to Daddy' only for the performance to mark her failed attempt at authentic age-crossing when the character smashes a mirror which reflects back to her, her older tragic self. By performing to excess both the eroticised body of the child female star whose 'erotic appeal … was inextricable from its supposed innocence' (Osterweil 2009: 1) and echoing the age-crossing of the adult female character whose creepy reenactment fails to faithfully capture her youth, the performers' teenage status in *The Hamilton Complex* again becomes even more visible, appearing at odds with but also in relation to these filmic references. These acts of age-crossing, intentionally it would seem, fail on the bodies of these teenagers too. As female-presenting teenagers that neither fit the mould of the young child star nor the older woman who plays the girl star she once was, the teenage performers appear instead to be self-reflexively marking performances of childhood innocence, such as these iconic film references, *as performance*.

Other roles that the young performers enact in *The Hamilton Complex* include dogs that typify the child's status as non-human, wild, and subservient particularly when the male bodybuilder asserts control over the performers by putting dog leads on them. Also, we see three of the performers echoing the Three Graces motif which encourages the viewer to locate the various subject positions available to these performers as both children who are presumably 'closer to nature' and females within Western art's on-going attempt to capture idealised feminine beauty:

> Children have traditionally been represented as closer to 'nature' than adults in their wildness, lack of civilized decorum but also their purity and innocence, supposedly uncontaminated by the influences of society. Infants and very young children in particular are often represented as the inferior Other contrasted to the ideal of the contained and controlled adult bodily Self which has achieved full growth and development and is able to deal rationally with others (Jenks, 1996, 2005; Prout, 2000).
>
> (Lupton 2012: 39)

However, rather than simply reinscribing these dominant historical representations of the child, or more specifically the girl-child that is being called upon by these specific references, the hegemonic representations of 'female', 'girl' and 'child' being referenced are continually interrupted by the performers' 'in-between' status as teenagers and mythical appropriations of in-betweenness through the figures of the zombie and the vampire. The performers abruptly transform into zombies, for example, after lying around the stage daydreaming in white flowing dresses and floral headdresses, whilst Kimya Dawson's song 'Utopian Futures' creates images of peace and spiritual growth in a world where capitalism is now dead and 'where the children grow with names they chose and genders all their own' as the lyrics tell us. Heads to the side, stares held for too long, and single arms held out as if their movements are controlled by another force, the young performers slowly move around the audience as quietly menacing zombies. The utopian world, it turns out, is just a dream for these female–girl–child–teenagers who are at once the child as a symbol of a heteronormative future that Lee Edelman observes (2004) and the evil child of the horror genre which originates with Puritanism via Thomas Hobbes (see Part I), both sexualised and asexual, neither fully adult nor fully child. The scene resolves itself when the outstretched arm of the zombie becomes the strumming arm for a collective air guitar rendition of *Here's to You*, an anthem of the 1970s human rights movement by Ennio Morricone and Joan Baez. What is suggested by this resolution is that the 'female–girl–child–teenager' is often denied her human status: instead, she is a doll; she is a non-human animal; she is an adult playing child; she is a symbol of futurity; she is the living-dead all at once.

As I have begun to suggest, however, as much as the montages suggest the performers' experiences of, and inescapability from, these hegemonic representations, these 'female–girl–child–teenagers' on stage *own* these representations and demonstrate them back to the audience to reveal our implicated-ness as meaning makers of these hegemonic and sometimes stereotypical tropes. One review captures this relational soliciting of the audience as an invitation to adjust our perceptions:

> the mere presence of these girls on stage reminds us that it is not women's freedom (to be themselves, to dress as they want) that should be curtailed, but rather the prurient way that they are perceived. What's required is a shift in perception: a piece of hair twirled or teeth biting a lip is not an invitation to something else.
>
> (Gardner 2016)

Throughout *The Hamilton Complex*, the performers navigate the fluid positioning of female–girl–child–teenager showing it to be discursively produced and experienced but simultaneously marking, refusing, and repurposing the dehumanising qualities that make them objects, animals, and zombie others. It does so largely by employing a self-reflexive trans*-age play strategy that marks the performance of innocence *as performance*. For me, this culminates in a redistribution of power *from* the hegemonic discourses of the female, girl, child, and teenager that ordinarily diminish or deny the humanity of the female–girl–child–teenager *over to* the performers themselves who dismantle, disrupt, and play with the supposed fixity of these discursive subject positions. Their playful disruption draws attention to the intersectional qualities of the female–girl–child–teenager, not only to illustrate how being interpellated as such works to dehumanise them, but also to reclaim and appropriate the very alterity this subject positioning affords, with all of its excess.

'Reading' Children's Bodies

So what can we learn from *The Hamilton Complex* about reading children and the bodies of the people we call children in performance? As this argument suggests, when we take a closer look at the way in which the work performs innocence, we are denied a simplistic, romantic reading of the child in a performance that instead calls for audiences to recognise the more nuanced, complex subject position of the female–girl–child–teenager and our implicated-ness as spectators within the negotiation of that subject position. In particular, *The Hamilton Complex* when approached from a feminist perspective, reminds us that not only children's bodies but more specifically cisgender, assigned female at birth bodies and female-identifying and female-presenting teenagers are often denied the status of human. The performance does this by inviting us to reflect on alterity and otherness in relationship to the materiality of the actual bodies we see on stage. Even against the backdrop of a choir ensemble that emphasises uniformity, with their identical costumes and shared anatomical youth, the spectator is nevertheless invited at the very opening of the show to observe the individual performers' different bodies *as* different from one another because of the extended time the performers stand in a horizontal line formation in close proximity to the audience. The spectator is given permission to look, even whilst being denied the fetishising gaze. We see significant height variations; some androgenous bodies; differently abled bodies and a single Black body amongst largely white or white-passing bodies. However, the differences between the performers' bodies are more pronounced and identifiable precisely because the audience is given time to observe. This looking is further marked by the performers' recognition of the potential gazes that perceive them through hypervisible gestures that are performed to excess and a text that calls attention to and calls out the paedophilic and patriarchal protectionist gaze.

Similarly, the way in which the performers' physical bodies align with or deviate from normative expectations of ability as well as gender and age is considered through the labour of the performer referred to as 'Queen' whose disability affects her mobility and speech. We are made aware of the performer's disability when she speaks into the microphone, is supported by the other performers to move around the space, and when she dances with the bodybuilder whose able-bodied status is explicitly exhibited throughout their duet via static, muscle-emphasising poses and demonstrations of physical strength. This duet is both beautiful and unsettling. Together, both performers navigate and draw attention to that ambiguous space, where the inequity of regimes of spectatorship renders some bodies visible, some invisible, and some hypervisible. Despite what reads as joy on the faces of both performers, the scene is haunted by the threat of coercion and exploitation, which ghosts much of the show, as this privileged white, male, able-bodied, adult figure dances alongside this female, disabled, teenage figure. The innocent in need of protection figure of the child starts to emerge with the duet's invitation to see a 'disabled body' being supported by an 'able body'. This is largely because the performer's disability is foregrounded as a difference against a bodybuilding physique that elicits a dominant reading of adult physical strength. However, the duet does not go so far as to encourage a perspective shaped by the medical model of disability that emphasises the harmful narrative of individual impairment in need of correction, because the normatively masculinised qualities of the bodybuilder are never positioned by the performance as desirable in its comparison with the skill and qualities of the performer who plays Queen. Indeed, the foregrounding of his individual physical strength is pitted against what reads as a far superior illustration of the strength of solidarity that is shown when all the young performers exit the stage with the performer who plays Queen using their hands to pull their bodies along the floor in the same way that she navigates the space throughout much of the performance. It is the strength of the collective identity of the female–girl–child–teenager that is being championed here.

Whilst *The Hamilton Complex,* does not necessarily insist on an intersectional reading that is also inclusive of race, there is 'a significant point [...] of coincidence between discourses of 'the child' and the lives of children' (Wallace 1995: 295) in the performance, which I would argue captures the 'material specificity' that Jo-Ann Wallace argues is absent from theoretical conceptualisations of the child. In one scene the colour of a performer's skin arguably intersects with the evolving female–girl–child–teenager subject position I am highlighting, to draw attention to the way in which innocence is normatively 'raced white' (Bernstein 2011: 4). Dressed in leotards that already privilege white bodies by claiming the colour 'nude' and covered in dirt stains, all of the young performers reference 11-year-old US child star Maddie Zeigler when she dances in Australian Singer-Songwriter Sia's music video for her song *Chandelier*. It is worth noting that in the original video, there is already an unheimlich, that is unhomely, quality to the dancer's appearance that the multiple 'Maddies' on stage also carry as they wear the dirty leotards. Reflecting on Zeigler's appearance in the music video, Alina Haliliuc notes:

> The child's presence is almost eerie, as if she was forgotten in a place that has none of the attributes of a 'home:' protection, care, or the presence of adult effort. This unfriendly dead space will soon be animated by the child's playful body and bouncy blond wig. Through a choreography of tireless frantic movement, Maddie tries to compose a supportive environment out of the abandoned objects of domestic care—beds, sofas, tables, and carpets—which reveal themselves as insufficient the more the girl animates them.
> (2019: 28)

In the absence of a male supporting dancer, which is common to the European ballet tradition that is referenced in Zeigler's repertoire of dance vocabularies, the choreography positions her as searching for support from the architecture of the space itself (ibid.). Rather than this sole figure in the music video who moves through an abandoned space and whose walls, furnishings, and objects fail to protect her, the collective 'Maddies' in *The Hamilton Complex* work against the video's dramatisation of 'a post-feminist neoliberal environment as a precarious "holding environment" for the youthful subject of talent' (ibid.). Zeigler's character in the music video for *Chandelier* presents the grim consequences of the postfeminist phallic girl (McRobbie 2009) who is both 'glorified for adopting masculine views of … risky behaviors' (Haliliuc 2019: 31) and simultaneously policed to 'observe norms of feminine embodiment that gratify the male gaze' (ibid.). The Maddies in *The Hamilton Complex*, instead, seem to be enacting the refusal of norms of feminine embodiment. One of the Maddies, instead, tells a story that thematically takes that idea of girls engaging in masculinised risky behaviours to its violent conclusion, whilst the performer simultaneously and unapologetically undermines normative feminine behaviour through her delivery of the story. This performer, dressed as a staged, reinvented version of Maddie, narrates the story of a girl who, alongside her father, murders and dismembers a number of families. Meanwhile, her intense and invested delivery simultaneously plays to and disrupts the stereotype of feminine embodiment as overly emotional. Another performer dressed as Maddie confronts her at the end of her story, asking 'why are you telling [the story] with so much emotion?' to which she replies laughing: 'I'm sorry that wasn't intended'. In short, she draws attention to the insincerity of her own storytelling thus signalling that the performers are evidently capable of self-reflexively *performing* norms of feminine embodiment and, in doing so, are actively disrupting regulatory gender regimes.

Whilst the spectator is not invited to read this storytelling performer's whiteness as significant, in the scene that follows immediately after this, we see all the Maddies lined up with the only Black performer, who is singing Daniel Johnston's song *Devil Town* into a microphone whilst still dressed as Zeigler in *Chandelier*. Against the backdrop of a barrage of images of performed heteronormative femininity (i.e. the virgin bride, the sexualised air hostess) that the audience has witnessed thus far – and which are shown to be tied up with childhood innocence and its potential sexualisation – I feel moved by the performer's song to retrospectively and mentally flick back through the performance's earlier images to notice whether they have indeed maintained the dominant perception of innocence as raced white. The performer sings: 'All my friends were vampires. I didn't know they were vampires. Turns out I was vampire myself. In the devil town'. Given especially how the performance draws the audience's attention to the materiality of the bodies onstage and their difference throughout, it is significant that the lyrics' reference to being positioned as a vampire – without one's knowledge – is sung by the only visible performer of colour on stage. For me, this scene reads as more than making visible the way in which perception dehumanises the female–girl–child–teenager then. Instead, as a solo which is voiced by this particular body, the moment arguably gestures towards a more oppressive marginalisation of the Black–female–girl–child–teenager as a subject category that is always already denied innocence by the white, male, patriarchal protectionist gaze.

The kind of othering suggested by this solo and performed by a Black female teenager, subsequently finds a glitchy visual language for a shared experience of alterity when all the Maddies start to shake in stiff, jerky movements reminiscent of a seizure. This shared action reads as an intentional and collective solidarity among the ensemble, where the inequities of age, gender, ability, and race that have been brought to our attention (albeit to varying degrees), are beginning to intersect in this moment and we, as audience, are potentially invited to receive them as such. It is *The Hamilton Complex*'s emphasis on the materiality of the performers' bodies as indicators of age and gender as well as (to a lesser extent) ability and race, which makes their employment of the *performance of childhood innocence* so effective as a strategy to remember and mark scripts of adult culture such as paedophilia. Moreover, the performance makes visible the gaze which denies that the bodies of the people we call children like adults' bodies are also 'ridden with semiotic, political, ethnographic, cartographic and mythical implications' (Gómez-Peña 2005). In other words, the performance reminds us that these performers are so much more than the adult projection of idealisation inherent in their personas' names ('Charity', 'Gift', and 'Hope' etc).

Contemporary performance, whilst challenging normative perceptions of innocence at the intersection of age and gender, is not yet sufficiently opening up a dialogue about the relationship between (the performance of) childhood innocence and race. There are very few examples of professional performances made with children in British and European experimental making contexts that critically explore issues of race and ethnicity. Furthermore, much of the work that currently dominates this performance landscape is often made with largely white and white-passing children for adult audiences, with only a few instances of work made with Black and global majority child performers. Some exceptions include Rimini Protokoll's *Airport Kids* and Andy Field and Beckie Darlington's *News News News* which are documented in Part III of this book by the performers themselves. However, in *Airport Kids*, much like *Five Easy Pieces* we see a subtle performance of childhood innocence being played out as it intersects with gender, age, and, specifically, national identity in order to refer to, but perhaps not fully attend to, *all* of the bodies of the child performers in the work as raced. We have seen, in *Five Easy Pieces* that the younger, white, gender-conforming performers are afforded innocence by the onstage character of the Director in a way that Elle Liza's teenage, mixed-race, androgynous body is not within the metatheatrical fictional world of the play. This staged negative treatment of Elle Liza (discussed in the previous chapter) is consistent with the treatment of the real-life assassinated figure she portrays, Patrice Lumumba, but whether the audience is encouraged to reflect consciously on the bias shown by the character of the Director, and perceive it as part of a larger discourse of innocence raced white, is unclear. Similarly in Rimini Protokoll's *Airport Kids*, a work made with eight 'global nomads' between 8 and 14 years old, there is a focus on national and geographic identity, familial relationality of the child performers, but not necessarily with direct reference to or implications for issues of intersectionality.

I want to be clear that this call to attend to the way in which the bodies of the people we call children signify in performance, just as much as adults' bodies is, of course, not an invitation to 'read' children's bodies in relation to abhorrent racial stereotypes or ableist tropes. Instead, I am foregrounding how the staging of white, white-passing, and Black and global majority heritage performers, who are also young, might invite a perspective that either intentionally or unintentionally preserves the hegemonic discourse of childhood innocence, which is raced white. The absence of practice and discourse in contemporary performance around innocence, race, and the performers we also call children, makes an intersectional, anti-racist approach more urgent, not only with regard to 'reading' young people and their bodies in performance but also when making work with them. By pointing towards the ways in which the *performance of innocence* intersects predominantly with gender and age in *The Hamilton Complex*, a future approach informed by feminist theory as well as the insights of critical race studies and anti-racist scholarship becomes necessary for providing a rich ground from which to analyse and make professional contemporary performance with young people in a way that acknowledges the complex and multiple subjectivities subsumed under the umbrella term 'children'.

At the time of writing, the politics of visibility surrounding the people we call children – beyond dominant narratives of paedophilia – are starting to gain more attention in the UK news media. This increased consciousness around young people's visibility in public life follows concerns expressed on social media and news media around the ableist and racist language used by teacher Kate Clanchy to describe her students in the Orwell prize-winning book *Some Kids I Taught and What They Taught Me* (2019). In the book, Clanchy characterises autistic children as 'jarring company' and uses racial tropes to describe one of her pupils as 'so small and square and Afghan with his big nose and premature moustache' (cited in Campbell 2021). The public arguments about the book both highlighted and simultaneously minimised prejudiced investment in 'reading' children's bodies as a mode of exclusion and othering. Frustratingly, the mainstream UK media has largely privileged the voices of white authors who defended the book, further contributing to the erasure of the position of writers and authors of colour, specifically Professor Sunny Singh and Monisha Rajesh, who took issue with the book's evident ableist and racist tropes (ibid.). Caught up in the narrative of 'cancel culture', what is missing from the public discourse about Clanchy's book and the arguments put forward that the author and the publisher have failed to fully address these concerns in a timely manner, is that children are always already marginalised subjects and that colourblind models of multiculturalism perpetuated by neoliberal discourse are not a sufficient answer to deal with the anxieties surrounding reading, writing, and speaking about the bodies of the people we call children.

Instead, *The Hamilton Complex* offers a felt, sensed, and embodied reminder of the role of perception in the process of making meaning from, with, and about children's bodies. Furthermore, what is needed now is for children to be given the space to perform, own, and/or resist modes of othering that may or may not align with how they present, identify, and experience the world. This is especially desirable in the current UK theatre context, given that the director of *The Hamilton Complex*, Lies Pauwel, was recently commissioned by the Royal Court to create a piece of work with transgender teenagers but where '[o]ne by one... her performers pulled out and the proposed show was dropped' (Trueman 2018). For Pauwels, this event is indicative of 'British fear' and 'British theatre's approach to participation' (ibid.). Paraphrasing Pauwels, journalist Matt Trueman also locates this problem as a lack of time given to participatory processes: 'Participation, for

Pauwels, isn't a passive thing. It requires trust on both sides, and that takes time to build up — time that British theatre too rarely affords' (ibid.). Whilst exploring the finer details of approaches to participation with people called children within British theatre is outside of the scope of this book, the fact that this commissioned work with trans teenagers has not been able to take place in a UK context, further marginalises trans experiences, limits the already restricted spaces for teenagers who identify as trans to perform and create work as collaborators and artists, and suggests that the professional British theatrical scene is not a space for teenage trans' work, play or experiences. There are exceptions, such as the Manchester-based art company *Trans Creative*, which was established in 2016 by transgender performer, activist, and theatre maker Kate O'Donnell and supports young trans artists and performers. However, the absence of trans children and work with trans teenagers in contemporary performance, is a question of deep inequity that is not separate from wider fears and anxieties around the people we call children, their bodies, and those who may anatomically be classed as 'children' but who do not fit the dominant narratives around what constitutes a child.

What is clear is that an intersectional approach to both making and analysing professional contemporary performance with children and young people is desirable, if not urgent, within the UK landscape. In order to develop this, I would argue that *The Hamilton Complex* offers some useful gender-based trans*-age performance strategies that demand that we consider how age-based and gender-based expectations, perceptions, and stereotypes are intimately linked. As I have argued, these strategies employ female-identifying and teenage-identifying bodies to powerfully enact the *performance* of childhood innocence to excess in order to re-member rather than appearing to forget sometimes harmful 'adult' cultural scripts. One specific strategy we can discern is young, female performers using trans*-age play to perform hyper-feminised professional adult roles that serve the interests of a heteronormative, objectifying gaze in a way that critically draws attention to rather than unproblematically eliciting that same gaze. Here the play between age and gender is staged in such a way that it works to facilitate an insightful parallel between the objectifying gaze directed towards a figure such as the 'air hostess' and the consumerisation and eroticisation of the figure of the innocent child therefore, dismantling this idealised figure as natural through a performative resistance to the emotional labour involved in both.

Another useful trans*-age strategy identified here is the use of ventriloquism. A common trope in the film horror genre, it is not uncommon to witness a child or teenage character (or child doll) mouthing the words of an 'adult', technological, animalistic, or other-worldly disembodied voice. *The Hamilton Complex*, as we have seen, draws on such filmic references by using a microphone that distorts the otherwise 'youthful' voices of the performers and red riding hood imagery that conjures the innocent/evil child commonly observed in horror films and its predecessor, the fairy-tale genre. However, what is distinct here is that the audience is aware that the script itself originates from the voices of the performers – the people we call children/teenagers underneath their hoods – who draw attention to the ventriloquism that haunts all of their action onstage (i.e. through the absent adult director/writer) by provocatively challenging the bodybuilder as a symbol of normatively-masculinised adulthood. A further trans*-age strategy that moves beyond the more binarised age-crossing we observed in the previous chapter is one that plays with the perceived in-betweenness of teenage identities that also *perform* childhood innocence in order to reveal its constructedness.

These strategies, largely through the performers' meaning-making with their own bodies and their critical relationship to the adult performer and live audience, evoke and destabilise the potential violence of the patriarchal protectionist gaze and reveal the way it intersects with gender and (to a lesser extent in this work) disability and race. The subjecthood of the performers is, therefore, not enabled through metatheatrical devices, as was arguably the case with *Five Easy Pieces*. Rather, it is the collective power of the performers and their shared subjectivities, which are negotiated through the figure of the female–girl–child–teenager (a figure that resists fixity to a single identity) that is determined by the reductive lens of patriarchal protectionism. If theatre and performance are going to take the people we call children seriously, we must avoid what in the context of university diversity and equality agendas Sarah Ahmed calls non-performatives; in this case, expressions that (ironically) 'give voice' to children and claim that they are affording children agency when really those samc speech acts '"work" precisely by not bringing about the effects that they name' (2006: 105). Through what I am calling its trans*-age strategies, *The Hamilton Complex* warns us that attempts to 'protect' children and young people do not need to come at the non-performative expense of denying that their bodies make meaning. Instead, it reminds us that the complex subjecthood and multiple identities of the people we call children are as open to change as those of their adult counterparts.

Notes

1 Credit: Video documentation and English subtitles used with kind permission of hetpaleis (hetpaleis & Sontag / Lies Pauwels, 2016).

References

Ahmed, Sara (2006) 'The Nonperformativity of Antiracism', *Meridians: Feminism, Race, Transnationalism*, 7 (1): 104–126.

Allen, Louisa and Toni Ingram (2015) 'Bieber Fever: Girls, Desire and the Negotiation of Childhood Sexualities', in Emma Renold, Jessica Ringrose and R. Danielle Egan (eds.) *Children, Sexuality and Sexualization*, London: Palgrave Macmillan, pp. 141–158.

Bernstein, Robin (2011) *Racial Innocence: Performing American Childhood from Slavery to Civil Rights*, New York and London: New York University.

Böhme, Gernot (2003) 'Contribution to the Critique of the Aesthetic Economy', *Thesis Eleven*, 73 (1): 71–82.

Butler, Judith (1993), Bodies that Matter: On the Discursive Limits of "Sex", London: Routledge.

Campbell, Lucy (2021) 'Kate Clanchy to Rewrite Memoir Amid Criticism of "Racist and Ableist Tropes"', *The Guardian* Tuesday 10 August 2021: https://www.theguardian.com/books/2021/aug/10/kate-clanchy-to-rewrite-memoir-after-criticism-of-racist-and-ableist-tropes (accessed 3 March 2022).

Carvajal, Doreen (1998) 'Barnes & Noble Vows to Stock Art Books Despite Indictments', *New York Times*, 20 February 1998: https://www.nytimes.com/1998/02/20/us/barnes-noble-vows-to-stock-art-books-despite-indictments.html (accessed 4 August 2021).

Clanchy, Kate (2019) *Some Kids I Taught and What They Taught Me*, Pan Macmillan.

Daily Mail (2021) 'Primary School Suspends Twitter Account After Woke Complaints That Vindaloo Video of Children Cheering on England's Footballers Showed "A Sea of Aggressive White Faces" and Promoted "Mindless Hooliganism"', 5 July 2021: https://www.dailymail.co.uk/news/article-9756641/Primary-school-deletes-Twitter-complaints-Euros-video-mindless-hooliganism.html (accessed 25 August 2021).

Duffy Katherine, Hancock, Philip and Tyler, Melissa (2017) 'Still Red Hot? Postfeminism and Gender Subjectivity in the Airline Industry', *Gender, Work & Organization*, 24 (3): 260–273.

Duffy, Bobby, Hewlett, Kirstie, Murkin, George, Benson, Rebecca, Hesketh, Rachel, Page, Ben, Skinner, Gideon, and Gottfried, Glenn (2021) 'Culture Wars in the UK: How the Public Understand the Debate': https://www.kcl.ac.uk/policy-institute/assets/culture-wars-in-the-uk-how-the-public-understand-the-debate.pdf (accessed 25 August 2021).

Edelman, Lee (2004) *No Future: Queer Theory and the Death Drive*, London: Duke University Press.

Furse, Anna (2020) *Performing Nerves: For Plays, Four Essay, On Hysteria*, Oxon and New York: Routledge.

Gardner, Lyn (2016) 'Young People Create Great Theatre but we Rarely Give Them the Freedom', *The Guardian,* 5 July 2016: https://www.theguardian.com/stage/theatreblog/2016/jul/05/hamilton-complex-young-people-create-brave-theatre (accessed 21 December 2021).

Germano, Isis (2018) 'So Cute, So Creepy', *Performance Research*, 23 (1): 44–51.

Gómez-Peña, Guillermo (2005) 'In Defense of Performance Art': https://www.pochanostra.com/antes/jazz_pocha2/mainpages/in_defense.htm (accessed 21 December 2021).

Haliliuc, Alina (2019) 'Sia's Strained Girl: Performing Persistence in Neoliberal Environments', *Gender Forum*, 71: 23–43.

Hetpaleis & Sontag / Lies Pauwels (2016) The Hamilton Complex video documentation of performance in Antwerpen, Belgium. Private link provided by Hetpaleis

Hochschild, Arlie Russell ([1983] 2012) *The Managed Heart: The Commercialization of Human Feeling*, Berkeley: University of California Press.

Holland, J., Ramazanoglu, C., Sharpe, S., & Thomson, R. (1994) 'Power and Desire: The Embodiment of Female Sexuality', *Feminist Review*, 46: 21–38.

Jenks, Chris (1996) *Childhood*, London: Routledge.

Jenks, Chris (2005) 'General introduction' in Jenks C (ed.) *Childhood: Critical Concepts in Sociology*, London: Routledge, pp. 1–22.

Kincaid, James (1992) *Child-Loving: The Erotic Child and Victorian Culture*, New York: Routledge.

Kincaid, James (1998) *Erotic Innocence: The Culture of Child Molesting*, Durham N.C: Duke University Press.

Linville, Susan E. (2007) 'Black Face/White Face: Keaton and Comic Doubling', *New Review of Film and Television Studies*, 5 (3): 269–284.

Lupton, Deborah (2012) 'Infant Embodiment and Interembodiment: A Review of Sociocultural Perspectives', *Childhood*, 20 (1): 37–50.

McGrady, Clyde (2021) 'The Strange Journey of 'Cancel,' From a Black-Culture Punchline to a White-Grievance Watchword', *The Washington Post*, 2 April 2021: https://www.washingtonpost.com/lifestyle/cancel-culture-background-black-culture-white-grievance/2021/04/01/2e42e4fe-8b24-11eb-aff6-4f720ca2d479_story.html (accessed 5 July 2021).

McRobbie, Angela (2009) *The Aftermath of Feminism: Gender, Culture and Social Change*, London: Sage.

Osterweil, Ara (2009) 'Reconstructing Shirley: Pedophilia and Interracial Romance in Hollywood's Age of Innocence', *Camera Obscura*, 24 (3): 1–39.
Prout, Alan (2000) 'Childhood Bodies: Construction, Agency and Hybridity' in Prout A (ed.) *The Body, Childhood and Society*, Basingstoke: Macmillan, pp. 1–18.
Russo, Mary (1994) *The Female Grotesque: Risk, Excess and Modernity*, London: Routledge.
Samuel, Henry (2016) 'British Photographer David Hamilton Found Dead in Paris', *The Telegraph*, 25 November 2016: https://www.telegraph.co.uk/news/2016/11/25/british-photographer-david-hamilton-dies-paris-police-source/ (accessed 4 August 2021).
The Foxhole (2021) 'Primary School's "Disgusting" Viral Video in Support of England Attacked by Woke Brigade', 7 May 2021: https://foxhole.news/2021/07/05/primary-schools-viral-video-in-support-of-england-attacked-by-woke-brigade/ (accessed 5 July 2021).
Trueman, Matt (2018) 'I Don't Like Acting. I Don't Like Theatre. I'm Too Cynical': Meet Risk-Taking Director Lies Pauwels', *Financial Times*, 17 October 2018: https://www.ft.com/content/b2c8abd4-d08f-11e8-9a3c-5d5eac8f1ab4 (accessed Wednesday 2 March 2022).
Wallace, Jo-Ann (1995) 'Technologies of 'The Child': Towards a Theory of the Child-Subject', *Textual Practice*, 9 (2): 285–302.
Warmoll, Chris (2005) 'Hamilton's Naked Girl Shots Ruled "Indecent"', *The Guardian*, 23 June 2005, https://www.theguardian.com/culture/2005/jun/23/photography.art (accessed 4 August 2021).

5 From Gender to Age

A New Approach to Reading Age in Performance

At the close of this section, I offer some thoughts concerning how (what I am calling) trans*-age strategies of children playing adults might further our understanding of reading and experiencing age play and 'age' in performance more generally. How might trans*-age strategies inform and allow for a more capacious approach to reading age whilst also signalling the wider political potential of playing with age in contemporary performance? This is where feminist, queer, and performance scholarship on gender and drag can offer some key insights. If cross-dressing, transvestism, and gender nonconformity are often used in performance as strategies for deconstructing normative gender categories, then I want to argue that trans*-age strategies such as age-crossing and age nonconformity equally contain within them the potential to destabilise socially accepted categories of age, from adult to child and all the iterations that lay in between and around these categories (baby, infant, pubescent, teenager, child, middle-aged, elderly etc). Age play's political potential *is* its destabilising quality. If we think about age as containing categories that can be 'crossed' or not conformed to – however fictional, discursive, temporary and yet *simultaneously meaningful these categories might be* – then we can also draw on terminology developed in queer, feminist, and drag communities and cultures to provide a language for articulating how age is being or could be perceived, practiced, and identified in performance. In other words, drawing on feminist and queer knowledges, experiences, and scholarship can lead us to novel ways of describing and understanding the complexities of trans*-age strategies in performance.

As a starting point, re-contextualising terms that have grown and evolved in feminist and queer communities enables us to ask: Is there an age equivalent to the notion of 'gender-disguise' (female disguised as male or male disguised as female) that Victoria Flanagan (2008) discusses in her analysis of cross-dressing practices in children's literature? Could age-disguise begin to articulate the conditions for the appearance of the adult disguised as a child and the child disguised as an adult in performance? Could gender-bending and gender fluidity allow for a discourse around age-bending and age fluid identities in theatre and performance? What does age non-conformity look and sound like in body-based performance practice? By intentionally appropriating the binarised assumption within the term 'gender reversal', we could arrive at a neologism 'age reversal'

DOI: 10.4324/9781003043072-7

as a useful description of a particular kind of shift from adult to child and child to adult beyond the commonly employed and potentially homogenising notion of transvestism within performance practice. If transgender refers to 'all identities or practices that cross-over, cut across, move between, or otherwise queer socially constructed sex/gender boundaries' (Stryker 1994: 251), then the expansion of this term through the asterisk means that trans*-age becomes an umbrella term to describe and explore identities and practices such as age-bending, disguise, reversal, crossing, fluidity, non-conformity in performances that breach or disrupt socially and discursively produced and recognised age boundaries. To position these identities and practices in relationship to the term trans* is a deliberate move to acknowledge that whilst we are focusing on arts-based practice – and specifically making and reading age *in performance* here - age is still intimately connected to both a performer's and a spectator's lived experience and regimes of interpretation that are no less real by virtue of them being always already mediated through the lens of performance.

A more nuanced language of bending, reversal, fluidity, disguise, and crossing in performance helpfully situates trans*-age strategies as part of *a continuum* of re/presentation that acknowledges the different ways that children play adults and adults play children from impersonation to mimicry to parody alongside more subtle appropriations, crossings, and doings. The need for more nuanced terminology also recognises that trans*-age strategies do not simply refer to people who are legible as 'children' playing people who are legible as 'adults' and vice versa. Instead, a nuanced approach can aid in describing something more specific and/or intersectional: 'teenagers' playing 'men', 'girls' playing 'white, heterosexual women', 'boys' playing 'mothers', or 'tweenies' playing occupational roles such as 'hairdressers'. This specificity includes the gender-related trans*-age strategies I discussed in Chapter 4, where the young performers in *The Hamilton Complex* (2016), are engaged in age play through the illustration of stereotypes of both adults and children via gendered, discursive, and historically and culturally-situated figurations of the girl, teenager, female, and child. Recognising trans*-age strategies as part of a continuum also includes examples that are akin to those instances of age play that I identified in works such as *Übung* (2001) by Josse De Pauw and Milo Rau's *Five Easy Pieces* (2016). In the former, we see age mimicry whereas in the latter the young performers are seen not just as 'demonstrating' adults within a metatheatrical context, but specifically representing, through age-crossing, adults in particular roles (police office, prime minister, king, parents) as outlined in Chapter 3, *The Child as Adult in Five Easy Pieces*.

The very notion of children 'playing' adults is itself called into question under this trans*-age umbrella when we take a closer look at the multiple ways that performance might utilise age-based strategies that, in turn, demand a new or different language to articulate this multiplicity. Children 'playing' adults in some performances includes a host of different approaches: parodying, demonstrating, illustrating, stereotyping, fictionalising, appropriating, enacting, embodying, and signifying through symbolic, iconic, or indexical representation. These different approaches can be missed or underestimated if we assume that the performers whom we also call children (and other related discursive identities) are either incapable of the intention to signify or are unknowingly signifying adult intentions. In a choreographic work entitled *Film with Hope* (2016), for example, we see a version of 'playing' that aligns more with what I would call age-bending rather than age-crossing. When adult artist Grace Surman collaborates with her daughter Hope we see both performers facilitate what reads as an intentional slippage through their actions between multiple binaries that ordinarily work to guarantee the naturalised and normalised adult/child hierarchy. These actions include bending hegemonic perceptions of adult/child that are ordinarily held up by assumed power relations between teacher/student, professional/amateur, human/animal, and parent/child.[1] Both Hope and Grace's age-bending is therefore different to the role playing we witness in *Five Easy Pieces* where we see a child demonstrating an adult profession or social role which does little or nothing to challenge the expectations associated with that role. Hope is not 'playing' a teacher or a parent. Instead, both her and Grace are engaged in behaviours that are suggestive of these positions *in dialogue with one another* in a way that bends the normative perception of these roles through the bodies that inhabit them. *Five Easy Pieces* instead deliberately crosses rather than bends our assumptions of social status according to a binarised understanding of child/adult relationships. The children in the play, unlike Hope, are age-crossing professions and roles that are not usually available to them outside of the theatrical space and/or are demonstrating them at a distance rather than bending the supposed fixity of normative perceptions of the adult as teacher, parent, and professional as *Film with Hope* does.

We also see age-bending, I would argue, in works such as Tino Sehgal's *This Progress* (2006). A specific example is where the performer who is 'a boy of about nine' asks audience members what progress is (Ridout 2007). Performance scholar, Nicholas Ridout recalls his experience of seeing *This Progress* alongside a friend in a way that captures something of the dialogic nature of age-bending I mentioned above. In this case, the relationality of age-bending takes place between performer and audience rather than between performers as it does in *Film with Hope* in direct response to the boy's question:

> The situation seemed to require an authentic response. To fake it would be condescending. There are strong ethical arguments against palming off comfortable clichés on young people. At the same time, I could draw upon the typical intellectual furniture of the left-leaning intellectual, offering recycled versions of creative destruction, summoning the ghost of the Communist Manifesto to intone, smugly, that "all that is solid melts into air". But how hollow would that sound? Not only would my nine-year-old interlocutor detect the humbug like bullshit on a stick, my friend would see right though it too [...] Eventually, we dredged up between us some basis for a conversation about the positive and negative values associated with progress, until, after a few minutes and a walk across the gallery space, we were introduced to a girl, somewhat older than the boy. The boy handed us over to our new

> conversation partner with a succinct summary of our views on progress, which was both so accurate and so damning in its glibness that I felt terribly ashamed of myself.
>
> (Ridout 2007)

This scene illustrates how the performance bends age expectations of the child, with a performer who shows himself to be more than capable of recounting the 'adult' version of progress offered by Ridout and his friend, beyond expectations of his years, but it also bends expectations of an age-appropriate response from the adult spectators too. Caught between the perceived expectations of both the child and the other adult spectator to offer an answer that sounds neither clichéd nor superficial, Ridout and his friend opt for a pros and cons reasonable response which fails to suffice. Had the young performer imitated an adult or more specifically an adult-associated role, in other words, had they age-crossed I suspect the feeling of shame might have been diminished or perhaps even non-existent for Ridout since it is largely his relationship to the performer as a child, the other adult, and his position as an adult that he is being interpellated to navigate here. Reflecting on the same performance some years later (although in response to a different iteration of the work in the Solomon R. Guggenheim gallery in New York in 2010), Antje Hildebrandt also notes that the children she encounters in Sehgal's work 'make me conscious of my own age. Their performance reflects back at me a certain idea of adulthood that does not sit comfortable with my own sense of self as adult' (2018: 111). This resonates with what I am suggesting about age-bending above specifically the relational aspect of bending, as for Hildebrandt, what creates an unequal power relationship is largely that the child 'knows the rules of the game better' and the expectation to be a 'good [gallery] visitor'.

Boris Charmatz's dance performance *Enfant* (2011), offers yet another version of trans*-age play. Children around 5 to 9 years old shift from playing limp, lifeless bodies being hoisted around the stage by adult performers to adopting adult-like behaviours and traits as they physically manipulate adult bodies onstage in an act I would describe neither as age-bending nor crossing but as age reversal. The language of reversal is more appropriate here given that the work is not inviting us to question the category of 'adult' or 'child' in the same way that I argue Surman's work does. Instead, the choreography dictates that the earlier section where we see a passive child being moved by active adults is simply reversed in the later section where the child becomes active and the adult becomes passive in terms of their physicality. The binary of 'adult/child' thus remains intact in *Enfant*, albeit reversed.

In the moment of meaning-making, one's reading of children 'playing' adults and vice versa, might also yield something that we have yet to imagine. I encountered such an unanticipated moment recently in *Shorty* at Soho Theatre in London (2023). The framing here was an adult performing (as) a child in the context of drag. In this solo work created and performed by Hester Stefan Chillingworth, we meet a 'non-binary drag child', Shorty. To describe what Chillingworth creates in the space as 'playing' Shorty is to imbue the performance with a sense of an actor/character relationship that fails to capture the complexity and intimacy of the relationship between artist and persona that is established onstage. The performance instead seamlessly interweaves the presences of both Chillingworth and Shorty. At times, the two are imbricated and layered over each other, and at other times the relationship is more fluid, moving seamlessly between artist and persona. Whilst, as an audience member, I was always made aware of both persona and artist – there is no appeal to suspend disbelief here – moments of indistinction are created by Chillingworth within the stageworld, where a third person seems to emerge. At times, the performance simultaneously encompasses both Shorty as a 'drag child' and Chillingworth as an adult performer/artist whereas at other times it gives rise to a third phenomenon more akin to the emergent category of a 'drag thing'.

Drag things have arrived on in recent years the counterpublic drag scene in resistance to the gender and class-based inflections of the mainstream 'drag queen' and lesser acknowledged 'drag king'. However, even whilst the capacious idea of a 'drag thing' embraces and welcomes gender expressions and lived experiences beyond binarised identity, as a descriptor 'drag thing' still feels reductive when applied to *Shorty* to the extent that the term participates in objectification through its reference to thingness. This is especially the case as the publicity material positions Shorty as a 'non-binary drag child' which problematises the easy identification of a 'drag thing' in Chillingworth's performance. Chillingworth's version of drag at the intersection of gender and age is perhaps closer to what José Esteban Muñoz has described as 'disidentification' in relation to the work of queer artists of colour (1999). As Kareem Khubchandani helpfully summarises in his own scholarship on drag, Muñoz's concept describes a practice that 'work[s] within and around the limits of expected identity performance to instead foreground critique, pleasure, and survival' (2023: 162). The way in which Chillingworth's drag practice intersects at the edges of expected age identity *and* gender identity performance in *Shorty* has the effect of inviting a deep empathetic connection, which at times for me was read and felt as critique, pleasure, and survival. Notably, a critique of the audience's expectations around age is made possible because of the ambiguity in perception that emerges when Shorty/Chillingworth asks 'how old am I?' and multiple audience members respond by assuming Shorty not Chillingworth is asking the question. This calling out of audience members' assumptions about which body, identity, person, and persona they are responding to at any particular moment critiques our age-based expectations about who ordinarily asks that kind of question.

Chillingworth also creates moments of pleasure in disidentification by developing a gestural vocabulary, comedic script, and mode of delivery via an adult body that does not infantilise Shorty as an adult-in-waiting. Instead, the gestures, script, and delivery take seriously Shorty's cultural location as a non-binary child; a location which cannot be easily 'identified' by an audience as the figure of the non-binary child has yet to experience legibility with dominant mainstream culture. Even whilst we witness a 'tantrum' that might at first glance suggest a reductive representation of a generic child, it is a meltdown that requests: 'stop looking at me', a demand that reads as if it is shared by both a non-binary drag child and an adult artist who opens the show with they/them pronouns and identifies as trans. Chillingworth's framing of their own identities and experiences shapes how we read the performance of the tantrum as it develops and oscillates repeatedly between 'stop looking at me' and 'look at me', which is available to interpretation as a shared call between artist and persona. More specifically, there is a sense in which Shorty appears to be taking pleasure in authorising what the audience should do (look/don't look), inviting us into a moment of real, material ambiguity in our own viewing habits (should I look? shouldn't I look?). The hypervisibility of a tantrum appears to provide an opportunity for the performance to navigate the politics of visibility of queer bodies whose legibility is so-often determined within a majority culture by a heteronormative gaze that marks queer and trans bodies as 'too' visible, not visible enough or, in the case of the transphobic gaze, harmfully renders trans bodies deceptive through their supposed 'invisibility'. Chillingworth and Shorty together own and author the hypervisibility of the tantrum to deny the heteronormative gaze any power to determine their legibility. Instead, we witness an adult body basking in the pleasure of a tantrum that adult bodies are not ordinarily afforded and a non-binary drag child foregrounding pleasure by defining themselves in a world where self-authorship and self-identification are so-often denied to both the trans community and indeed the people we call children. This is age and gender disidentification working in *Shorty* to foreground survival against the limits of expected age and gender identity within a wider transphobic context that maintains and privileges binarised gender.

I want to propose that the language of fluidity, crossing, disguise, bending, reversal, and disidentification has the potential to enrich our understanding of the continuum of age play practices that can be observed across a number of contemporary performance, dance, and live artworks. It is through this language that we can imagine new possibilities for thinking, spectating, and practising through this continuum as scholars, audiences, and makers. In particular, I want to suggest that identifying strategies under the trans*-age umbrella, as opposed to potentially homogenising different kinds of age play as 'age transvestism', can aid poststructural readings that attend to the complexity and situatedness of meaning-making in performance, considering issues of intention, perception, context, polysemic signifiers, and historically, culturally and politically situated modes of reception etc. Having proposed the expanded potential of terminology that is most commonly associated with gender to help conceptualise trans*-age strategies as a continuum of age play, how does this expanded understanding therefore affect and inform how we read 'age' more generally in performance?

What Is Age?

What do I mean by age? We can think of age in a number of different ways from anatomical age to age as a socially produced category to age as a set of citational practices. The body that participates in age-bending, fluidity, reversal, cross-aging, and disidentification through trans*-age strategies has the potential to problematise the naturalised conflation of (perceptions of) anatomical age with age as a category that is socially produced and culturally and historically negotiated. By 'anatomical age' I do not wish to essentialise, rather I am interpreting this category as one's perceived and/or 'known' biological age as it is made legible in a performance and/or via the performance's surrounding publicity materials or documentation. To clarify this point, it is helpful to return to Judith Butler's well-known discussion of drag as illustrative of gender performativity in order to draw some initial similarities between their theory and perceptions and re/presentations of age in performance.

> The performance of drag plays upon the distinction between the anatomy of the performer and the gender that is being performed. But we are actually in the presence of three contingent dimensions of significant corporeality: anatomical sex, gender identity and gender performance.
>
> (Butler [1990] 1999: 175)

To layer age over Butler's reading of gender is to open up the possibility for trans*-age play in performance as a practice that calls age itself into question:

> The performance of *trans*-age strategies* in performance play upon the distinction between the anatomy of the performer and the *age* that is being performed. But we are actually in the presence of three contingent dimensions of significant corporeality: *anatomical age*, *age identity* and *age performance*.

Just as hegemonic masculinities and femininities are under interrogation in practices of drag – even whilst drag might sometimes reaffirm gender norms – trans*-age strategies can call into question normative categories of adult and/or child to reveal age as socially produced and iteratively naturalised. As drag often plays 'upon the distinction between the anatomy of the performer and the gender being performed', so too does age play have the latitude to enact a slippage and a simultaneous recognition of the perceived anatomical age of the performer *and* the age of the character or persona being performed.

Mapping age onto Butler's observations about gender is productive because it foregrounds 'three contingent dimensions of significant corporeality' that can be understood as follows when we see children playing adults and vice versa in performance:

1. 'anatomical age', that is, the *perceived* biological age of the performer's body onstage, which is predominantly indicated to an audience through physical appearance, voice, and movement among other marked signifiers;
2. 'age identity', which I am interpreting as the performer's/character's/persona's age as it is identified as a discursive category through reference to established social labels such as baby, toddler, pre-pubescent, teenager, child, millennial, middle-aged, old-aged etc. Age identity therefore describes an assumption about the performer's and/or the persona's/character's discursive age; and

3 'age performance' which like gender performance is the citational practice of ritualised acts within the everyday which produce a particular age or age group that is legible as such. Age performance is useful in the context of reading age within performance practice because it refers to those *acts* that are indicative of or that begin to confirm a performer's and/or persona's and/or character's anatomical age and age identity.

By imitating age, as some drag imitates gender then, I propose that age play has the potential to 'reveal the imitative structure of [age] itself' (Butler 1990: 137–138, my addition). So, by developing an age-based version of Butler's contingent dimensions of corporeality, my intention at the close of this section is to offer a deconstructive methodological gesture to consider how the imitative structure of age itself might be explored, revealed, and/or challenged in performance practice more generally. However, as I have already argued trans*-age strategies in performance do not simply belong to the realm of 'imitation' so it is important to revise Butler's dimensions of corporeality for the context of performance practice, in order to recognise that the imitative structure of age might be open to revision not just through practices of 'imitation' but through age-bending, fluidity, reversal, non-conformity, crossing, disidentification etc. *in performance.*

We can describe this additional level of interpretative work *in theatre and performance*, which is not accounted for in Butler's formulation, as the quotation marks that are placed around the work to acknowledge that 'this is a performance'. The presence of these quotation marks, I would argue, necessitates an additional fourth dimension of corporeality to be added to my appropriation and layering of Butler's theorisation here. This fourth dimension serves to acknowledge the way in which the body is marked by a performance that contains within it the possibility to disrupt or reaffirm the citational practices that work to produce 'age' as given and natural in an everyday context:

4 'The performance of age' (as distinct from age performance) describes *theatrical or other body-based performance forms that are marked as performance and have the potential to align with or deviate away from the historically-situated ritualised practices that produce age-based norms (see age performance above).*

As Geraldine Harris has argued, the intelligibility of performance depends on the 'legible presence of the quotation marks, which, as described by Butler, the process of performativity as citation operates to conceal in "everyday life"' (1999: 76). In performance then, it is the legible presence – what I am calling the 'performance of age' here – rather than the concealment of these quotation marks that offers potential to facilitate a re-imagining of an otherwise fixed and non-negotiable alignment of an age norm with a performer, character, or persona.

What I propose then is that, like gender, age is 'performatively constituted' (Butler 1990: 25) but in performance there is the possibility to draw attention to this through the performance of age. To be clear, the idea that age might be performatively constituted does not mean that age is not experienced and felt as a lived materiality. Neither does acknowledging age as performatively constituted seek to devalue or ignore the violence, discrimination, and systemic disadvantages one might face at different stages of life for either complying or not complying with age-based norms. Instead, to acknowledge age as performatively constituted seeks precisely to recognise where age-based norms operate through citation in order to maintain harmful patriarchal protectionist logic, to perpetuate and justify age-based discrimination, and to support structures of power that dehumanise, limit, and police the people we call children's subjectivity and freedom to practise agency in the world. The performer, as a subject in the world, is performatively constituted by acts that signify a particular age or ages. However, by virtue of the legibility of the performance *as* performance, the subject, as a performer, exists within a context where age can be negotiated through the legibility of those quotation marks that are ordinarily hidden to naturalise age norms. So, *in performance* - that is, through the fourth dimension of corporeality 'the performance of age' - there is potential to disrupt the ways of 'doing age' that have been socially acquired through the repetition of acts ('age performance'), which align with an accepted category of age ('age identity') that fits with age-based norms. It is through performance that this disruption is potentially available to be recognised as such by a spectator and therefore age-based norms are open to reinvention.

It is important to note that, whilst gender is constituted as 'doing' by Butler, they do not equate this doing with an agent who chooses to 'put on' a particular gender: gender performativity is 'not a doing by a subject who might be said to pre-exist the deed' (ibid.) instead gender performativity is determined by a set of ritualised acts that are established in relation to a subject.[2] However, as Kathy Dow Magnus reminds us '[f]or Butler, the fact that the subject is *constituted* by social discourse does not mean that the subject is *determined* by social discourse' (2006: 83).[3] If we suppose age operates in a similar way to the way in which Butler argues gender works then, the subject exists in relation to ritualised acts that produce age-based norms which constitute but do not determine the subject. Performance, with its legible quotation marks, therefore, offers a place where the 'conditions that produce and limit us prove malleable' (Butler, cited in Magnus 2006: 101) and it becomes possible to challenge or resist the citational practices that work to produce and fix 'age' as natural.

Whether or not we recognise the people we call children *in performance* as subjects who can challenge age's citational practices depends on how a performance negotiates these four dimensions of corporeality (anatomical age, age identity, age performance, and the performance of age) *but also* how, in turn, audience members read these dimensions. If, for example, the performance of age uses legible quotation marks to facilitate the performer's deviation away from or challenge to age-based norms, there is no guarantee that this will be read as such, since an audience member's perception of the performer's anatomical age and/or their age identity, may limit the extent to which they believe the performer, especially one called 'child', to be capable of exercising agency and subjecthood. Undoubtedly, the everyday repetition of age-based norms through ritualised acts that work to secure their appearance as natural are also operating in performance to the extent that reception is shaped through those very norms that naturalise children as not yet fully formed rational subjects and as blank slate humans. Whether we see the people we call children as having the capacity to challenge the conditions that limit them has already been shaped by iteratively repeated age-based norms in everyday life.

However, by appropriating, revising, and reimagining Butler's dimensions of corporeality in drag in relation to age performativity and the performance of age in contemporary performance, we not only have the beginnings of a method for interrogating how trans*-age strategies operate in current and future body-based practice that negotiates these dimensions of corporeality, but also a way of attending to the relational act of interpretation that takes place when reading age in performance. To approach age in this way opens up the possibility of thinking about the people we call children as aged *and* gendered, sexed, and racialised subjects who participate in re/presentations that inevitably negotiate majority culture. It also reminds us that, to dismiss these significant dimensions of corporeality risks ignoring the potential that some children and/or their performances have in perpetuating and, moreover, resisting expected identity norms.

Notes

1 For a detailed analysis of *Film with Hope* in relation to age transvestism, see Senior (2018).

2 Seyla Benhabib has famously contested Butler's framing of the subject as an effect of language, arguing that it is limited because it softens the importance of 'intentionality, accountability, self-reflexivity, and autonomy' (1995: 20–21).

3 Although Magnus agrees with Benhabib that Butler 'unduly restricts the notion of agency and discounts the possibility of more radical acts of initiation, creativity and social transformation' (Magnus 2006: 90) she also notes in Butler's later work, namely their Adorno Lectures (2003), they develop a more 'extensive and empowering notion of agency' (Magnus 2006: 91).

References

Benhabib, Seyla (1995) 'Subjectivity, Historiography, and Politics: Reflections on the 'Feminism/Postmodernism Exchange' in Seyla Benhabib, Judith Butler, Drucilla Cornell, and Nancy Fraser (eds.) *Feminist Contentions: A Philosophical Exchange*, New York: Routledge, pp. 107–126.

Butler, Judith ([1990] 1999) *Gender Trouble: Feminism and the Subversion of Identity*, New York: Routledge.

Butler, Judith (2003) Kritik Der Ethischen Gewalt. Adorno Lectures, 2002. Frankfurt am Main: Institut für Sozialforschung an der Johann Wolfgang Goethe-Universität.

Flanagan, Victoria (2008) *Into the Closet: Cross-Dressing and the Gendered Body in Children's Literature and Film*, New York and London: Routledge.

Harris, Geraldine (1999) *Staging Femininities: Performance and Performativity*, Manchester and New York: Manchester University Press.

Hildebrandt, Antje (2018) 'The Child as Art Object in Tino Sehgal's Ann Lee, Ann Lee & Marcel and This Progress – A Reflection', *Performance Research: A Journal of the Performing Arts*, 23 (1): 109–112.

Khubchandani, Kareem (2023) *Decolonize Drag*, New York and London: OR Books.

Magnus, Kathy Dow (2006) 'The Unaccountable Subject: Judith Butler and the Social Conditions of Intersubjective Agency', *Hypatia*, 21 (2): 81–103.

Muñoz, José Esteban (1999) *Disidentifications: Queers of Color and the Performance of Politics*, Minneapolis: University of Minnesota Press.

Ridout, Nicholas (2007) 'You Look Charming. You Look Enchanting. You Look Dazzling. You Look Breathtaking. You Look Unique. But You Don't Make an Evening', Tate Website, 1 September 2007: https://www.tate.org.uk/tate-etc/issue-11-autumn-2007/you-look-charming-you-look-enchanting-you-look-dazzling-you-look (accessed 30 January 2024).

Senior, Adele (2018) 'Age Transvestism' in Contemporary Performance and Live Art with Children', *Performance Research: A Journal of the Performing Arts*, 23 (1): 26–36.

Stryker, Susan (1994) 'My Words to Victor Frankenstein Above the village of Chamounix: Performing Transgender Rage', *GLQ: A Journal of Lesbian and Gay Studies*, 1: 237–254.

Part III

Experiencing Children

6 Queer(ing) Methodologies

Part three turns to queerness to rebalance the inequity of the lack of space and time given to documenting children's voices and experiences within the current contemporary performance and performance studies scene. It asks: How do we attend to the lived and relational experiences of children as performers and collaborators in contemporary performance? How can we foster their potential as co-researchers and archivists to self-represent in post-performance contexts? And, in doing so, how can we develop approaches that not only negotiate children in performance as makers and carriers of meaning but also as bodies and historically-situated subjects with their own embodied experiences?

These questions feel urgent for many reasons. First, my own encounters as an audience member of performances that include people we call children have increasingly demanded new ways of describing the sometimes-complex embodied interactions with and experiences of these works. The many knowledges acquired from these performances can provide a useful starting point for addressing some of the challenges that arise from the questions above. In the case of Britt Hatzius' *Blind Cinema*, which I explore in the next chapter, I turn to queer phenomenology as a means of attending to the relationality of these experiences and problematising the embodied and intimate encounters sometimes available in performance with the people we call children. The shift to a queer, body-based critical framework is largely a direct response to the particularities of my embodied experience as a pregnant person encountering *Blind Cinema*. This critical approach also felt necessary because the children who performed in the work are not framed through the visual-centric economy that so-often dictates professional practice with children. Instead, the young performers are foregrounded as breathing, feeling, living bodies in a closer, intimate embodied relation with the audience than much of the theatre I have discussed in the book thus far. The performance, in many ways, urges us to attend to the people we call children as bodies with complex lived, material, and embodied realities. As such, Sarah Ahmed's queer phenomenological approach (2006) becomes useful for unpacking *Blind Cinema* alongside theories of intimacy developed in dialogue with one-to-one performance practice (Johnson 2012, Heddon *et al.* 2012, Wake 2017, Zerihan 2006) as well as recent research on Autonomous Sensory Meridian Response or ASMR and whispering to articulate the particularities of this embodied experience (Andersen 2015, Li 2011).

DOI: 10.4324/9781003043072-9

Secondly, whilst previous discussions of children within the fields of performance and theatre have been useful for considering how the presence of children in live performance intersects with theatrical fictions and the theatrical economy, the lived experiences of the people called children themselves have been largely overlooked in scholarship on contemporary performance. Children in performance have been considered 'stubbornly real' (States 1985: 37), 'theatrical hazard[s]' and metaphors for (real) risk (Orozco 2010: 82, 84), and 'uncanny' when their assimilation into the fictional world of a performance and/or the professional world of the actor is incomplete (Ridout 2004: 60). Josh Abrams further develops the idea of the child on stage as 'a marker of the space of affective labour' in a way that begins to address the people we call children as bodies in the present moment of performance (although he also draws on a performance where children are not physically present). He convincingly argues that the theatre's insistence on a presence that resists linear teleology coupled with the child's symbolic resonance as potentiality and futurity, offers 'a new way of envisioning the political' (Abrams 2013: 202). Whilst Abrams' thesis takes into some consideration the child's bodily and relational presence and how that 'breaks the link of signification' for the audience, the methodological, embodied, and material effects of body-based and relational encounters with children in performance on both analysts and the people we call children themselves, has yet to be fully explored.

Thirdly, and on a related point, theories of the child within the academy often fail to account for what Jo-Ann Wallace calls the 'material specificity' of actual children (1994: 298). This is the case in a number of disciplines that privilege childhood as a social construction at the expense of considering the actual people we call children, such as in childhood studies or theories of childhood akin to Lee Edelman's work (2004), that arguably 'empty the child of matters related to its physical embodiment' (Dyer 2017: 295). Poststructuralist theories of the child, Claudia Castañeda also observes, are limiting in their positioning of the figure of the child as 'a site of possibility and potential' (2002: 169). Castañeda summarises:

> [T]he child is figured as the embodiment of becoming rather than being (Deleuze and Guattari), as the site where thinking becomes possible (Foucault), as the condition that throws "man" off course (Lyotard). Within feminist theorizations of the subject via psychoanalysis, the (girl) child is figured as the ground of subject making.'
>
> (2002: 167)

Through queering methodologies, by which I mean adopting queer-led approaches such as Sarah Ahmed's queer phenomenology (2006) as well as queering existing methodologies of research, I hope to deliberately interrupt normative approaches to reading and researching children that are led by adult privilege, where adult privilege is understood as the norm of 'us[ing] the child as a pre-subjective other that we can inhabit or know as theorists' (Castañeda 2002: 168). To queer adult privilege, instead, is to start from a position that deliberately challenges the idea of the child as 'the subject yet to come-not yet literate, not yet capable of reason, not yet fully agential' (Wallace 1994: 298). A queer reading of children in performance and queer-informed research *with* children, I argue then, is careful not to approach the people we call children as the site for adult (researcher's/spectator's) desires of 'transformative change' (Castañeda 2002: 158). Instead, it is concerned with embracing a multitude of experiences of being with children in performance and research precisely in order to shake up our existing 'adult' methodologies alongside making space for the 'specific materiality' of the people we call children that are routinely ignored when theorists use the child to understand and confirm adult subjectivity (Wallace 1994: 288). As performance is a body-based practice, I would argue that it is therefore a fruitful place to attend to the child as, what Castañeda calls, an emergent and contextualised figuration that is both embodied as well as material-semiotic.

I use the term 'queer' to capture the methodological attitude of the last part of this book, not to fix queerness as an identity for researcher and/or researched, but instead in a way that borrows from a position Judith Butler articulated almost three decades ago, but which still resonates in a contemporary context, where queer is imagined as:

> a site of collective contestation, the point of departure for a set of historical reflections and futural imaginings [...] never fully owned but always and only redeployed, twisted, queered from prior usage.
>
> (Butler 1993: 19)

In this respect, my interest in queering approaches to researching children's appearance and participation in contemporary performance aligns with more recent attempts to develop 'a queer methodological approach to child development and education [that] can more generally disrupt teleologically constructed narratives of growth that require a developmental sequence which culminates in normalcy' (Dyer 2017: 292). Following Dyer, I am particularly interested in queering as a way of making space for 'more expansive ways to account for children's deviances from normativity' (ibid.: 293) in both performance and post-performance contexts. As such, my approach aligns with the work of recent performance scholarship that has been directly informed by queer theory (Germano 2018), although my focus in Part III is more on process or post-performance analysis, whereas the emerging literature focuses mainly on performance analysis. For me, queering also involves asking how we attend to actual children's deviations from cultural norms within these contexts as well as attending to our own deviations. Taking into consideration my own positioning as an audience member, researcher, and sometimes co-researcher alongside people we call children, in this final part of the book I notice the ways in which performance might create relational affects that queer in their ability to undo rather than fix identities. Instead of reifying the child/adult binary then, my interest in queer approaches deliberately takes its lead from the performance strategies I have outlined thus far that work to destabilise it. After all, just like adults, the people we call children queer and participate in queer representations and are or have queer bodies, queer identities, queer narratives, and queer lived experiences.

Building on the book's strategies for reading performances where the 'child [is] queered by innocence' (Stockton 2009: 12) and performances that dismantle the notion of the child as a fixed age-based identity category, my approach is informed by Hannah Dyer's assertion that '[a]pplying queer methods of analysis to studies of childhood can help to queer the rhetoric of innocence that constrains all children and help to refuse attempts to calculate the child's future before it has the opportunity to explore desire' (2017: 292). Similarly, I propose that adopting queer methods or queering existing methods of analysis that we regularly apply to adult bodies in theatre and performance studies can assist in moving beyond a reading of the child as a placeholder for potentiality and as always already 'stubbornly real'. To bring queerness into analytical relation with young performers in the context of contemporary performance is instead to shift towards recognising that children are queered by innocence, that both on and off stage some people we call children identify as queer in terms of their gender, sexuality and/or other aspects of who they are, and that theoretical abstractions of the child are problematic in that they often assume whiteness. For example, whilst Lee Edelman is clear that his thesis is not about actual children in the world (2004: 11), José Esteban Muñoz importantly critiques Edelman's theory for the way in which it 'accepts and reproduces [a] monolithic figure of the child that is indeed always already white' (Muñoz 2009: 95). To focus on the materiality of the voices and the bodies of children as they are made available to the audience member of *Blind Cinema* and to make space for the thoughts and experiences of actual young people who have participated in contemporary performances, is to foreground the way in which performance and performance research might deliberately undermine this conflation of the people we call children with the child as a white monolithic figure.

As such, following a queer phenomenological reading of *Blind Cinema*, Chapters 8, *Growing Sideways Together* and 9, *The Child as Researcher and Archivist* disrupt this white monolithic figure to prioritise contributions from young people themselves, the majority of whom are people of Black and global majority heritage and have performed within the context of professional contemporary performance and dance. In *Growing Sideways,* I collaborate on post-performance and post-process research with two young people who participated in the work of London-based company Fevered Sleep: Sorrel Barnes, who performed in *Men and Girls Dance* in Brighton at age 9 in 2016, and Zina Abaraonye, who was involved in research and development work for *We Are Not Finished* in 2019 at age 13. The dialogue between myself, Zina, and Sorrel emerges from a research commitment to queering a normative approach to researching with children, which is shaped by a developmentalist approach that privileges a limited perspective of 'growing up' that ends with adulthood. Such a perspective ignores the myriad other ways that the people we call both children and adults might 'grow' both separately and together. Instead, the chapter aims to attend to our individual and shared 'sideways growth' as it pertains to 'the width of a person's experience or ideas, their motives or their motions' (Stockton 2009: 11). Whilst Stockton's notion of growing sideways emerges through a reading of the 'ghostly gay child' in literature, film, and television, who challenges the dominant narrative that children 'grow up' to full developmental stature, the chapter offers a practical working through of Stockton's notion of 'lateral contact' (ibid.) between 'adults' and 'children' within the context of contemporary performance. In doing so, it responds directly to Zina and Sorrel's more nuanced position than 'child' as cisgender, female-identifying adolescents (Zina is 14 and Sorrel has just turned 13 at the time of writing) who participated in professional performance during their childhood and tween years. As such, the chapter charts a meeting that evolves from, rather than against, our mutual experiences of transition to ask: what can I/we learn from young people about what it means to be a (pre)teenager making performance with a professional theatre company and what collaborative potential might the metaphor of the 'teen' offer within the current paradigmatic shift away from research *on* children to researching *with* children in the field of performance studies?

The next chapter, *Child as Researcher and Archivist*, shares post-performance documentation by the young performers who appeared in Andy Field and Beckie Darlington's production of *News News News* at Contact Theatre, Manchester in March 2022, which was gathered during a two-day workshop at the children's primary school. The performers' archive of their post-performance experiences is also accompanied by some questions I posed to the (adult) artists, that are queered by patriarchal protectionist assumptions and content that we might ordinarily encounter when adults interview children but instead are asked of the adult artists. To contextualise the documentation, I offer an accompanying commentary in the margins as a series of autoethnographic reflections. These reflections help to situate the game I created for the workshop to encourage the performers to take up the dual role of researcher and archivist but also to explore what lateral contact might mean in this school-based context and with a number of performers in comparison to the trio-based research process Zina, Sorrel and I had established. The marginalia also helps to locate a key concern: How useful is appropriating both existing approaches to positioning children as researchers in childhood studies (and its related disciplines) and research methods that are commonly reserved for adults in performance studies in the post-performance archival process? The chapter echoes the workshop structure, culminating in a child-authored manifesto on 'working with children in performance' that the performers consented to be disseminated in this book and with an international audience of other child performers/makers and adult makers and pedagogues as part of an ASSITEJ-funded symposium at Fundus Theatre in Hamburg, Germany in 2022. In supporting the production of a manifesto – and breaking with the historical trend of adult-led manifestos – I am interested in generating a meaningful interjection in research *with* children that not only positions the young performers as researchers but also explores the activist potential of their research activities.

In summary, the following pages offer an exploration into what a queer methodological approach to 'reading' children and researching *with* children in contemporary performance might look and feel like. It queers a normative reading of children beyond their apparent extra 'presence' in performance by creating space for the people we call children to attend to their own material specificity, should they wish to, so that in the future we might consider how this specificity intersects with representations of the 'child' that they navigate in performance. In doing so, this final part of the book builds on the reparations of scholarship (James, Jenks and Prout 1998) that have taken issue with research *about children without children* and has since paved the way for a framework that has been absent from academic literature for too long: children's self-representation. It also, however, recognises and aims not to repeat the limitations of such 'attempts to represent children as agentic social actors' where 'the child is simultaneously erased and occupied by the adult author's figuration of the child as a theoretical resource' (Castañeda 2002: 143). Indeed, the focus is only on 'agency' in this section, to the extent that the activities create the conditions for agency to be exercised by all participants rather than agency as something adults always already possess and simply 'give' to the people we call children. This is not to disregard the structural disadvantages that often limit children's access to exercising agency and the way in which these oppressions maintain and perpetuate adult privilege. Indeed, recognising agency as something that is done rather than something one has, is a means of challenging this adult privilege. Instead, putting a queer phenomenological approach to work and privileging the perspectives of young performers is a deliberate attempt here to queer the predetermined idea of the child as a 'social actor' within childhood studies of the global north, which problematically relies on the reductive assumption of this actor as a unitary masculine and rational subject (Walkerdine 1988; Burman and Stacey 2010).

References

Abrams, Josh (2013) 'Affective Presents/Effective Presence: Intensity, Futurity, and the Theatrical Politics of the Child' in Matthew Causey and Fintan Walsh (eds.) *Performance, Identity and the Neo-Political Subject*, Abingdon: Routledge, pp. 201–14.

Ahmed, Sara (2006) *Queer Phenomenology: Orientations, Objects, Others*, Durham and London: Duke University Press.

Andersen, Joceline (2015) 'Now You've Got the Shiveries: Affect, Intimacy, and the ASMR Whisper Community', *Television & New Media*, 16 (8): 683–700.

Burman, Erica and Stacey, Jackie (2010) 'The child and Childhood in Feminist Theory', *Feminist Theory*, 11 (3): 227–240.

Butler, Judith (1993) 'Critically Queer', *GLQ: A Journal of Lesbian and Gay Studies*, 1 (1): 17–32.

Castañeda, Claudia (2002) *Figurations: Child, Bodies, Worlds*, Durham and London: Duke University Press.

Dyer, Hannah (2017) 'Queer Futurity and Childhood Innocence: Beyond the Injury of Development', *Global Studies of Childhood*, 7 (3): 290–302.

Edelman, Lee (2004) *No Future: Queer Theory and the Death Drive*, London: Duke University Press.

Germano, Isis (2018) 'So Cute, So Creepy', *Performance Research*, 23 (1): 44–51.

Heddon, Deirdre, Helen Iball and Rachel Zerihan (2012) 'Come Closer: Confessions of Intimate Spectators in One to One Performance', *Contemporary Theatre Review*, 22 (1): 120–133.

James, Allison, Chris, Jenks and Alan Prout (1998) *Theorizing Childhood*, Allison James, Chris Jenks, and Alan Prout (eds), Cambridge: Polity Press.

Johnson, Dominic (2012) 'Ecstatic Intervals: Performance in a Continuum of Intimacy' in Maria Chatzichristodoulou and Rachel Zerihan (eds.) *Intimacy Across Visceral and Digital Performance*, Basingstoke: Palgrave Macmillan.

Li, Xinghua (2011) 'Whispering: The Murmur of Power in a Lo-Fi World', *Media, Culture and Society*, 33 (1): 19–34.

Muñoz, José Esteban (2009) *Cruising Utopia: The Then and There of Queer Futurity*, New York and London: New York University Press.

Orozco, Lourdes (2010) '"Never Work with Children and Animals": Risk, Mistake and the Real in Performance', *Performance Research: A Journal of Performing Arts*, 15 (2): 80–85.

Ridout, Nicholas (2004) 'Animal Labour in the Theatrical Economy', *Theatre Research International*, 29 (1): 57–65.

States, Bert O. (1985) *Great Reckonings in Little Rooms: On the Phenomenology of Theater*, Berkeley: University of California Press.

Stockton, Kathryn Bond (2009) *The Queer Child or Growing Sideways in the Twentieth Century*, Durham and London: Duke University Press.

Wake, Caroline (2017) 'The Ambivalent Politics of One-to-One Performance', *Performance Paradigm*, 13: 163–173.

Walkerdine, Valerie (1988) *The Mastery of Reason*, London: Routledge.

Wallace, Jo-Ann (1994) 'De-scribing *the Water Babies:* 'The Child' in Post-Colonial Theory' in Chris Tiffin and Alan Lawson (eds.) *De-Scribing Empire*, London and New York: Routledge.

Zerihan, Rachel (2006) 'Intimate Inter-actions: Returning to the Body in One to One Performance', *Body, Space and Technology*, 6 (1). http://doi.org/10.16995/bst.174

7 The Embodied Child of *Blind Cinema*

> *If orientation is about making the strange familiar through the extension of bodies into space, then disorientation occurs when that extension fails. Or we could say that some spaces extend certain bodies and simply do not leave room for others.*
>
> (Ahmed 2006: 11)

Disorientating. This was my experience of *Blind Cinema* by Belgium-based artist Britt Hatzius. *Blind Cinema* (2017) begins with a slow walk of mainly adult audience members into a small cinema auditorium at the Cornerhouse in the centre of Manchester, UK. We are here as part of the Flare Festival. The programme tells us to expect to be blindfolded; that behind us there will be 'a row of children who, in hushed voices, describe a film only they can see'; and that these 8 to 11 year olds will be seeing the film for the very first time. Walking into a cinema space to see performance work is not a familiar experience for me. The chairs invite a longer stay – they are comfortable and low to the ground. This is not a theatre space. As my hands touch the fabric of the armrests, a flutter of memories of sitting in a local cinema with friends of the past arrives unbidden. My body registers and remembers the cinema space specifically as a body that was scripted as a girl from birth and immediately calls my attention to it as a gendered space: a place of open secrecy, of touching and being touched in those so-called formative years.

Sara Ahmed might refer to this opening description as the background. The experiences I describe on entering the cinema-performance space constitute the circumstances against which the cinema screen appears as the object that one is ordinarily orientated towards when seeing a film. In *Queer Phenomenology: Orientations, Objects, Others*, Ahmed explains that the background is that which is often marginalised to the edges of phenomenological analysis in order for phenomenology to face and '*to sustain* a certain direction' (2006: 31). By way of example, she draws on Edmund Husserl's intentionality towards the writing table in his home study. She demonstrates how, within the phenomenological tradition of attending to an object of the consciousness, Husserl's perception of the table he encounters in the present, necessarily relegates the domestic sphere behind and around him to the background. By foregrounding those objects and bodies that are not simply unacknowledged but often actively demoted by the phenomenologist, Ahmed draws our

DOI: 10.4324/9781003043072-10

attention to the politics of bracketing off what veers away from 'straight' perception. In Husserl's case, this bracketing has problematic political implications in the sense that it is indicative of who is afforded the space and time to write:

> We can think… of the background not simply in terms of what is around what we face, as the "dimly perceived," but as produced by acts of relegation: some things are relegated to the background… in order to keep attention on what is faced. Perception involves such acts of relegation that are forgotten in the very preoccupation with what is faced.
>
> (Ahmed 2006: 31)

Husserl's orientation towards the table, alongside passing references he makes to other objects that he 'co-perceives' in his surroundings in the first volume of *Ideas* (1969), notably his children heard playing nearby, ignores the dependency of his writing on the domestic work carried out 'to keep the desk clear' whilst he writes (Ahmed 2006: 30). For Ahmed, phenomenology has traditionally orientated itself towards some objects and not others and so it reveals itself to be, in this instance, a gendered practice. It is no coincidence that Husserl's children are part of this domestic scene and subsequently consigned to the background, since we could add nuance to Ahmed's claim in the epigraph and propose that *children's bodies, in particular, are not extended by certain spaces*. The traditional philosopher's space, such as Husserl's study is one example of this, where the children play at a distance from his work and his attention to his own perceptions. *Blind Cinema*, I will suggest, explores through practice this claim that children's bodies are not extended by certain spaces.

Following Ahmed, I attend to the background that is ordinarily 'bracketed out' of Husserlian phenomenology in my reading of *Blind Cinema* throughout this chapter. In particular, I want to propose that the specificity of the affective, embodied, and sensory moments of performance with the children in this piece demand, and can be explicated by, drawing on the insights of queer approaches to phenomenology. In particular, Ahmed's work on queer 'orientations' offers a means of unpacking the disorientating experience of this performance. Such disorientating spatio-temporal aspects include: the absence of the visual; the intimacy of the whispering; the close physical proximity to the children; the children's interpretive work as they attempt to make sense of what they are seeing on the screen; the fluidity and lack of fixed meaning that is evoked by their descriptions; the viscerality of the warmth and smell of the performer's breath; the signifying work of their dialects; the absence of gender fixity and racial identification; and the continual 'failure' of meaning-making in the performance.

With the help of scholarly writing around intimacy (Johnson 2012), one-to-one performance (Heddon *et al.* 2012, Wake 2017, Zerihan 2006), and recent research on Autonomous Sensory Meridian Response or ASMR and whispering (Andersen 2015, Li 2011), I argue that these disorienting strategies of *Blind Cinema* queer a 'straight', by which I mean a 'straightforward' normative, orientation towards the dominant image of children on stage as innocent in need of protection; an image which is sustained by the patriarchal protectionist gaze I discussed in part II.[1] I begin by considering the way in which the work both orientates and disorientates me towards the child as a vulnerable subject and what this implies about the kind of responsibility and care this performance demands. The kind of intimacy *Blind Cinema* evokes is then explored and followed by a discussion about the role whispering plays in foregrounding both the child as a body and also my own embodied response as an audience member, which is contrary to the dominant ways in which the bodies of the people we call children are often offered up to the nostalgic, protective, and eroticising gaze discussed in previous chapters. I then go on to consider this embodied response by examining the way in which the blindfold denies visual access to the performer's body and thus breaks with the dominant optical mode through which both cinema and performance audiences regularly and normatively experience children in film and onstage. The final section of the chapter considers how the directionality of the bodies of the young performers, and the use of space in *Blind Cinema*, operates to resist the tendency towards othering children in public spaces (Cele and van der Burgt 2015). In summary, *Blind Cinema* creates a performance space which 'extends certain bodies' in a space (Ahmed 2006), that is, the bodies of the performers we call children, when ordinarily it does 'not leave room' for them. It does so, I propose, not through orientation but conversely through acts of disorientation that might in turn inform the methods through which we archive the lived, embodied, and relational experiences of children as performers and collaborators in contemporary performance more generally.

(Dis)Orientating Oneself

We are told to put on our blindfolds. Then, quiet falls around us. It's too quiet. After a few moments, we hear bodies moving up the middle aisle and then eventually brushing past the seats behind and in front of us. I am around 19 weeks pregnant and become increasingly aware that nobody else around me knows: not my colleague and friend who is seated adjacent to me, not the person sitting on my other side, and not the performers in front or behind me. I feel exposed. My vulnerable body sits still, sight removed, as if held hostage. I feel something creep up to my ear. Relax. It's just the funnel – we were warned about this in the preamble. I lean into it. I can hear the breath of the performer. They feel extremely close and then, a haze of light enters my blindfold. The film has begun and the whispers descend upon the room, into my ear, and all around, filling the senses. They begin to describe what can be seen on the screen with a gentle but nervous voice. I listen intently. It becomes clear the performer is not scripted.

For each audience member, the performance comprises three of these one-to-one encounters with three different young performers whispering into their ear. Alongside these one-to-ones, the constant soundscape of the other performers whispering into their respective funnels towards the ear of their own designated audience member can be heard, although what they are saying is too faint to decipher. I refer to this setup in the writing that follows as 'one-to-one-to-all' to capture something of both the individual and collective experience of the other one-to-ones generated by the sea of whispering that accompanies the improvised narrative offered to my own ear through the funnel. This one-to-one-*to-all* format seems to echo the intensity and politics of responsibility Rachel Zerihan identifies in one-to-one performance more generally (2006), whilst not participating specifically in the signature 'alone time' with a performer. My responsibility is to sit and listen, whilst their role is to speak. The set-up has all the trappings of one-to-one works that begin or end with the audience member romanticising about the intimacy of the engagement between performer/audience but the collective experience of hearing the other performers' witnessing and relaying the film to their assigned listener plays an important role in the affective experience of *Blind Cinema* to cut through any attempt I might make to idealise the intimacy encountered.

Whilst the form resists the idealisation of the intimacy of one-to-one performance, I inevitably project vulnerability onto the people we call children who labour around me. This projection is, in part, a consequence of my pregnant body, which is, in Ahmed's terms, a bodily orientation that creates the conditions of possibility for a line to be drawn; an extension of my body in space as a care-giver, a position that is further emphasised because of the makers of meaning who stand behind me, creating and unfolding 'the work' in the moment of its iteration. I interpret their vocalisations as vulnerability. Two out of three of the performers assigned to me frantically and nervously scrabble around for a meaning that they can translate for my listening ear, at least at the beginning of their individual encounters with me before they settle into the act. I recognise their effort as a moment of care: for me and for the performance 'to work'. At the same time, I am not only an audience member in this moment but also an audience-researcher, a subject position that, to some extent, appropriates the institutional ethics procedures that demand the categorisation of children as 'vulnerable subjects'. The discourse of the child as innocent in need of protection steadily creeps up and folds its way into my reading of the work.

However, the intensity of the one-to-one aspect of *Blind Cinema* emphasises a sense of co-experienced vulnerability that requires the kind of care common to one-to-one performance practice more generally, among adults. I interpret the gentleness of the funnel arriving at my ear, for example, as the performer's recognition of my own vulnerability as a blindfolded participant. Care in one-to-one performance, Caroline Wake helpfully notes, is often dialogic: 'while the performer owes the spectator a duty of care, the reverse also applies, especially when the artist is vulnerable' (2017: 167). In *Blind Cinema,* I similarly feel I owe the performer a duty of care not only because I read the performer's initial struggle with finding a verbal language for the visual event that they see in front of them as vulnerability, but because of the *intimacy* generated through this shared encounter. This intimacy is both specific to me and the person standing behind me but it is also shared, albeit differently by the other one-to-one pairings around us. The physical closeness of the performer to my body and the assumption of trust that they are not going to suddenly shout or accidentally jolt the funnel into my ear both contribute to the intimacy of this moment and the care it seems to require from them and me to listen and to avoid distracting them by taking visible or audible pleasure in, or concern for, their struggle.

Unlike one-to-one performances that presume or invite the spectator to be 'a performing spectator' (Heddon *et al.* 2012: 122), *Blind Cinema* promotes a physical and verbal inactivity on the part of the audience. In this work, one is only a participant to the extent that they agree to sit quietly, listen, and imagine. Yet, the invitation to listen to a child's voice inevitably heightens my responsibility to try and understand, reassure, and encourage. I thus find myself nodding along when the performer asks a question that we both know (according to the rules of the performance space) I am not supposed to verbally respond to. I laugh when they laugh, even if I do not find what they are relaying particular funny. There is undoubtedly more pressure to be a good audience when young performers are involved. That said, willing a performance to work is not particular to child/adult one-to-one interactions. The need to please is so common in (adult) one-to-one performances that Helen Iball refers to it as 'giv[ing] good audience' (Heddon *et al.* 2012: 124). Nevertheless, my responsibility is genuine to the extent that I recognise the performer's struggle to improvise. It is a struggle I am acquired to seeing in contemporary performance and this prior embodied knowledge of the performers' struggle enables me to appreciate the artistry of their engagement as both generous and risky. I begin to see them, or rather, experience them less as vulnerable children and more as artists and cultural producers.

Children and Intimacy

Blind Cinema is a pleasant encounter, but it is not a comfortable one, predominantly because the form makes me constantly aware that a child performer is working in the service of me, the adult audience member. Nicholas Ridout, drawing on performances that also include children, has called one-to-one works where there the performer is invested in the performance of labour rather than its representation 'service economy performance' (2008: 130). Knowing both that they are not being paid for their participation and that I am not paying for their 'service', since the performance is free, complicates the categorisation of this work in Ridout's terms. There is certainly an emotional investment from them – or at least I assume this investment exists because of the exertion and commitment I hear in their voices – with a potential risk of failure for the performers to communicate 'effectively'. Despite the tension this creates, or perhaps because of it, I enjoy the sensation of the performers whispering in my ear. The dialectical clues in their whispering voices align with my prior knowledge that these performers are from local Manchester-based schools – St Brigid's RC Primary in Beswick and Beaver Road Primary in Didsbury I find out later – and the cues bring a comforting familiarity to the experience. Yet, a feeling of uneasiness still exists in response to their emotional and bodily labour, highlighted in the performers' audible effort to find the words to describe what they are seeing on the screen.

The pleasant kind of interaction experienced in this work resonates with the 'convivial' encounters that art critic Claire Bishop recognises and critiques in 'relational art' of the 1990s, although it should be noted she is predominantly referring to work exhibited in corporatised art settings (Bishop 2004: 56). Whilst

Blind Cinema takes place within a non-corporatised, non-profit festival context, it shares some aesthetic commonalities with relational art practices theorised by Nicolas Bourriaud (1998) in terms of their intersubjective qualities and emphasis on collective creation rather than individual consumption of meaning through detached opticality (Bishop 2004: 61). *Blind Cinema*, which is the antithesis of 'detached opticality' because of its imaginative investment in something that the audience cannot access visually, exists only in a one-to-one dialogue between both the young performer and adult audience member who collaboratively co-author the work through interpretive interactions with the screen, sound, and each other. Although *Blind Cinema* does not follow the DIY aesthetic evident in Bourriaud's relational art, the cinema functions like the already established cultural spaces of the paradigmatic works he cites, such as the museums and art gallery contexts of New York-based artist Rirkrit Tiravanija. This parallel with relational art is significant because the cinema space's regimented seating which favours the optical and the conventional expectation of silence it demands of cinema-goers creates the ideal environment for *Blind Cinema* to inject an arguably more participatory experience of togetherness in comparison to the average cinema-going experience.

As an audience member then, I am still bound to the expectation of silence in this performance space but there is nevertheless a strong sense of community which emerges from the form: the blindfolded audience members sharing the anticipation of experiencing cinema without sight; the performers co-experiencing rule-bound communication; and the little pockets of one-to-one encounters bearing a mutual, shared act of interpretation. Like relational art's attempt to 'erode the distinction between institutional and social space' (Bishop 2004: 56) *Blind Cinema* hosts a social form of art that echoes the predominantly 'positive human relationships' said to emerge from aesthetic relationality (ibid.: 62). The content of the film that these child performers are describing, for example, is neither upsetting nor distressing and the delivery is not overtly provocative which therefore situates the intimacy of this work in the realm of the 'pastoral' (Johnson 2012: 90).

Paradoxically, however, the conviviality of *Blind Cinema* is experienced in such a way that shakes the 'pastoral securities of nationally and internationally sanctioned intimacies' that Dominic Johnson argues are refused in (adult) performances that deliberately engage in discomfiting intimacies (2012: 92). Here, Johnson is referring specifically to what he calls 'ecstatic' performances that problematise and challenge an untroubled definition of intimacy as a pleasant interpersonal interaction between two people (ibid.: 89). Whilst the performances he discusses, in line with the wider literature on intimacy and one-to-one performance, refers exclusively to adult performers and spectators, Johnson's reworking of the notion of intimacy is nevertheless useful for thinking about an experience of intimacy between a 'child performer' and 'adult spectator' that is already highly politicised. Rather than accepting intimacy as 'two people coming together in a politically neutral way' (ibid.), Johnson helpfully proposes that intimacy exists on a continuum, citing the socio-legal fight for same-sex marriage as an example that some intimacies are celebrated whilst others are 'disparaged, stigmatized or criminalized' (ibid.). In performance practice, he suggests that this continuum slides:

> from the heavy depths of solitude, to the solitary pleasures of ecstatic narcissism, to the convivial shortcomings of pastoral intimacies, to a promiscuous ecstasy and its troubled erotics, to, finally, abuse and its destitutions.
>
> (Johnson 2012: 100)

If we accept a continuum of intimacy in these terms, we can acknowledge that the moment of a child whispering into the ear of an adult whom they do not know in *Blind Cinema* is not the kind of intimacy we ordinarily celebrate and yet at the same time it is 'sanctioned' in this work (by the festival organisers, the teachers, the parents, the audience etc.). I am as much a stranger to the performers as they are to me. My strange(r)ness carries with it political resonance in this context, where societal norms assume and dictate that intimacy between a child and an adult whom they do not know should be approached with caution and suspicion. The British legacy of the 'stranger danger' discourse used in campaigns and government information films of the 1970s and 1980s arguably still persists in the wider socio-political context in which the performance takes place and I carry this discourse with me into my experience of *Blind Cinema*. This is not because of the potential for any real danger to the children involved, but because of the uniqueness of this experience of sanctioned intergenerational intimacy between adult and child strangers.

In this regard, *Blind Cinema* shares the discomfiting intimacy of Mammalian Diving Reflex's (MDR) *Haircuts By Children* (2006) without the physical risk or aspect of touch present in the latter work. *Haircuts* is a performance in which a group of children aged 10–11 from Parkdale Public School were trained to cut hair and gave free haircuts to willing spectators across different locations in Toronto. Indeed, the description of *Haircuts* by Broderick Chow and artistic director of the company Darren O'Donnell parallels, almost word for word, my experience of *Blind Cinema* in terms of strange(r) intimacy:

> Creating an affective environment controlled entirely by children generates a strange and awkward intimacy between stylist [performer] and client [spectator], where both must navigate a spatial and social proximity that our culture conventionally forbids.
>
> (2014: 148)

As the tension created by *Haircuts* demonstrates, the power relationship between adult and child is already assumed to be unequal in the majority of social interactions with the people we call children, not excluding *Blind Cinema*, with questions of their ability to consent, know, and understand what they are participating in always already haunting child/adult encounters. *Blind Cinema* plays with this societal questioning of the child's competence by continually shifting the balance of power: from the adult audience that is served by the young performers in the name of art to the young performers who both hold the funnel as a literal and metaphorical microphone and decide what to edit in and out of their narration. Furthermore, the largely inactive adult audience is, in a poetic reversal of roles, 'seen and not heard', seated and blindfolded yet simultaneously in the position of the consumer whilst the children work – with audible effort – to produce the content.

Blind Cinema, therefore, sits firmly in the middle of Johnson's continuum, characterised neither by an experience of solitude that desperately seeks or misses another person nor by an encounter in which I am 'overwhelmed by their proximity' (ibid.: 89). However, unlike the relational art that Bishop argues avoids more complex modes of participation in favour of encounters that are celebrated for their assumed intrinsic democratic appeal (2004: 67), *Blind Cinema* is the embodiment of the idea that 'the central region of the intimate continuum may itself be crowded by political difficulties' (Johnson 2012: 90). The performance demonstrates through its form that this kind of intimacy *is always* politically resonant, even whilst it occupies the centre. Along with the power relations and alterity of both performer and audience member suggested above, *Blind Cinema* overtly announces the politics of its intimacy as something other than the familial and sentimental intimacies we are accustomed to where child/adult relations are concerned through whispering. The act of whispering plays an important role in dismantling normative modes of perception and reception of the people we call children in contemporary performance here and therefore demands further exploration to unpack its potential socio-political significance in Hatzius' piece and beyond.

On Hearing

As I sit here in this hybrid cinema-performance space, my body recalls past experiences of occupying similar spaces as a child as well as in my later adult years: the frustration of other viewers' incessant whispered interruptions during a film; the welcome whisper of a shared personal joke; the erotic whisper of a lover's private promise; and the curiosity of my first child's inquisitive whispers as he looks to me for confirmation that I share his understanding of a performance or a film we are seeing together. Only, *this* time, whispers are allowed. They are simultaneously both public and private. The warmth of the breath of each performer is felt on my neck and ear and triggers a gentle tingling sensation down my spine. I am the child here. I laugh under my breath as my body remembers the tickle of my own mother's breath on my infant neck and all the times my own whispers have caused shivers for my own children.

Xinghua Li tells us that whispering 'bears the imprint of domesticity or femininity and is seldom related to publicity' (2011: 20). In *Blind Cinema*, this imprint is felt specifically as memories of mother/child interactions both past and present. However, the intimacy and privacy of this experience revisited in a very public space is somewhat disconcerting. In place of the mother, the young performer's whispering breath seems to create an audible vibration that is felt through and around the funnel. It is a resonance that is embodied. It comes from and belongs to the body of the performer and affects a different kind of physical intimacy to that of the mother, one's own children, the friend, or the lover.

The kind of physical intimacy that *Blind Cinema* invites is a sonic intimacy that is felt in and through the body. From a physiological perspective, whispering is 'first, *a lack of vibration of the vocal cords*, second, *an excessive flow of breath* and third, *an intimate reception by the ear*' (Li 2011: 21). The lack of vibration of the vocal cords in the whispering voice, however, does not necessarily mean that the voice is experienced as disembodied. The excessive flow of breath and the attention the ear pays to each in- and out-breath foregrounds the child's body as a living, breathing body. Indeed, following Adriana Caverero's (2005) proposal that the voice reveals something of the inner corporeal self, Li suggests that whispering 'carries overwhelming clues about the interior movement of the whisperer's lungs, chest, palate, teeth and lips' (21). *Blind Cinema* foregrounds these embodied aspects of the voice of each of the child performers through this gentle act of whispering into a funnel; an act which garners my attention towards them, often at the expense of the filmic content they describe which I struggle to remember post-performance. The specificity of the way each performer smacks their lips together; the particularities of the mouth forming consonants and vowels; and the differences in speed of delivery are all suggestive of bodily movement unique to the individual whisperer. The funnel turns my attention towards these movements and away from the cinema screen to which we are normally proximally and acoustically oriented in this space.

If these aspects of bodily communication that are available through the whisper are taken as indicative of self-revelation, research from Carnegie Mellon University conversely suggests that whispering is an ineffective means of expressing the self:

> Voiced fricatives and stops lose their voicing. Nasals become faint. Regular tonalities of the speech mostly disappear … Vocal signatures of the speaker, such as age or accent, also become harder to detect. So do the paralinguistic cues like pitch or intonation, which communicate the speaker's emotions, moods or attitudes. Suffering from a loss in the knowledge of the body.
>
> (cited in Li 2011: 21)

Whilst vocal signatures and tone may be more difficult to ascertain through a whisper, the performers' whispers are not, contrary to this research, without emotion, mood, or attitude. The sound of hushed laughter, the sharp in-takes of breath, the use of emphasis, and, of course, content ('oh… what *is* that?') indicate emotional material such as humour, surprise, investment in the film, as well as uncertainty. In addition, the paradox of anonymity afforded by the whispering voice is that it arguably offers the whisperer a form of vocal self-expression that they might ordinarily shy away from in another public context. As the artist comments:

> This whispering is something quite special. It cancels out somebody who has a loud voice, and therefore maybe has more authority. With the spoken voice

> there is immediately a hierarchy of voices whereas with whispering you take away that hierarchy. Those kids who are less inclined to stand on stage and speak up suddenly are in a very different position where they can hide in the dark. They're anonymous.
>
> (Hatzius 2017)

The anonymity of the whisperer coupled with the inability to be seen by the audience permits the performer an extension of an embodied self in a hybrid space that references cinema and performance spaces that otherwise do not 'extend' children's bodies *as bodies* in the widest possible sense of the term. In other words, whereas mainstream theatrical forms and popular cultural forms of seeing the people we call children performing often participate in a romanticised, nostalgic, and/or sexualised gaze, it is difficult to romanticise the child in *Blind Cinema*, to feel nostalgic for a past childhood, and to sexualise any perceived innocence (Kincaid 1998). This is mainly because innocence is not a dominant referent in this performance. One would be reaching to experience nostalgia as a blindfolded audience member listening to a child describe an abstract film as part of an arts festival. Undoubtedly, dwelling on the memories of the mother/child interaction I discuss above might perpetuate a sense of nostalgia, but any attempt to maintain such a nostalgic reception is undercut by the public and collective whisper of voices that prevent the experience from being reduced simply to a private familial-like exchange.

Instead, we are offered only a glimpse of the young performers as thinking bodies, through reference to their embodiment and the imaginative workings they share in the moment of the performance unfolding. There is, of course, the potential for the audience to equate this interaction with the idea of the child as a blank slate, who is progressing to full adulthood. But, again, this idea of children heading towards so-called completeness is undermined by the spectator's futile attempts to arrive at a complete, fixed meaning of either the performer or the film being described. We, the child performer and the adult audience member, both share in the feeling of being unfinished and incomplete in this hermeneutic game, always failing to make it make sense. Similarly, the erotic gaze encouraged by some depictions of the innocent child is denied by the absence of the ocular in this work. Instead, visuals are replaced by an arguably more complex relationship based on closeness through sound that has the potential to trigger a physiological response in the form of hairs standing on end or sending shivers down the spine of the listener.

In this way, *Blind Cinema* shares similar affects to those generated by the popular online trend, Autonomous Sensory Meridian Response or ASMR, also known as the Whispering Community (Andersen 2015). The intimacies of ASMR videos, which involve audio, visual, or haptic stimuli such as instructional role-play tutorials on self-care or repetitive actions like putting on latex gloves, are intended to trigger a 'relaxing, shivering sensation for the viewer' (ibid.: 683). Like ASMR, which is often experienced in the privacy of the listener's own home but is shared as part of a large networked online community, the performance facilitates a private encounter in an otherwise public space. In contrast to *Blind Cinema*, however, the physiological affects of ASMR are created by content that draws largely on heteronormative roles of care, which are mainly gendered as stereotypically female and often delivered by female-identifying and female-presenting people in soft, slow, whispered voices. At the same time, the Whispering Community is at pains to claim that the experience is one of relaxation as opposed to being driven by sexual desire, although recent research suggests that sexuality plays a significant role in ASMR practice (Waldron 2017). As *Blind Cinema* neither participates in the gendered care roles of ASMR videos nor the voyeurism of the distant privacy of the performers' actual or performed domestic settings, the emotional content of the performance is not experienced as a sexualised or erotic encounter despite the potential physiological effects of whispering (ibid.). Instead, it is friendly in tone and echoes what Nitin Ahuja identifies in clinical-based settings within both ASMR role-play and real-world scenarios as '[t]he proximity of two people in an unthreatening space [as] an event of immediate synaptic consequence' (Ahuja 2013: 450). Similarly, the thinking body of the performers that we encounter in this work denies the 'empty innocence' James Kincaid suggests shapes constructions of the 'modern child':

> [T]he instructions we receive on what to regard as sexually arousing tell us to look for (and often create) this emptiness, to discover the erotic in that which is most susceptible to inscription, the blank page.
>
> (1998: 16)

Blind Cinema, in other words facilitates intimacy but importantly avoids reiterating sexualised representations of children as a blank page to be 'inscribed on' that are common in mainstream culture. However, the type of intimacy it shares with ASMR might still be perceived as what Lauren Berlant and Michael Warner call 'nonstandard intimacy' (1998: 558), a term that Joceline Andersen borrows to describe ASMR practice. Andersen argues that ASMR 'makes public a kind of intimacy that, in heteronormative culture, is exclusively the private experience of the couple' (ibid.) and, therefore, is necessarily consigned to being perceived as a non-standard transgressive intimacy, even as its followers would claim otherwise. Likewise, *Blind Cinema* makes public an alternative kind of intimacy based on whispering that carries with it the association of the largely private familial, domestic context, but which is problematised by the fact that the performer and audience do not know each other in this public context.

By exploiting the ability of whispering to 'question[s] some key assumptions about the relationship among voice, body, space and power' (Li 2011: 20), the form of the performance – performers we call children whispering to an audience of adult strangers – begins to challenge normative interactions with children which we might expect to see in mainstream theatre or cinema spaces. This is neither the child performer of Matilda wowing us with their triple threat skills nor is it our nephew playing a donkey in the school nativity. The collective of whispering voices from the young performers' bodies that create them, resists what Rachel Zerihan has called the 'compulsive monogamy' of one-to-one performance (2009: 4). In other words, *Blind Cinema* retains the form of the individual experience of a one-to-one performance whilst the collective whispering undermines the potential exclusivity of the one-to-one encounter. Whilst the political potential of whispering as a performance strategy is not the focus of this work, whispering's presence in a public arena with children, signals towards its prospective usefulness, namely its radical and ethical potential beyond the theatre festival. As Li argues:

> [T]his is how ideology reigns – through whispering. Unlike the coercive shouts, yells or screams, the ruling whisper wields a hegemonic, soft power and sneaks into our social unconscious without being questioned. To take the whispering power back, let us save this privileged means of communication for the disenfranchised and the marginalized.
>
> (2011: 32)

The people we call children often experience public space as a marginalised and excluded group. In terms of both form and content, the young performers' collective whispering to adults then – as part of the one-to-one-to-all format of *Blind Cinema* – has the ability to speak back to this hegemonic power during a time of 'volume politics' (ibid.). A key question then is whether contemporary performance with the people we call children can model strategies of resistance for wider contexts in ways that acknowledge the potential for an ethics of otherness and responsibility at the core of whispering as a form of communication where 'there is always a listening ear' (ibid.: 23).

On Not Looking

The child who speaks into my ear tells me that something that looks like a monster appears on the screen. They offer descriptions of colours and shapes rather than focusing on characters and narratives. They don't overlay meaning or suggest subtext. As the next child approaches my ear, they offer little sense of the figure and the ground of the film. A ball is bouncing and there's a chair. It sounds as though they are watching a surrealist cartoon but I become more interested in enjoying the sounds of their whispers than the content. This voice is both the same but different from the last whispering voice I heard. It is slower, less energetic. Are they a boy or a girl? I can't tell and then I feel frustrated by my own binarised question and the need to know and to name them. I listen more carefully.

The imaginative vision on offer in *Blind Cinema* is partial and not fully formed. It resists completeness. There is a failure to categorise, to name what is seen (by the child) and what is heard (by the adult). In short, there is no colonising gaze here: neither with the young performer nor with the adult listener. Nevertheless, *Blind Cinema* turns the 'spectator-owned' (Zerihan 2006) aspect of many one-to-one performance practices on its head. Whilst this is a co-authored piece in the sense that it 'harness[es] the imagination of the spectators' (Grau 2003: 205), ownership of the spoken material sits firmly with the young performers because the audience member is not permitted to speak back. There is no obvious attempt, for example, to 'dislocat[e] the central position of the author' (ibid.). Instead, as a participant, you have a feeling of being held hostage by the performer, a role that is amplified by the visual deprivation courtesy of the blindfold around your eyes.

The blindfold has several disorienting effects that, I would argue, facilitate an alternative reading of children's bodies from mainstream performance and filmic practices, that depend on the romantic, nostalgic, fetishizing, and voyeuristic gaze. This is because blindfolding audience members in this space has the effect of resisting 'established conceptualisations and manifestations of the [cinematic] gaze… where looking (from a distance) is associated and inscribed with various hierarchies of power and control' (Lindner 2012). If looking is regulated by normative visual economies that promote the white, male, heterosexual, able-bodied perspective – specifically within the mainstream cinema space that is referenced by the site-specificity of this piece – then the removal of sight is arguably a direct challenge to the way the cinema space and screen ordinarily orientates visual reception in line with this dominating gaze. Following film theory's attention to the gendered and racialised aspects of the heteronormative gaze with its acts of voyeurism and fetishism (Lindner 2012), the removal of optical vision from one's experience of a performance with the people we call children has the effect of foregrounding the *absence* of signifiers of gender and race that are ordinarily offered up for visual consumption.

If this is the same gaze that Donna Haraway has suggested in her essay 'The Persistence of Vision' 'signifies the unmarked positions of Man and White [in] scientific and technological, late-industrialized, militarized, racist, male-dominated societies' (Haraway 1997: 283) then denying a visual encounter with the performers, relies instead on other means of knowing and meaning-making beyond the violence of this gaze. The removal of sight from the whole audience and the way this sight usually orientates towards a gaze that 'replicate(s) dominant symbolic structures and power hierarchies' (Lindner 2012), is a reminder that we often depend on visual markers of gender, race, sexuality, class and I would add here *age* in our reading of child performers as much as adult performers. To counter the way the gaze makes assumptions related to identity, *Blind Cinema*'s use of the blindfold foregrounds the situatedness and embodiedness of making meaning with and about children by denying the spectator access to a gaze that differentiates, whilst simultaneously claiming to be neutral. Instead, the performance employs a one-to-one form that promotes 'intimacy as visceral closeness and phenomenological responsiveness' (Zerihan 2006). As Zerihan argues the politics of the gaze are intimately tied to performance as an embodied practice:

> Bodily presence in terms of embodied corporeality and proximal closeness mark important strategies for continuing to interrogate the politics of the gaze in performance, pressing into individual / cultural / political narratives and their openness to dialogue, fuelling my refusal to allow the corporeal body to "become obsolete" from contemporary performance works.
>
> (Zerihan 2006)

In *Blind Cinema*, it is precisely the elimination of sight in the otherwise visually-oriented practices of performance and film viewing, that through its negation opens up questions of the politics and ethics of the gaze in contemporary performance with the people we call children. When we are asked to remove our blindfolds at the end of the performance, the visual 'reveal' of the young performers – standing on a stage in front of a cinema screen – draws attention to them as gendered and racialised bodies. By drawing visual attention to these bodies through the reveal, this moment puts into practice Lindner's claim that:

> vision and technologies of vision, including cinema [and here I would add performance] have very real and material implications. They discipline and shape bodies, relations between bodies, and bodily experiences.
>
> (Lindner 2012)

Before the blindfold is removed, there is no visual anchoring from a cinema screen or theatre stage to offer these performers' bodies up to the white, male, heteronormative, eroticising, patriarchal, protectionist gaze. *Blind Cinema* rather encourages audience members to encounter their own bodies and the bodies of the performers as *bodies in relation within space*, specifically, we are invited to consider how they announce (or do not announce) themselves through non-visual means. This experience of the body in space not only includes what we have already discussed as the young performer's body declaring itself audibly through a whisper but also the body's directionality, the distance between one's own body and the bodies of others, the space the body occupies, and the way in which it is therefore orientated. *Not* looking in this context, therefore, emphasises the body as spatially situated and deserves further attention to ascertain how the use of space in *Blind Cinema* re-orients both the bodies of the people we call children and also the bodies of the people we call adults. If, as I am suggesting, non-visual strategies are able to reorient audiences' relationships to the child and the bodies of the people we call children to account for their (shared) embodied experiences, then, to borrow from Lindner, this proposal could have 'very real and material implications' for thinking about how visual and non-visual strategies might be employed in future performance practice with young performers to disrupt the normative way in which the bodies and bodily experiences of the people we call children are shaped and disciplined by dominant visual economies.

Re-Orienting Bodies

Sarah Ahmed considers how different ways of being orientated within the world invite different orientations towards objects and others. She argues that 'bodies come to have certain orientations over time and [...] come to be shaped by taking some directions rather than others' (2006: 58). Inevitably, I am unable to know what orientations these diverse performing bodies – with their attendant individual, political, and cultural histories – have come to take over time. I can assume, however, that the majority of their experiences of performance in their life so far, as performers and spectators, have often been orientated towards the face-to-face directionality of nativity plays, pantomimes, or local dancing or drama school shows. In turn, we can make the same claim about the (mainly adult) audience members of *Blind Cinema,* whose orientations towards children's bodies in performance prior to this moment will have mainly followed this face-to-face relationship. If we adopt Ahmed's parlance to describe this normative directionality as a 'straight' or 'straightforward' (2006: 79) encounter with children in performance, then *Blind Cinema* offers a different literal and metaphorical directionality through its alternative spatial configuration of performer to audience.

In this piece both performer and audience assume a front-facing position – with performers standing behind seated audience members – which counters the ordinarily straight encounter with children as performers in mainstream theatre. Whilst the performer standing behind the audience is at a visual advantage both in terms of sight and spatial positioning, this arrangement nevertheless enables a shared proximal closeness. The average height of the young performers coupled with the funnel directed towards the audience member's ear, means that this configuration is felt as more of a horizontal experience – perhaps akin to a side-to-side arrangement in a one-to-one performance – in contrast to the average cinema/theatre-going experience. Discussing preferred alternative terms for describing one-to-one performances, such as one-for-one, one-on-one, or one-with-one, Wake draws attention to the effects of physical proximal distance and direction between performer/artist and spectator on the latter's reception of the work. She elaborates on what the spatial configuration of performer to audience might imply about the mode of the work, for example, that it is convivial in a side-to-side arrangement and perhaps more confrontational in a face-to-face (2017: 165). The spatial set-up of *Blind Cinema* certainly contributes to the sense of conviviality of this encounter, as discussed earlier. However, it also deliberately moves away from the straight encounter, as one that is characterised by the adult either physically looking *down* on and/or looking *at* the people we call children.

Whilst what I mean by 'straight' encounter from adult to child implies sexuality, my use of the term here is concerned largely with drawing attention to the normativity of the gaze that dominates mainstream visual economies and that can be further nuanced through reference to the ocular-centrism that *Blind Cinema* appears to resist. As I suggested in the chapter on *The Hamilton Complex*, the bodies of the people we call children in performance are often framed in relation to the notion of 'to-be-looked-at-ness'. Laura Mulvey discusses this directorial and spectatorial trend predominantly in relation to dominant representations of female bodies in classic Hollywood films in her seminal essay 'Visual Pleasure and Narrative Cinema' (1975) but it is helpful to consider the scopophilic aspects of the patriarchal gaze as part of the straightness of the encounter that is often encouraged by hegemonic representations of the child. I am not alone in aligning Mulvey's theory of what she calls the male gaze with the dominant reception of children in mainstream representational art forms:

> Concerning the spectators, as well as the adult characters in films about children, feminist theories on male scopophilia and the female image, as

> elaborated by Laura Mulvey (78), Teresa de Lauretis and Ann Kaplan, for example, can be displaced onto an "adults-looking-at-children" pattern. Ann Kaplan's question: "Is the gaze male?" (23–25) then becomes: "Is the gaze adult?" Since there are no child filmmakers (except, perhaps, as amateurs in certain experimental high schools), the child represented in films necessarily takes on the role of an ethnographic subject, filmed as opposed to filming, analysand rather than analyst, signified, not signifier. The result is frequently a false, sentimental portrayal of children as seen by adults.
>
> (Colvile 1990: 445)

For Giorgiana Colvile, the active/male and passive/female binary that Mulvey argues organises male-dominated 'ways of seeing and pleasure in looking' in classic Hollywood films can be put to work to recognise the parallel active/adult and passive/child binary common to representations of the people we call children within cinema. With the exception of some contemporary performance, dance, and live art practice, dominant representations of children within theatre can also be said to follow this pattern, since the child is often written (not writer), authored (not author), produced (not producer), artwork (not artist), directed (not director). So, by recognising the straightness of the gaze that *Blind Cinema* works against, I am extending Covile's idea of the child as signified (not signifier) and analysand (not analyst) in films to the wider context of theatre and performance practice and scholarship that has largely ignored what, after Colvile, we might call the 'adult gaze' in performance – with the exception of Isis Germano's scholarship (2018). I nuance this gaze in my discussion of *The Hamilton Complex* to instead consider how that performance is simultaneously eliciting and disrupting a patriarchal protectionist gaze. To also think of the dominant gaze as 'straight' is to imply the different ways in which the 'adult gaze' might show up in performance as white, male, abled-bodied, patriarchal as well as erotic, judgemental, and nostalgic (Senior 2018). It is the straight(forward)ness of the adult gaze that is being disorientated and denied by this horizontal, side-to-side spatial configuration in *Blind Cinema*.

A further aspect of the disorientating effect of this side-to-side interaction, is that it potentially offers the performers a way of being in a public space that the bodies of the people we call children are not ordinarily granted. In turn, *Blind Cinema* offers audience members a means of experiencing the people we call children in performance, beyond the straight(forward) adult gaze. To substantiate this claim, we must first acknowledge that the bodies of those we call children often occupy public spaces differently from adult bodies. Linda McDowell and Jo Sharpe, for example, argue that '[t]he body, its size, shape, gestures, the space it takes up, those masculine and feminine norms which mean that men sprawl and women don't; the differences in physicality that construct and reflect gender norms create ways of being in space' (1997: 203). If (perceived) differences in physicality both shape and reproduce gender norms then we might also say that the difference in physicality between (most) adults and (most) children both construct and reflect problematic *age norms* that then contribute to the ways both children and adults not just occupy space but shape how they are permitted to occupy space. These age norms are problematic to the extent that they suggest that age and perceived competence go hand in hand, so that 'the younger the children, the less competent they are viewed by adults' (Cele and van der Burgt 2015). I am not reiterating essentialised notions of bodily difference, here, but rather addressing the way in which the people we call children, as well as adults, experience perceived and discursively constructed differences between 'adults' and 'children' as 'an embodied politics of difference' (Cele and van der Burgt 2015). Indeed, actual bodily differences in height and weight are often used as a means of othering 'the child' in many contexts and along with other bodily aspects (such as shape, appearance, gender, and performance) are important signifiers *for* children in the construction of *their* own social identities (James 1993).

Research on young people's bodies in public spaces, and specifically children's experiences of their own bodies in particular public contexts, is still in its infancy. However, drawing on empirical research conducted within the fields of geography and education on children's bodily strategies for negotiating public spaces, Cele and van der Burgt (2015) suggest that the people we call children 'actively negotiate both a physical body and a discursive body in their use of public spaces, and this affects both their spatial patterns, social interaction, and identity processes' (ibid.: n.p). In the absence of specific research on the embodied experiences of young people who occupy theatre and cinema spaces in particular, Cele and Van der Burgt's work offers useful insights for the field of performance studies to reflect on the people we call children's relationships with their own bodies and adults in public spaces, such as that afforded by *Blind Cinema*.[2] In particular, child participants in Cele and van der Burgt's research expressed feelings of being marginalised and excluded from public spaces, and this, in turn, correlated with their lived experiences of being considered visible or invisible by the adult community they encountered. Similarly, earlier research on the relationship between children's geographies and their political lives demonstrates that 'children are often ignored, punished, or expelled for embodied practices that do not signify (quite literally) in the world of adults' (Mitchell and Elwood 2012: 801).

If children's experience of public space often tends towards them being othered (Cele and van der Burgt 2015) and the child's body is central to both being perceived as other and is also used creatively by children to negotiate a sense of belonging that alleviates this sense of exclusion (ibid.), then what does this public context of *Blind Cinema* do to a dominant perception of the child as 'other'? In other words, whilst I can neither know nor comment on the performers' individual or collective embodied experiences of this work, I can speculate on how *Blind Cinema* negotiates this treatment and perception of the child as other in public space. First, this tendency towards othering the child is refused in the performance because of the heightened presence of the performers' bodies as complex, emotive, and thinking bodies, rather than bodies that can be easily spectacularised and objectified. Second, the form resists allowing the adult to 'ignore, punish, or expel' children for their embodied practices – the particularities of the whispering voice, the smell of the breath, the feel of the breath, and the different ways in which each child performer interprets the film – disrupts a 'straight' orientation towards othering the child.

At the same time, the dramaturgical configuration of adult audience/child performers as us/them, does not permit me as an audience member to reduce 'them' to 'the same'. Instead, they seem to hold the space with their improvised dialogue and as 'bodies out of place' (Ahmed 2006: 61) that appear to command the space by literally occupying the aisles in-between the seats. Importantly, the work asks me to experience *the potential* for their othering, rather than to other them, in the sense that I am invited to think about how welcome their bodies are (or are not) in this festival/performance/cinema space and how they occupy it in a way that is materially different to my own occupation of the space (as cisgender female, researcher, pregnant, mother, performance scholar, regular arts festival-goer). I am not encouraged to *other them* by essentialising the supposed differences between us. Furthermore, when the blindfold is taken off and the children stand in their school uniforms, I am aware of how this experience of being blindfolded, spatially situated side-to-side, and whispered to by young performers as embodied subjects has interrupted the straight adult gaze that might ordinarily position them in relation to the primary school age identity that their uniforms would ordinarily indicate.

Along with the use of space, the funnel becomes what Ahmed might call a reorientation device, that is, a means of orienting ourselves differently towards the child's body in performance. For Ahmed, for example, using 'the [kitchen] table that supports domestic work to do political work (including the work that makes explicit the politics of domestic work) is a reorientation device' (Ahmed 2006: 61). The work of UK-based performance artist Bobby Baker is exemplary in this regard, making visible Ahmed's notion of reorientation in practice. Baker, for example, takes domestic objects from and within the kitchen to reorient our taken for granted assumptions of them as simply supporting domestic work and repositions these objects politically in order to enable 'a feminist protest at the lack of social transformation in women's lives' (Aston 2000: 17). Since children's experiences of the world are rarely explicitly acknowledged to be shaped by inequalities perpetuated by adults and the straight adult gaze, the notion that adult relationships towards the people we call children need to be reoriented often goes unremarked, even in the face of legislation on 'children's rights' (UNCRC 1989). Henry Giroux draws attention to the contradiction in adult's publicly professed concern for children's safety, a perspective that still holds over two decades later, when he considers the North American context in which '[m]ost of the violence waged against children is by adults; this includes the 2,000 to 3,000 kids, many of whom are middle class, who are murdered annually by family members and friends' (2000: 16). Whilst I am not claiming that *Blind Cinema* can address the wider systemic and historic oppressions faced by the people we call children, the funnel creates an embodied experience for the audience member that extends the bodies of actual people we call children in a cinema-performance space, where it would previously have been oriented towards the straight adult gaze. This micro-political intervention of the funnel is significant because the adult gaze is sustained on a macro-level by 'the influence corporate culture now wields in redefining the terms through which children's experiences and identities are named, understood, and negotiated' (Giroux 2000: 16).

Whilst for Ahmed, issues of orientation, disorientation, and reorientation are predominantly related to gender, sexuality, and racism, and specifically racism as an 'ongoing and unfinished history, which orientates bodies in specific directions, affecting how they "take up" space' (2006: 111), I would suggest that ageism and age-related bias with particular regard to children, also orientates bodies in certain directions rather than others. The strategies discussed throughout encourage and demand a reorientation towards the bodies of the people we call children by queering the straight adult gaze, where queer is '*whatever* is at odds with the normal, the legitimate, the dominant' (Halperin 1995: 62). In doing so, *Blind Cinema* offers the people we call children the possibility for their 'bodies to inhabit spaces that do not [ordinarily] extend their shape' (Ahmed 2006: 62):

> When [children's] bodies take up spaces that they were not intended to inhabit, something other than the reproduction of the facts of the matter happens. The hope that reproduction fails is the hope for new impressions, for new lines to emerge, new objects, or even new bodies…
>
> (Ahmed 2006: 62, my addition)

One of the lines to emerge from the arrival of children's bodies as something other than a signifier of sexualised innocence, potential for evil, incompetence, or as an unfinished adult is new ways of being with the people we call children in performance, and hopefully, by extension, in everyday experiences. This way of being is one that is mindful of the relational aspects of encounters with young people and recognises and respects both the alterity and the shared aspects of their embodied and discursive experiences.

Conclusion

To address the disorientating effects this work had on me as an audience member, I have turned to a queer phenomenological approach that recognises the importance of embodied experience but also deviates away from the traditional phenomenological practice of perception from the white, male, heterosexual, able-bodied position that Ahmed critiques. To attempt to speak from this latter position would have ignored the bodily aspects of my specific encounter with the work and shored up the straight, normative, adult gaze which is denied by the affective aspects of this performance. Alongside a rich history of phenomenological analysis of performance as an embodied experience[3], phenomenological approaches to film analysis share the assumption that we 'see and comprehend and feel films with our entire bodily being, informed by the full history of and carnal knowledge of acculturated sensorium' (Sobchak 2004: 63).[4] Although Vivian Sobchak emphasises that some films and, indeed, specific genres of film invite more explicitly affective experiences than others, I agree with film scholar Katharina Lindner that our openness to an embodied engagement with the world and aesthetic experiences is inevitably shaped through our previous encounters with practice that invites a kinaesthetic or tactile meeting:

> We are likely to be more open to the tactile or kinaesthetic dimensions of the cinematic experience if we have a particular history of tactile or kinaesthetic engagement with the world – that is, if we have come to embody a particularly tactile or kinaesthetic way of being-in-the-world. The 'sense-making capacities' of our bodies might also be more readily engaged if we are not provided with traditional cinematic pleasures or points of engagement.
>
> (Lindner 2012: np)

The tactile engagement that has been afforded to my body as a performance scholar over the years undoubtedly shapes my encounter with *Blind Cinema* as a rich sensory and embodied experience. Yet, at the same time, it is the performance's denial of the traditional cinematic pleasure of identifying with a character on the screen and its refusal to offer the primary point of engagement through the optical lens, that moves me to attend specifically to my bodily engagement with(in) this work. Whilst my sense-making capacities may well be more attuned to the kinaesthetic experience of live performance – because of my iterative return to performance over the years – there are aspects at work in *Blind Cinema*, as we have explored, that demand an embodied encounter with the cinema-performance hybrid experience on offer but particularly with regard to the embodied experiences of the performers we call children in this practice. It is perhaps no surprise, then, that Hatzius began the process by focusing on audio descriptions for non-sighted people because of her frustration as a film-maker and visual artist with visual imagery (Hatzius 2017). In that move away from the visual and towards the audience's auditory experience, she has created a work that offers some key strategies for engaging differently with the people we call children in representational spaces such as theatres and cinemas. Indeed, the optical privilege signified by the adjective 'spectator' itself comes under strain in this work.

The performance strategies identified throughout the chapter thus work to destabilise the straight, adult gaze in practice. These predominantly include whispering, the blindfold, and funnel as disorientation and reorientation devices, and the lateral contact between performer and audience. What these strategies point towards is a set of tools that utilise voice, objects, and space to foreground both the child performer's body *as* embodied and the audience member's experience of children in performance as an equally affective, embodied encounter. What remains to be seen is how the content of the work, specifically the film's thematics, could push the politics of this intervention against dominant ways of reading and experiencing the performers we call children even further. As my descriptions throughout the chapter recount, the content of the film became almost insignificant within the moment of performance. Yet, in thinking about future practice with young people, there is an opportunity to move the content as well as the form towards a greater recognition of what – over twenty years ago – James *et al.* (1998) were calling for in the sociology of childhood: '*both* an appreciation of the importance of embodiment *and* the active role of children in apprehending and constructing their social world through that embodiment' (162).[5] In short, I wonder what would happen to the relations of power if children had written, collaborated on, or directed the film. Or, if there was more at stake in what the film was asking of them, which moved into creating an environment for their social, cultural, and political lives to be extended through their 'anonymised' bodies in the socially and culturally regulated context of the cinema space. I return to this question of anonymity in the conclusion.

If the idea of an embodied experience of children's bodies is troubling for the reader, then let me put you at your ease by admitting that it is deliberately so. In performance studies, we are comfortable with thinking and writing about intimacy, risk, and embodied experiences in relation to adult makers and spectators. The lack of critical scholarship on how we encounter the people we call children in performance practices outside of an applied drama context, however, is a startling omission. As this book attests, the bodies of those we call children are raced, classed, gendered, sexed, contextualised, historically-situated, and politically resonant. Adults are often in a position of power (as theorists, artists, directors, spectators etc.) to contribute to the framing and shaping of the reception of bodies in relation to these and other complex iterations of the lived body and, therefore, we have the opportunity to either challenge or sustain hegemonic models of representation and interpretation where children are concerned. *Blind Cinema* signals towards a practice that resists hegemonic models by foregrounding the bodies of the performers we call children as corporeal entities that share an intimate relationship with audience members' own embodied experiences. In doing so, the performance has an important set of disorientation strategies to offer both scholarly and artistic communities that put into practice Ahmed's claim that 'risking departure from the straight and narrow makes new futures possible' (2006: 20–21). Indeed, what new performance futures have we yet to imagine with the people we call children? Whilst I have indulged in my own experiential engagement with this work, the performer's experiences of their own embodied practice in performance, however, are yet to be articulated. The following chapters seek to address this absence by giving space to the people we call children to discuss their experiences of making and performing in professional contemporary performance.

Notes

1 For Ahmed, the idea of straightness is informed by sexuality and specifically the proposal that '[t]o become straight means that we not only have to turn towards objects that are given to us by heterosexual culture, but also must "turn away" from objects that take us off this line' (ibid: 21). *Blind Cinema* resonates with Ahmed's theory not directly in

terms of sexuality, but because it orients the audience to a different directionality that does not follow the straight line of sight that audiences have become accustomed to when encountering children in performance.

2 This research is based on ethnographic fieldwork in Stockholm, Sweden, and Bournemouth, England with children aged 8–11, which is the same age as those participating in *Blind Cinema*.

3 Influenced by philosophical thinkers such as Edmund Husserl, Martin Heidegger and Maurice Merleau-Ponty, theatre and performance studies has an extensive relationship to phenomenology including substantial works by Stanton Garner (1994), Alice Rayner (1994) and Bert O States (1985). For more recent examples of phenomenological approaches to making and analysing performance, see *Performance and Phenomenology: Traditions and Transformations* (Bleeker *et al.* 2015).

4 For further examples of phenomenological analyses of film see Barker (2009) and more recently Lindner (2012) who offers a queer phenomenological reading of queer cinema and specifically Jordan Scott's 2009 film *Cracks*.

5 In an academic context, this has since been taken up by scholars such as Sue Ellen Henry (2014) who examines how the relationship between corporeality and social class are 'co-constructed' in children's lived experiences, specifically in the US school context. However, there is still much work to do.

References

Ahmed, Sara (2006) *Queer Phenomenology: Orientations, Objects, Others*, Durham and London: Duke University Press.

Ahuja, Nitin K. (2013) '"It Feels Good to Be Measured": Clinical Role-Play, Walker Percy, and the Tingles', *Perspectives in Biology and Medicine*, 56 (3): 442–451.

Andersen, Joceline (2015) 'Now You've Got the Shiveries: Affect, Intimacy, and the ASMR Whisper Community', *Television & New Media*, 16 (8): 683–700.

Aston, Elaine (2000) '"Transforming" Women's Lives: Bobby Baker's Performances of "Daily Life"', *New Theatre Quarterly*, 16 (1): 17–25.

Barker, Jennifer (2009) *The Tactile Eye: Touch and the Cinematic Experience*, Berkeley: University of California Press.

Berlant, Lauren and Michael Warner (1998) 'Sex in Public', *Critical Inquiry*, 24 (2): 547–566.

Bishop, Claire (2004) 'Antagonism and Relational Aesthetics', *October*, 110: 51–79.

Bleeker, Maaike, Jon Foley Sherman and Eirini Nedelkopoulou (2015) *Performance and Phenomenology: Traditions and Transformations*, New York and London: Routledge.

Bourriaud, Nicolas (1998) *Relational Aesthetics*, Dijon: Les Presses du Réel.

Caverero, Adriana (2005) *For More Than One Voice: Toward a Philosophy of Vocal Expression*, trans. Kottman PA, Stanford, CA: Stanford University Press.

Cele Sofia and van der Burgt Danielle (2015) 'Children's Embodied Politics of Exclusion and Belonging in Public Space' in Kirsi Kallio, Mills Sarah and Tracey Skelton (eds.) Politics, Citizenship and Rights. Geographies of Children and Young People, Singapore: Springer.

Chow, Broderick D.V. and Darren O'Donnell (2014) 'Young Mammals: The Politics and Aesthetics of Long-Term Collaboration with Children in Mammalian Diving Reflex's The Torontonians' in Victor Emeljanow and Gillian Arrighi (eds.) *Entertaining Children: The Participation of Youth in the Entertainment Industry*, London: Palgrave Macmillan, pp. 147–166.

Colvile, Giorgiana (1990) 'Children Being Filmed by Truffaut', *The French Review*, 63 (3): 444–451.

Garner, Stanton (1994) *Bodied Spaces: Phenomenology and Performance in Contemporary Drama*, New York: Cornell University Press.

Germano, Isis (2018) 'So Cute, So Creepy', *Performance Research*, 23 (1): 44–51.
Giroux, Henry A. (2000) *Stealing Innocence: Youth, Corporate Power and the Politics of Culture*, New York and Basingstoke: Palgrave.
Grau, Oliver (2003) *Virtual Art: From Illusion to Immersion Massachusetts*, trans. Gloria Custance, MIT Press.
Halperin, David (1995) *Saint Foucault: Towards a Gay Hagioraphy*, Oxford: Oxford University Press.
Haraway, Donna (1997) 'The Persistence of Vision' in K. Conboy, N. Medina and S. Stanbury (eds.) *Writing on the Body: Female Embodiment and Feminist Theory*, New York: Columbia University Press, pp. 283–295.
Hatzius, Britt (2017) Interview with the Author, Flare Festival, Manchester, Wednesday 5 July 2017.
Heddon, Deirdre, Helen Iball and Rachel Zerihan (2012) 'Come Closer: Confessions of Intimate Spectators in One to One Performance', *Contemporary Theatre Review*, 22 (1): 120–133.
Henry, Sue Ellen (2014) *Children's Bodies in Schools: Corporeal Performances of Social Class*, New York: Palgrave Macmillan.
Husserl, Edmund (1969) *Ideas: General Introduction to Pure Phenomenology*, trans. W. R. Boyce Gibson, London: George Allen and Unwin.
James, Allison (1993) *Childhood Identities: Self and Social Relationships in the Experience of the Child*, Edinburgh: Edinburgh University Press.
James, Allison, Chris, Jenks and Alan Prout (1998) *Theorizing Childhood*, Allison James, Chris Jenks, and Alan Prout (eds.), Cambridge: Polity Press.
Johnson, Dominic (2012) 'Ecstatic Intervals: Performance in a Continuum of Intimacy' in Maria Chatzichristodoulou and Rachel Zerihan (eds.) *Intimacy Across Visceral and Digital Performance*, Basingstoke: Palgrave Macmillan.
Kincaid, James (1998) *Erotic Innocence: The Culture of Child Molesting*, Durham N.C: Duke University Press.
Li, Xinghua (2011) 'Whispering: The Murmur of Power in a Lo-Fi World', *Media, Culture and Society*, 33 (1): 19–34.
Lindner, Katharina (2012) 'Questions of Embodied Difference: Film and Queer Phenomenology', *NECSUS: European Journal of Media Studies*, 1 (2): 199–217.
McDowell, Linda and Jo Sharpe (1997) 'Introduction: Body Maps' in *Space, Gender, Knowledge*, London: Arnold.
Mitchell, Katharyne and Sarah Elwood (2012) 'Mapping Children's Politics: The Promise of Articulation and the Limits of Nonrepresentational Theory', *Environment and Planning D: Society and Space*, 30 (5): 788–804.
Mulvey, Laura (1975) 'Visual Pleasure and Narrative Cinema', *Screen*, 16 (3): 15–27.
Rayner, Alice (1994) *To Act, to Do, to Perform: Drama and the Phenomenology of Action*, Ann Arbor: University of Michigan Press.
Ridout, Nicholas (2008) 'Performance in the Service Economy: Outsourcing and Delegation' in Claire Bishop and Mark Sladen (eds.) *Double Agent*, London: Institute of Contemporary Arts, pp. 126–31.
Senior, Adele (2018) 'Age Transvestism' in Contemporary Performance and Live Art with Children', *Performance Research: A Journal of the Performing Arts*, 23 (1): 26–36.
Sobchak, Vivian (2004) *Carnal Thoughts: Embodiment and Moving Image Culture*, Berkeley: University of California Press.
States, Bert O. (1985) *Great Reckonings in Little Rooms: On the Phenomenology of Theater*, Berkeley: University of California Press.
UNCRC (1989) United Nations Convention on the Rights of the Child: https://downloads.unicef.org.uk/wp-content/uploads/2010/05/UNCRC_PRESS200910web.pdf?_ga=2.236163779.333501690.1552479510-1520726232.1552479510 (accessed 13 May 2019).

Wake, Caroline (2017) 'The Ambivalent Politics of One-to-One Performance', *Performance Paradigm*, 13: 163–173.
Waldron, Emma Leigh (2017) '"This Feels So Real!": Sense and Sexuality in ASMR', *First Monday*, 22 (1). https://doi.org/10.5210/fm.v22i1.7282
Zerihan, Rachel (2006) 'Intimate Inter-actions: Returning to the Body in One to One Performance', *Body, Space and Technology*, 6 (1). http://doi.org/10.16995/bst.174
Zerihan, Rachel (2009) 'Live Art Development Agency Study Room Guide on One to One Performance': https://www.thisisliveart.co.uk/resources/one-to-one-performance-2009/ (accessed 14 May 2019).

8 Growing Sideways Together

Zina Abaraonye and Sorrel Barnes on *Men and Girls Dance* and *We Are Not Finished*[1]

> *[C]hildren grow sideways as well as up… in part because they cannot according to our concepts, advance to adulthood until we [adults] say it's time.*
>
> (Kathryn Bond Stockton 2009: 6)[2]

When Zina, 14, asks me, 'Do you ever get scared that your adolescence is completely gone?', my initial response is to question the category of adolescence. If adolescence is a marker of biological and physical transition from childhood to adulthood, I respond, I certainly don't fear the loss of puberty, the painful and hyper-visible acne, or the embarrassment of being asked for identification when buying alcohol. As a teenager, I never embraced (and indeed rarely used) the term adolescence. The term always felt strange in my mouth, like I was echoing the words of my GP (General Practitioner) or some other health professional. I recognised it largely as a scientific description that attempted to define a whole host of changes that we are supposed to go through during those 'difficult years'—emotional, bodily, social, cultural—that the term 'adolescence' inevitably failed to capture. Worse still, as a young person I quickly learned that variations of the term could be wielded by adults as an attack on, or an excuse for, my behaviour: comments on my maturity such as 'I'm tired of this adolescent behaviour' or 'typical adolescence' were often delivered and met back with an obligatory eye roll. The idea of adolescence felt and still feels reductive; a snapshot of a more complex life that was not experienced as delineated stages of development.

From a developmentalism perspective, the assumption that the end of adolescence is marked by the termination of one's physical growth and full cognitive development depends on an ableist logic that one is somehow 'finished' having passed through puberty. Whilst the days of being mistaken for an underage alcohol consumer are certainly over for me at 40 years old, the idea that adolescence might be 'completely gone' is undercut by a sense of perpetual transitioning I share with my young collaborators, Zina aged 14 and Sorrel aged 13, at the time of writing this. Suffice to say, my adulthood has been marked through a series of transitions: from pre-pregnant to post-pregnant body, from childless adult to parent, from single to married, and so on. Performance too has fostered a thirst for sitting in liminal

DOI: 10.4324/9781003043072-11

and often ambiguous spaces of transition. As I get to know Zina and Sorrel, I am keen to discover what transition means for them in relation to their experiences taking part in work by London-based company Fevered Sleep, with co-artistic directors Sam Butler and David Harradine. For Sorrel, this involved performing in *Men and Girls Dance* in Brighton at age 9 in 2016, whilst more recently Zina participated in research and development work for *We Are Not Finished* in 2019 at age 13.

This chapter charts the meeting of a cisgender female academic (at the time of writing) and two young cisgender females at moments of mutual transition, including a shift in age from pre-teen to teen. It is the beginning of a dialogue that attempts to reclaim both a wider (less normative) and a more specific (context-dependent) understanding of the shift from pre-teenage to teenage years, sometimes referred to as the 'tween' years. What can we learn from young people about what it means to be a (pre-)teenager making performance with a professional theatre company? What collaborative potential might the metaphor of the 'teen' offer within the current paradigmatic shift away from research *on* children to researching *with* children in the field of performance studies (Senior and The Institute for the Art and Practice of Dissent at Home 2018)? We did not start with these specific questions in mind. Instead, they grew as we began listening to one another. Together, Sorrel, Zina, and I planted the seeds for a way of working that widens the reductive definition of teenage adolescence. This was done by moving away from the prevailing and limiting discourse of the child as 'growing up' and towards the more inclusive metaphor of 'growing sideways' (Stockton 2009: 11).

As the adult academic tasked with leading our small team of what I regarded as artist-researchers because of the various knowledges Zina and Sorrel brought to the process, I find Kathryn Bond Stockton's notion of 'growing sideways' useful because it 'suggests the width of a person's experience or ideas, their motives or their motions, may pertain to any age, bringing "adults" and "children" into lateral contact' (ibid.). My approach to collaborating on this research, therefore, takes issue with the assumption that 'growing up' means 'an end to growth when full stature (or reproduction) is achieved' (ibid.). Instead, my investment in this notion of growing sideways is driven by a fundamental question: how can performance and performance scholarship foster this lateral contact? So, I put Stockton's framing to work as a methodological approach for doing research *with* these young collaborators in the hope of acknowledging our shared vulnerabilities, collective not-yet-knowing, and even our mutual strangeness, whilst simultaneously recognising the unique vantage points and experiences from which we speak as subjects that are (and this list is not exhaustive) classed, gendered, and raced.

Although this section recognises and is part of a larger commitment in my own work to address the absence and marginalisation of the people we call children's voices from performance and dance studies literature, this collaboration should not be mistaken for an attempt to 'give voice' to children or young people as marginalised subjects, with its colonial and classist resonances. Instead, the focus on this notion of growing sideways attends to *what might be excluded from and suppressed within the sociology of childhood* when it turns its attention away from the child as object of research and towards them as a 'social actor'

(Burman and Stacey 2010: 230). Whilst our intergenerational collaboration owes some debt to the childhood studies' turn towards the child as an 'actor' and 'agent' who is capable of shaping their own cultural and social worlds and experiences, I want to propose that growing sideways together actively recognises the limitations of this child as 'actor', who is based on a rational subject bound to Western masculinist individualism (Walkerdine 1988). I am gifted with the opportunity of working with two young females who already sit in tension with this rational subject, particularly in the uncomfortable teenage space between 'children' and 'adults'. So, I aim to lean into the uncertainties and ambiguities that our collaboration throws up, seeking to find modes of lateral contact between us that sit beside but resist conforming to normative modes of adult/child relationships as experienced/inexperienced, protector/protected, fully formed subject/not-yet subject. As I have warned against in earlier chapters, these binarised frameworks are especially problematic when they position young people as vessels into which we (adults) pour our infantilising fictions, feelings of nostalgia, and reductive claims of childhood innocence.

To locate and nurture this lateral contact, what follows is a series of excerpts from email exchanges with Zina, transcribed semi-structured conversations between myself and Sorrel conducted via an online conferencing platform, alongside some photo-elicitation and poetic writing offered by Sorrel via email. The dialogue that these moments generate, in turn, poses questions about the politics of collaboration with young people across art and the academy, touching upon issues of agency, subjectivity, autonomy, control, ownership, and power, although they are not always named as such during the exchange. The chapter therefore offers a methodological approach to doing post-performance research with the people we call teenagers in a way that intends to foster our mutual attempts to grow sideways in dialogue with one another.

Un/Knowing

Recognising the pervasive conceptualisation of the 'fully grown up' rational actor discussed previously—which also hails me as 'the adult' in this collaboration—I start our conversation from a position of both un-knowing and not-yet-knowing: a vulnerable but arguably necessary position for the adult academic researcher. In an attempt to create the conditions for Sorrel and Zina to exercise autonomy, I simply ask them: What do you want to do? This is where my collaborators serendipitously arrive at a set of methods (from Sorrel) and a theme (from Zina), which eventually leads to the question from Zina that opened this chapter and sparked its thematic focus on the (pre-)teenager in contemporary performance:

Sorrel: Things I might want to do…

- Writing about my experience in response to questions you ask or just general questions
- Examples of other children or projects that we've heard of that relate to what we're doing

- Diary entries of my time in the theatre—performance atmosphere, after the last show especially
- Examples of a typical day
- Photographs of us working in performance
- Lists and bullet points of our experiences

Zina: What I want to research and document is why teenagers are so miserable.

I share with Sorrel and Zina a rough visual map for how we might each inform and be informed by the other collaborators' interests, with the multidirectional arrows acknowledging the potential for lateral relations between us:

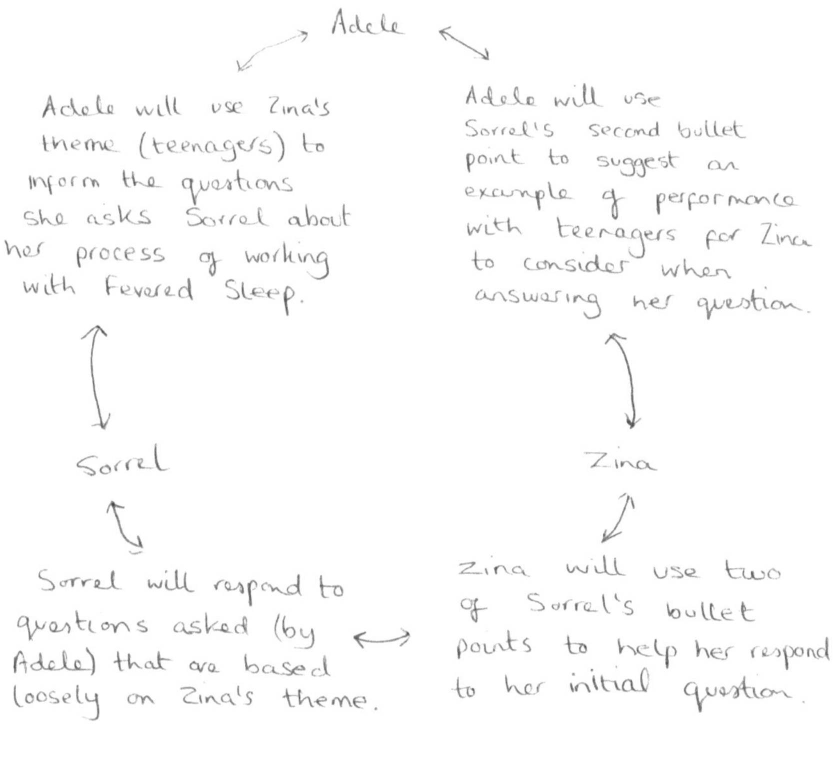

For Sorrell, the process develops in alignment with her interest in responding to questions that I pose and discussing photographs of her performing. For Zina, we move in relation to but also sideways to her theme of teenagers. So, following the prompt in the visual map above, Zina's question about adolescence that opens this chapter is a direct response to a short video clip which I select and share with her because of her interests in teenagers. The video is an excerpt from *Once and For All We're Gonna Tell You Who We Are So Shut Up and Listen* by Ontroerend Goed as well as a theatre review of the performance (Logan 2008). We then allow the process to grow over a few weeks, so that Zina's initial response to her prompt, which is to create 'A Day in the Life of a Teenager', is met with a creative constraint that I impose based on the stereotypical idea of the teenage years as both rebellious and lazy. Namely, I ask Zina to create a different kind of diary entry that resists describing her day in terms of how productive she has been. This opens up a written conversation between us that is documented in the pages that follow.

Girlhood

Adele: So I'm intrigued by the title *Men and Girls Dance* and particularly as a woman recalling, during different stages of my life, being called a girl and that raising lots of different emotions for me. I see when you talk about the work you refer to yourself and the other young performers as girls. What does the word 'girl' mean to you, because when you talk about it in the writing you refer to yourself and the other young performers as girls?

Sorrel: I mean, we were all young and I think the name of the show went really well with it because it was nine girls and eight men I think—or ten, I'm not entirely sure—but I think there were more men than girls. They were older men in their twenties, thirties and we were like between 9 and 10, 10 and 11. So, obviously 'girl' is for a young female, and I think that class of word is for like toddlers to young women, which is the end of teens ... When you're 18 you're an adult; people would generally call you an adult then. Then you can be called a woman. But if you're younger than that you're a teenager or a child and I think that would be classed as girls.

Adele: So, do you have a different relationship to that word 'girl' now compared to when you were in *Men and Girls Dance*—or maybe you didn't really need to think about it very much—or is it just the same?

Sorrel: It just felt normal [to be called girl]. Like, if I was called anything else ... I don't know what else I could have been called. To me, 'girl' is what you call a group; it's plural. If it's just one girl you're not going to be like, 'Girl, come over here' ... so it's like a class of someone, what they're classed as.

Adele: Like a category.

Sorrel: Yeah.

Adele: I remember being called a girl as an adult and being really angry, being infuriated by that, in a way that I wouldn't be as a child.

Sorrel: Yeah. When you turn 18 and you're like, 'No, I'm an adult now, please call me a woman. I've just had eighteen years of my life, please call me a woman'.

Adele: Yeah, that's it! Does it bother you now if people call you a girl?

Sorrel: No, I don't think so because I've only just turned thirteen. I don't really class myself as a teenager because I'm at that early stage. I've only just turned thirteen. But I don't think that would bother me. No, no.

Adele: It's interesting. I think it can be used as a weapon when you're a young adult woman. It can be infantilising, like somebody else's authority is being pressed down onto you … So, you were being framed as girls and they were being framed as men and we know from the copy of the show that they were male professional dancers and you were girls who danced for a hobby, non-professionally. So, you're kind of framed by those categories. I was wondering whether you got to be anything other than a girl in that work?

Sorrel: They would call us girls when they were just addressing the girls, but I think they may have also called us dancers to get everyone's attention. So, they wouldn't be like, 'Men and girls, can you look at us?' They would be like, 'Dancers, can you look at us or everyone?' It was really cool because we were really young and like, 'Oh my gosh, we're being called dancers. That's so cool!'

Adele: So, in the process, you were called dancers. Do you think that in the performance itself, you were anything other than a girl there? Were there other parts of your identity that you were able to explore?

Sorrel: In the performance, I was thinking, 'I know how to get these things right' so I wasn't really thinking about who I was. But, also, I had all my fellow peers around me and I was thinking, 'She's going that way; I need to go this way.' So I wasn't really thinking about who else I was.

Authority

Adele: Do you feel that at any point in the process, you had some authority, or took the lead?

Sorrel: In *Men and Girls Dance* we were paired. I was paired with this dancer called Luke I think, and we were doing a section of the performance where it was all lifting and jumps, so we had to try and make our way around our man and we had to do different lifts to get from one place to the other but not touching the floor. So, it was all our [the girls'] ideas. I controlled the whole thing. 'So, we can go from here to there, then we can go back to there'. Also, we were put in groups for the main dance; it was called the 'spaces dance' and we were put into groups of three. This wasn't for the whole dance—it was me, a girl, a man—and he had the structure that we were supposed to work around, and we could create this ourselves.

Adele: Your memory is amazing!

Sorrel: I didn't know I remembered all this.

Adele: As you say, there was a structure. There was a constraint: 'Don't touch the floor'. But you felt like you had some freedom within that. Do you feel like that freedom ever moved into you feeling like you had authority over anything, whether that was over other dancers or the choreography itself, or your own body?

Sorrel: With the play thing, where we had to start in one place and end in another, I choreographed that. Somewhat in the other dances when we were choreographing them, I was bringing my ideas from that and incorporating them into the other. That was my bit in the dance, and I was like, 'That's me'. I feel like I had the authority for that, the control over what goes on there. There was also another bit in the show where they put on music and we just did anything on the stage, anything at all. We could stand at the front of the stage and just stare at the audience. We could partner with one of the men and jump across the stage however we wanted to. We could sit down. We could do one of our dances. We could do anything on the whole stage. That was all improvising, so when it got to that point I was like, 'OK, what do I want to do here? Maybe I want to do some of this, some of that'. So that was also all my decision and all the other girls' decisions. We could do something together or on our own. I felt like that was our control because obviously Sam and David [the Artistic Directors] were in the audience and they couldn't really do anything about it [laughs] and we were here like, 'This is our freedom. This is what we get to do now. This is ours'.

Adele: Did anyone really play with the freedom that you were given in that section, like really push it or plan and talk to each other at the beginning about what you might do? Or did you just let it happen in the moment?

Sorrel: Well, when we had breaks, we said, 'Imagine if we all did this. Imagine if we all came together and did a huge dance like a flash mob or something'. But at the time I think we were all like, 'This has to go right; it can't look stupid'. So we didn't do anything like that. We just let it go, and did what we felt was right, what came to mind.

Adele: So, you thought about being resistant [laughs] but didn't. I'm just thinking about what my 7 year old son might do with that kind of freedom now—I think he would really run with it [laughing]. But, that's interesting that you didn't go through with it. There was a feeling that you wanted this to work, so there's a sense of obligation but also a sense of community I should imagine with the other people you were dancing with.

Capitalism

30 January 2021
Dear Adele,
Sorry it's taken me so long to get back to you, online school is hitting harder the second time around. Since your last email before Christmas, I've been trying (and often failing) to evaluate my days not by means of how much I've achieved—as capitalism would define me by—but by how I've felt. Admittedly, the first time I tried, I felt like I had nothing to write about. I had no idea how to describe my day, which was a good one, not by its productivity, and furthermore, no idea how to lead a 'good' day that wasn't rooted in productivity and bettering myself or 'doing

something' as I always hear said. I eventually settled for writing about my emotions, and how I felt during the day which should arguably decide the outcome of how successful a day was. This is what I wrote the first time:

> *Today was a really nice day. I got an email from Adele (who I'm working with on the Fevered Sleep Project book) asking me to try a week where my diary entries aren't centred around productivity, so here goes. 9am didn't happen. I slept happily until 11 and enjoyed the weather. I read before breakfast, we watched Small Axe and ate banitsa [a traditional Bulgarian pie] which was nice. Small Axe is really good. I went on my computer sometime afterwards and had a blast. I felt very relaxed throughout the day. I played Sims and listened to Evermore by Taylor Swift. I loved it. Especially the song about Taylor killing a cheating murderer. We watched Modern Family + Community during dinner which was fun. I wish Jeff + Britta ended up together on community. Before going to bed, I listened to Rumours by Fleetwood Mac. At least cocaine worked for them. Also I got into G64's Connections play! I'm a really big part!!! Georgie, Louis. Adelka, Ksenia and more are also in!!!!*

Reading back on that, I can see how I still managed to pinpoint my day by the things I achieved, although it is an improvement from basically everything I did beforehand. I actually talked about how I felt throughout the day, which is something I used to never consider. I kept this up for longer than a week. Although I get lazy with it, I do try and focus my daily evaluations on my emotions throughout the day over the productive things I've achieved. I think it's better this way because when you look on the long-term, a good, happy life isn't necessarily productive or socially considered successful. It's the simpler things that give us happiness and contribute to a good life.

Reading your response to my question [see the introduction to the chapter] gave me a lot more certainty on life and growing up. As a teenager, I'm constantly learning and changing. Of course in school, but one of the greatest joys in my life is constantly gaining more perspective, getting wiser, so to say. Because there's so much of this at my age—I hardly think I'm anything like the person I was three months ago—there's this scary, burdening feeling that all this growth and change abruptly stops the day one turns eighteen. That's another thought instilled by capitalism, that the world will be at your beck and call the moment you become an adult. That's when you become smart and you have it all together. There's no more room for change, growth, journey. Only a 9–5, marriage, two kids, and a prayer that you won't be given the divorce subplot.

I've written quite a lot here, and I hope I'm not too annoying by linking everything back to capitalism. I think that's when I first began thinking of myself as smart, when I decided I hated capitalism and this world a bit. That's also when I think we grow up. Sure, as children, we know that there are bad things in the world, but there's a shift when we start consciously thinking and actually seeing it. Learning about politics and seeing how unfairly it affects us seemed to have woken me up. Waking up, referring to my way of seeing the 'shift' like something out of the

Matrix. Take the red pill and properly wake up and consciously see the veins and ligaments of a system so many suffer every day under, or take the blue and see it and understand it through a clouded lens.

This email has been a massive brain dump.

Ironic because another brain dump I did was in December 2019 when I was 13. It was at one of Sam & David's workshops called *We Are Not Finished,* as if I were drunk, I stood up in front of a few teenagers, two adults, and a bunch of seven-year-olds and ranted about how much I hated the world. Picture this while keeping in mind that I'm not very good at arranging my thoughts. Much better now, certainly not then—when I barely had a grasp of what I even hated. This is what I wrote about it after.

03 *December 2019*
I ranted about everything wrong in the world.

Very detailed.

I remember it all coming out like mumble jumble, but everyone clapped and agreed with me, seeming impressed. As a person who usually keeps most of their feelings in, it felt great to let it all out and feel that other people agreed with me.

This entire email reeks of teen angst and anger, but the truth is, despite living with the burden of seeing the world for what it 'truly is' (quotes because that sounds extremely pretentious and I am an extremely pretentious person) I'm quite a happy, calm person. Maybe due to the knowledge that I can't do anything to change it—which should anger me more than it does, I'm secretly a very lazy person. While thinking like an adult, I still find moments where I enjoy life, feeling like a kid. For example, during *We Are Not Finished,* me and my friends there all brought blankets and made a blanket fort. David and Sam said they'd expected that of the younger ones. It was nice to feel like a child, compared to constantly being treated like an adult. I hope this has been somewhat helpful (or at least interesting). I think it's intriguing toying with the feeling of wanting to be, feeling like, and being treated like an adult, while still craving the ease and simpleness of childhood. I'm sure if I thought long enough, I could link this too, with capitalism.

Have a great morning/afternoon/evening! And more after that.
Zina

In/Equ(al)ity

Adele: One of the interesting things about the show, of course, is your relationship with the men, the male partners. How did you feel dancing with men?

Sorrel: It was really fun because obviously they're all professionals and they've done cool shows and are working with so many amazing people. They were all very strong so it felt like they were our canvas and we could do whatever we wanted because they could do anything. We could ask them to lift us up in the air as high as we wanted to because they could do it. It was really cool because obviously it's my first time working with famous—well not famous—professional people who have had so much experience and so much background.

Adele: You mention they're professionals. I guess the question then is can you ever be equal?

Sorrel: Yes, I definitely did feel equal to them because at the start, we were all sitting on the stage, the audience were walking in and we were making a massive newspaper blanket. The girls sat on one side of the newspaper and the men sat on the other and the newspaper was in the middle, but we were [sat] quite far away. One girl had to make a position then the men had to copy. It was really good because they were copying us and we were copying them and it felt very equal. We were incorporating our ideas into one big thing. Also, I think because when most people think 'professional' they think, 'Oh my gosh, they must be so good' but obviously the girls didn't have much experience—we weren't really great dancers—but in some bits of the show in the improv the men weren't doing everything amazingly. We were all being silly: not doing things perfectly, not having the perfect posture, not having the perfect technique. So, it showed we were equal—not unprofessional girls and professional men, but a mix.

Adele: Were there any moments of inequality?

Sorrel: Mmmm … I don't know. Maybe when like … [pause] I don't know because most of the show was all of us together and I'm trying to think about bits in the show with us separated because in the show we were all either in groups with the men or altogether doing the same thing, apart from the start but I don't feel like that would be inequality. No, I don't think so.

Non/Professional

Adele: Do you still consider yourself a non-professional even though you were in a professional theatre show?

Sorrel: I think so, because obviously I'm very young and there are so many young professional dancers. But I don't really know … I haven't really thought about that. I still class myself as a young, as a really young person. Also, I don't think I'm an amazing dancer. I think I'm just an alright dancer. So, no I don't think I would.

Adele: I'd like to talk a bit more about professionalism because it's often tied to wage and being paid to do something. I just wondered whether you were paid to do *Men and Girls Dance*.

Sorrel: No. When I auditioned I was really young so I didn't actually think about that. Maybe if it was now I may have thought, 'Am I going to get paid for this? Is this something I'm going to get paid for?' But at that age, I wasn't thinking about that. I was just thinking, 'Oh my gosh, I'm going to be on stage I'm going to be in a show' … So, you'd also class yourself as a professional if it's your job. And you're getting paid for something you love. Well, you might not love it but if you're getting paid for a job you're a professional.

Un/Certainty

I share with Sorrel a photo of her in a performance space being held in a foetal position by a male-presenting performer. She is resting in his arms and against his chest. She faces away from him and towards the camera, with a microphone in her hand. She wears purple leggings, grey trainers, and a patterned top. He wears a mustard t-shirt and black casual trousers.

Sorrel: Wow, I look so young! In this photo, I'm being held by Kip and I have a microphone in hand and I'm describing what I can see, hear, feel, and smell. I think this was taken in the middle of the performance, so I would've been a bit tired but not shattered. Getting held like this felt really cool because you felt safe but then also like you were about to fall. I think whilst I was talking, Kip wasn't just holding me in the same position but I think he was moving me all around and holding me differently so I could see from different views and describe different things. There was a change in the way that I performed because in dance classes you stand in rows whereas here you could stand anywhere and everywhere.

Adele: What's interesting to me is always those tensions between freedom and control, feeling empowered and feeling powerless, giving and taking. I like how you describe this photo where you're being held by Kip and that this made you feel both safe and unsafe at the same time, as if you were going to fall. Were there any other moments in the rehearsals or the performance itself that created tension between two things that we might think of as opposites: freedom/control, safety/risk?

Sorrel: Yes, definitely. This is quite literal. So, in the performance, we had to pick up the newspaper blanket but none of the audience knew that when we lifted it up and put it back down, one of the men from the back went under it, lay on the floor, and put it over him. We'd rehearsed it but onstage it looked like improv—it kind of was—but we knew it was going to happen. He was called Nick. He stood up suddenly, and we were playing chase around the stage when he was covered in this newspaper. So, we were all screaming onstage and running around, and he was chasing us. I think I was the smallest, so I was chosen. All of the girls ran off the stage, and I'd still be there, and I would go forward and touch him but purposefully, and he'd grab me in and spin me, just keep spinning me everywhere he was lifting me, behind, around, everywhere. We had rehearsed it so many times and each time we had rehearsed it he said, 'You just need to let go a bit more because it's easier for me to spin you around' and I was like, 'Oh my gosh, OK it's going to be fine. I know he's not going to drop me' but whilst that was happening I was

> like, 'Oh my gosh, I'm going to fall. He's going to chuck me'. I was so scared and every time he'd say, 'Just let go a bit. It's OK, I'm not going to drop you I promise'. In the performance I was literally not holding him at all, and he was just spinning me everywhere and it was so fast and I was really scared. Obviously, I did know that he wasn't going to drop me, but then I had that certain feeling 'what if he's going to drop me' so that was kind of like safe and unsafe.

Un/Finished

10 February 2021
Dear Zina,
I'm in floods of tears after reading your email. First, at the thought of how difficult things must be for you at the moment. We often hear in the media about the effects of online learning and homeschooling on young children and parents but there doesn't seem to be a public narrative of/for the experiences of teenagers, at least in the UK, at the moment. I'm sorry about this. Us adults need to do better. But thank you for taking the time out of the pressures of schoolwork to write such a generous and careful email. Secondly, I'm crying because I keenly share your insights on productivity and how difficult it is for us all to step back from thinking about our lives in terms of a series of tasks, jobs, and economically 'useful' achievements, whether these are paid or unpaid. You're not alone here! For me, having to juggle parenting and caring for two young children alongside a full-time job during the last year, has (sadly) only emphasised life in terms of how productive I am and how productive I am given permission to be in the context of a pandemic. The success of my career is often measured in relation to a series of goals and indicators that I have to meet if I want to go for a promotion for example and these don't stop because of a pandemic. Just as your lessons, curriculum, and preparation for exams continue. I don't know about you, but that feels unfair to me; that we should carry on as normal when the situation is anything but normal.

What I really like about your reflections here, is that everything you did with your day was what you wanted to do and was not in the service of self-development for economic or profit-driven outcomes: you slept in, you read, you ate good food, you watched some tv and a film, you played a computer game, you listened to music. The philosopher Alan Watts says 'you play the piano, you don't work the piano'. It's a gentle reminder of the importance of play and resisting living a life of necessity towards a set of outcomes. I'm sure that by setting aside a goal-oriented mindset, you learned a lot that day, perhaps in a way that might constitute some small but meaningful act of opposition to a culture that frames us as 'lazy' or 'useless' unless we are economically productive. I don't know about you, but watching *Small Axe* certainly widened my perspective on the diversity of the experiences of West Indian immigrants throughout the 60s, 70s, and 80s, the police brutality, the subjugation and discrimination, the protest and activism, the music—oh the music—and what it might mean to be 'free'. We elders are not necessarily wiser because we are older. But, if I'm being a good elder I feel compelled to say there are spaces that value the critical thinking, listening, and empathy you developed during your day of play.[3] I know that these qualities are valued by Fevered Sleep.

I think one of the interesting tensions with theatre and performance, especially in the context of your interest in capitalism, is that it operates at the intersection between work and play. In simple terms, an audience pays whilst the performers work for them. Historically speaking, theatre performers have been called 'players' (rather than workers notably), and this strong association with play carries through into the professional practice of companies like Fevered Sleep for whom 'making work' is a form of serious play. No matter how much we theatre-folk might frame our skills and experiences in terms of the love for our craft or volunteer our unpaid labour to get a show on its feet, the economic conditions of this play/work are ever-present and I think they are further complicated when we invite young people into this context. Theatre has a complex history of child labour. How we think about the economic conditions of production are tied up with this open-ended distinction between work and play and can affect and be affected by whether you're seen as professional or amateur, paid or unpaid, experienced or inexperienced. I note that you are being paid for your contribution to this essay, which is an important commitment on Fevered Sleep's part to financially recompense you for your labour on it. If only all professional companies instituted this policy when working with under 18s (and over 18s for that matter). But it made me wonder whether being paid to do it might change your relationship to the task. Do you see it as work, play, or both? Does being paid affect what you feel able to say here? Do you self-censor, I wonder? In the interests of transparency, I'm waged, so I'm not being paid a fee for my work here, but I do see this contribution as part of the research I'm contracted to do, so I too am being recompensed in that sense.

I'm also really interested in, as you so beautifully put it, 'wanting to be, feeling like and being treated like an adult'. I think some adults might feel this too. Sure, they have adult privileges, but the desire to want to be perceived as a 'together', rational, fully formed 'grown up' is strong. I think the idea of the adult is a fiction though! This term 'adult' depends so much on what we understand a child to be. If as adults (and perhaps teenagers!), we can distinguish ourselves from what we think a child is (or should be), then we know what constitutes an adult and vice versa. In other words, I think the idea of the adult is wholly dependent on what we think a child is. The problem is that children and young people don't have the power to decide when you stop being a child and become an adult. Adults and the institutions, rituals, and laws they uphold decide that. In the eyes of the law (or most legislation), you're an 'adult' when you reach 18. Although, it's interesting that in England and Wales children as young as 10 can be convicted of a crime—which means very young children are deemed criminally responsible, even whilst they don't share in the same voting (or other) rights afforded to adults. In Sweden, you can't be convicted of a criminal offence until you're 14, and in Portugal, it's 16, so we have the lowest age here in England. Then we have child development studies, which has had a significant impact on what we consider 'normal' development from childhood (through adolescence) to adulthood. Some of my favourite writers, Jackie Stacey and Erica Burman, say that the idea of growing up that child development has offered us is based on 'an ideal-typical white, middle class childhood that is also culturally masculine'. Apart from experiencing white privilege, I don't feel like this idea of 'normal development' would have fairly represented me as a working-class girl, growing up in Huddersfield.

So adults decide what a child and an adult is … Where does the teen/ager fit in? The idea of a teenager seems to trouble a clean distinction between adult and child as they are no longer a child and not yet an adult. This is why I liked your prompt at the beginning of the project to think about teenagers. Perhaps this ambiguity about the teenager (not child and not-yet-adult) is why there's some policing of your play when you recall den building during the R and D sessions: we (adults) don't expect teenagers to build dens. I'm intrigued by the idea that there are certain kinds of play that we are or are not permitted to do once we reach certain ages. At the same time, we (again, adults) might write off some very real and material fears and anxieties that teenagers experience as 'teen angst'. So, we expect you to be responsible and play to your age, but then we infantilise or marginalise your fears, anxieties, and experiences. Although, perhaps the idea of teen angst, for a teenager, is an important way of identifying and sharing those fears with one's peers? You tell me. It's interesting though that we don't talk about 'adult angst'; that would be too vulnerable for us adults. For sure, you don't suddenly stop feeling fearful, anxious, and insecure after your 18th birthday.

I asked Sorrel the other day what she would include if she had to write a set of rules for how theatre/dance companies should work with 8–11 year olds (this was the age range for the show that she was in). What do you think? If you had to come up with some rules or advice—perhaps in relation to what we've been talking about (productivity, payment, work, play, adult/child relations, fears, vulnerability, rights, censorship, economics, perceptions of age-based on class, race, gender etc.)—what might it include?

Apologies for the VERY long email. Maybe it's conveying some of my adult angst ☺ I don't know. In any case, I hope it resonated with you and that you might be up for responding to some of my questions/thoughts. Looking forward to your response.

With best wishes,
Adele

p.s. big congrats on the G64 Connections play! Enjoy …

Transformation

Sorrel:

Transformation meant change …
Transformation was me feeling different about my life.
Transformation was an emotional change.
Transformation was me discovering my love for theatre.
Transformation was me changing my mindset.

Transformation was discovering what my body can do.
Transformation was working with other people.
Transformation was leaving my comfort zone.
Transformation was my leap of faith.
Transformation was me using my body in different ways.
Transformation was me working towards a goal.
Transformation was me stretching and challenging myself.
Transformation was feeling the thrill of performing.
Transformation was that this was a milestone in my life.
Transformation was being treated like a professional.
Transformation was being moved to tears.
Transformation was a deep change in who I was.
Transformation is me now doing 7 hours of dance a week.
Transformation was a change for life.

Adults[4]

Adele: It sounds like your life has been full of theatre before *Men and Girls Dance*.

Sorrel: Yes, definitely. Since very young we've been going to pantos, going to theatres, going to see my dad's shows, my uncle's shows.

Erin [Sorrel's mum who is sat off to the side]: You've seen lots of Rambert, Ballet Boys, and things that Luke or Kip might have been in, but none of us quite expected what you have been part of.[5] That was unchartered territory.

Adele: What was it that was unchartered? Was it the subject matter—was it 'Men' and 'Girls'?

Erin (Sorrel's mum): I think it's what you touched on about a level-playing field. Often you might have a version of events where there's a child professional in Matilda or something like that but there's something about children being seen and perceived as children or girls, as you say. That turned it on its head because that's what I thought and worried it was going to be like. There was this really interesting levelling experience where you would come back and talk about how David and Sam had talked to you, and you'd have sessions where you'd never be separated from the male dancers. Everything was absolutely collaborative and genuinely was real as opposed to 'we think we're doing that but that's not what's happening' and that includes the way that Sam and David used language. You felt so challenged.

Sorrel: Yeah. [nods]

Loss

> *'Teen'*
>
> *From the middle English 'tene', from Old English 'tēona' meaning injury, grief and misery, where 'tēona' is akin to Old Norse 'tjōn', which means loss or damage*
>
> (Merriam Webster 2021)

Adele: Did anyone lose or find anything during the creative process?

Sorrel: I think we all found our love for dance, being able to move our bodies differently and using it in creative and inventive ways. I found that being treated like a professional and having our own choices in the performance and not just being told what to do was incredible. I found that there were bits of the final performance that were my idea and that was just amazing to feel that and to have found that confidence in putting ideas forward. On the last performance, I found a completely different energy; I realised that I didn't want this to end. All I kept thinking of was how my life was never going to be the same again and how I would never feel that feeling of joy again.

Erin: I am going to say one thing which you won't say, I don't think. [turns to Sorrel] Is that OK …? Can I say it … about coming home after the last show?

Sorrel: Oh yeah.

Erin: What I can only describe as a process of grief after finishing the last show. There's a kind of rite of passage in the goodbye at the end, which is really important about how you hold that final space and the level of emotion that had been felt onstage and the level of emotion that the audience were giving back that was really heightened because of the subject matter or because of people being challenged and because of the joy. So you [to Sorrel] felt all those things.

Sorrel: Also because you spent so long on it and it was all over.

Erin: So, it wasn't about the performances. The process had taken weeks and the relationship and trust … all I can describe in our house was grief and bereavement and you, age 9, never having felt those feelings before but you coming up the stairs on the last night, sobbing uncontrollably and you said, 'What am I going to do? What am I going to do?' and I said, 'What tomorrow or next week?' thinking you were tired, and you said, 'No, with the rest of my life' because it had been all-consuming and that levelling experience with those relationships you've never encountered with that intensity before. Anyway, I'm sorry I'm just jumping in … I had to get my two-penny worth in Adele. [laughter]

Adele: Us adults are always interfering, aren't we? [laughter]

Erin: Sorry, I was told specifically to sit outside of the screen and not to interfere. [laughter]

Work/Play

28 February 2021
Dear Adele,
I'm glad you resonated with my email, I think I experienced the same insight with your reply actually. My entire world revolves around simplicity and ease and while I so desperately don't want to be an adult, I only have a faint idea of what it might be like. As mad as it is to say, your email reminded me that adults are as complex as children, with their own responsibilities, demands, and ideas. That may just be me though, I always find it interesting to realise that other people, in general, have lives and brains as complex as my own.

In terms of the step between teenhood and adulthood, I wanted to ask almost what it's like being an adult. Our entire lives up to 18 are preparation for what we'd like to do as adults, but then what? What now? I feel like I'm constantly dreaming and aspiring, whether I pursue anything I want, or not. I can't imagine that one day I'd be set, in a set job, maybe with a set family with nothing more to hope for or want. It feels like an end, at least for me who never wants to leave my luxuries and unemployment. I think it's this rebuttal that forces me into my competitive, productive mindset, as I'll eventually have to work. As an adult, do you still get those dreams and aspirations, 'what I'd like to be when I'm older', however ambitious?

I enjoy the ties between work and play on this project because I consider it work but it feels like play. The compensation is definitely one of my indicators but I think that even without it, I'd consider this as a sort of work. Other extracurricular projects that I don't get paid for I still consider as work because there's usually something to be benefited off it, and not usually for me. From this, the benefit is a BOOK!! An actual book that I am a part of which still doesn't feel entirely real. From my drama play, the benefit is actually just the experience with my friends and being able to work towards something. So I guess when there's something to gain, I consider it work.

I don't know if I'm right when I say this but 'teen angst' seems like a simplified explanation to the complexity and the problems that teenagers actually face. For any angst to be somewhat taken seriously, we, of course, as a society, would have to actually care about mental health.

I thought about what rules might be included when working with children but honestly, my mind feels blank. I was only 11 three years ago but I feel like I cannot remember what that was like at all. Maybe my only advice would be to keep their experiences completely wholesome. At that age, almost nothing can hurt you. Or maybe things can and I just don't consider it. I wonder.

Thank you for your insightful emails! Have a lovely day/evening!
Zina

Futures

Adele: What do you imagine a show called *Men and Teenagers Dance* might look like?

Sorrel: Imagining the show *Men and Teenagers Dance*, I think it would be very different. It would be less enthusiastic because in my performance we were all very little, so it was easy to lift and throw us around and we had loads of energy, whereas most teenagers are usually tired and sometimes grumpy. The structure of my performance was how it suited us and how we wanted it to look and feel. However, in the teenagers' one, it would be different depending on how they want it to look and feel. Being a teenager now, and looking back on the performance, I think I would prefer it to be different. I also think teenagers look at themselves differently and are more aware of how they look and feel, so when I did my performance we were at the age when we didn't care about how we looked and we just cared about what was going on around us and being excited for what was to come. I think I would also want the costumes to be different because in my performance we were all in random clothes, which I did love, but I think I would want to be in something similar to everyone but not exactly the same, so something that you can express yourself in but something that you can all see that we're all connected. I also think it would've been very cool if David and Sam let the girls come all together and brainstorm and create our own piece of choreography, purely from just our ideas, something that showcases all our personalities and talents.

Adele: I'm curious now you're a teenager—actually I know you said you don't feel like one so I'll rephrase the question—now you're thirteen if you had to write a set of rules for a professional theatre and dance company about how to work with pre-teenage children say 8–11 like you were in *Men and Girls Dance*… is there anything you think it should definitely include?

Sorrel: I don't really like rules because I feel they're too limiting but I think if there was one thing to say I'd say it would be: 'hear their ideas, hear them out' because some of them will be crazy or impossible to do but I'd say, 'Still listen to them and take them in and as many as you can try and incorporate them' because if you're trying to create a piece that's like say, *Men and Girls*, then you want to incorporate as much of the girls' ideas or boys' ideas towards that piece and you want to make it as much theirs as yours. Obviously, make it safe. Safe, as in, they're not going to get hurt.

Adele: Do you think that kind of advice would be the same for a group of teenagers?

Sorrel: Yeah, it would definitely be the same, because I was young so we followed their instructions, but maybe being older you'd feel a sense of power where you'd be like, 'No actually I think we should really do this' but I think the rules would still stay the same.

Growing Sideways

Stockton argues that the pervasive discourse of the child as 'growing up' in a linear and fixed fashion is a 'short-sighted, limited rendering of human growth' (2009: 11). Whilst her references are to the 'ghostly gay child' and children's queerness as explored in the fictional realms of film, TV, and literature, her analysis has implications for the 'sideways movements that attend *all* children, however we deny it' (ibid.: 3). This includes, I suggest, actual children/(pre-)teenagers involved in professional performance practice. How do we navigate the discursive, symbolic, and material conditions of the young people we (as adult artists and scholars) work alongside and the power dynamics common to all intergenerational work, even whilst pursuing a non-hierarchical relationship? Just as *Men and Girls Dance* does not shy away from both the pleasures and the discomforts of (the perceptions of) 'men' and 'girls' dancing together in the UK in the twenty-first century, the dialogues, email exchanges, and creative writing presented here enact a horizontal connection that intends to raise both pleasurable and uncomfortable questions: questions about the shared anxieties and positive feelings around affective relationships between adults and children, gender, in/equity, free/paid labour, non-/professionalism, power(lessness), and (lack of) authority.

The dialogue on girlhood, for example, allows a mutual sideways movement away from both the discursive subject position of 'girl' available to Sorrel within the performance and the neutral observer/interviewer available to me within the academy, which is instead deliberately undermined by my gender-interested responses. As we have seen, the discursive hailing of Sorrel as a 'dancer' during the *Men and Girls Dance* rehearsal process offers her a way of both moving *and* thinking about herself as a dancing body within a professional community. Alongside the embodied invitation of the improvisational choreographic practice she describes, Sorrel is perhaps able to explore this dancerly identity as an alternative to the boundaries of gender that were imposed by the premise of a performance that names her 'girl'. At the same time, the positioning of the young female performers in the work as a group of 'girls' invites the audience to negotiate an arguably more expansive perception of masculinity beyond the paedophilic connotations espoused by the popular news media when men and girls are positioned in relation to each other. However, this reimagining of male subjectivity in the performance is arguably only possible *in relation to* the performers' identification as 'girls' and renders the category of 'girl' unavailable for the kind of identity reframing that is afforded to the male adult bodies onstage. Whilst, of course, *Men and Girls Dance* does not set out to reimagine different modes of subjectivity for contemporary girlhood or to explore the extensive diversity of girls' lives, the residual relational tension created by the foregrounding of bodies onstage as either 'men' or 'girls' echoes the complex discursive conditions haunting all intergenerational collaborations. During our exchange, for example, neither Sorrel nor I can step outside of our subject positions, especially as the disciplinary frameworks they belong to reward us for our continued participation as the 'right' kind of subject. I am very aware of the privilege afforded to me as a white cisgender female (at the time of writing), which permits me to ask questions that may not be available to other interviewers. However, we can sit beside these subject positions to acknowledge, comment on, or interrogate them with a methodological approach that shifts to accommodate different or emerging relational subjectivities beyond simply the 'impartial interviewer' and the 'girl' or the 'teenager'.

To do this, an approach to sideways intergenerational collaboration cannot simply be self-reflexive—or autoethnographic—for the 'adult'. Instead, it has to explore methods and modes that permit sideways growth—as 'something that locates energy, pleasure, vitality, and (e)motion in the back and forth of connections and extensions that are not reproductive' (Stockton 2009: 13)—for *all* collaborators. This chapter has attempted to create a space for this kind of horizontal rather than vertical growth by embracing the potential of Zina's theme of the teenager so that some of its attendant meanings guide the interview and letter-based content: from the etymological origins of 'teen' as loss, grief, and misery to its contemporary associations with transition, transformation, change, and rebellion. Similarly, Sorrel's self-selected method of describing photos from the performance—as a form of child-led photo-elicitation—generated descriptions of bodily, emotional, and relational responses that were not necessarily visible in the piece itself. Furthermore, the letters between Zina and myself offered Zina a stake in writing the interregnum experience of the (pre-)teenager, whilst we both intermittently occupied the positions of questioner and respondent through an on-going, unfinished, and, as Stockton might say, mutually energetic, pleasurable, vitalizing, and emotional dialogue.

Undoubtedly, this kind of collaboration is complex political territory, since there is always an asymmetrical power relation, especially where co-authorship is desirable but the responsibility lies firmly with the adult, as one might argue it should. However, in order to meet young collaborators laterally, the responsible adult does not necessarily need to be the rational, fully formed 'grown up' that Stockton dismantles; just as we would not want to reduce the vast experience, knowledge, and questions Sorrel and Zina bring to this contribution on account of the lack of vertical, upward growth and development suggested by their ages. Instead, it is only through an ethical gesture of openness, vulnerability, and not-yet-knowing on the part of the adult that our shared experiences, here as artists, researchers, children, teenagers, female-identifying people, and humans, can flourish and grow. Growing sideways together.

Notes

1 An earlier version of this chapter is published in *Love and Not Knowing* (Cull Ó Maoilearca and Pell 2024). I would like to thank Laura Cull Ó Maoilearca and Performance Research Books for kindly permitting me to reproduce the material here. Also, many thanks to Fevered Sleep's Artistic Directors Sam Butler and David Harradine for facilitating my initial contact with Zina and Sorrel and their parents, sharing performance documentation with me, and for allowing the research process with Zina and Sorrel to unfold freely. Most of all I would like to thank Zina and Sorrel, who gave me permission to use their words here and have helped me to grow sideways.

2 I would like to thank Isis Germano who first introduced me to Kathryn Bond Stockton's work, when she discusses the notion of 'growing sideways' in relation to the dramaturgy of Lies Pauwels' *Het Hamiltoncomplex* in *Performance Research* (2018).

3 I am drawing on Dar *et al.*'s recent description of the 'good elder' as a custodian who creates 'transformative spaces that, at least temporarily, level power dynamics among students, administrative staff and academics to create and cherish collective methodologies for survival' (2020: 7).

4 In line with the project's university-approved research ethics application, which took into consideration issues of safeguarding and the one-to-one nature of the research, all communication with the young people involved in this chapter, whether written or verbal, included a nominated parent.
5 Luke and Kip are two of the adult performers who appeared in *Men and Girls Dance.*

References

Burman, Erica and Stacey, Jackie (2010) 'The Child and Childhood in Feminist Theory', *Feminist Theory*, 11 (3): 227–240.

Cull Ó Maoilearca, Laura and Luke Pell (2024) *Love and Not Knowing*, Aberystwyth: Performance Research Books.

Dar, Sadhvi, Liu, Helena, Martinez, Angelina and Brewis, Deborah N. (2020) 'The Business School is Racist: Act Up', Organization, 28 (4): 695–706.

Germano, Isis (2018) 'So Cute, So Creepy', *Performance Research*, 23 (1): 44–51.

Logan, Brian (2008) 'Edinburgh Festival: Once and for All We're Gonna Tell You Who We Are So Shut Up and Listen', *The Guardian*, Friday 15 August: https://www.theguardian.com/culture/2008/aug/14/edinburghfestival.onceandforall?CMP=gu_com (accessed 30 January 2024).

Merriam Webster (2021) https://www.merriam-webster.com/dictionary/teen (accessed 19 March 2021).

Senior, Adele and The Institute for the Art and Practice of Dissent at Home (2018) 'On Children', *Performance Research*, 23 (1): 1–4.

Stockton, Kathryn Bond (2009) *The Queer Child or Growing Sideways in the Twentieth Century*, Durham and London: Duke University Press.

Walkerdine, Valerie (1988) *The Mastery of Reason*, London: Routledge.

9 The Child as Researcher and Archivist

Documenting *News News News*

This chapter foregrounds the experiences of performers aged 10 and 11 who participated in *News News News* at Contact Theatre, Manchester in March 2022. *News News News* is a 'a television news show made by children for adults, recorded in front of a studio audience and broadcast live on the internet' (Field and Darlington n.d.). It includes filmed footage of the young performers interviewing a local Member of Parliament, members of the public, and academics on self-selected issues such as homelessness and climate change. An archive of reflections on the performers' experiences of participating in this work was collected and recorded as part of a two-day research workshop that I facilitated at their Manchester school.[1] A selection of the documentation from the workshop is included here with some interview material that was gathered separately from the adult creators of *News News News*, Andy Field and Beckie Darlington. The research was informed by two main aims which arise from acknowledging the absence of either child-led or child-informed documentation on (the people we call) children's participation in contemporary performance within the academy, particularly by young people of Black and global majority heritage. The first aim was to re-position the performers as researchers and archivists of the professional performance they participated in, in order to help create a child-informed record of their participation. Secondly, the overall project set out to put into practice Royona Mitra's invitation, following Chelsea Kwakye and Ore Ogunbiyi's call in *Taking Up Space: The Black Girl's Manifesto for Change* (2019), to 'make space' as 'an act of decoloniality' in the academy (Mitra 2019). It did so by foregrounding the overlooked experiences of mainly Black and global majority heritage performers who made up the young cast of *News News News*.

The project's attempt to practise 'giving up space' in research *with* children is a deliberate recognition of my positionality as a white author who is able to pass as cisgender and the power that affords me to relinquish the space I have to the people we call children and specifically to children of colour in order to foreground perspectives that have so far been marginalised within the context of professional contemporary performance in the UK and its associated scholarship. What I am not claiming is that making space affords an equal footing for the young performers cited below. Even whilst my approach, as mentioned previously, is acutely conscious not to repeat historical classist and colonial attempts within the academy to

DOI: 10.4324/9781003043072-12

'give voice' to marginalised subjects and communities (Jackson and Mazzei 2009), I am still the sole author of this book and the curator of the pages within it, which affords to me the privilege, for example, of selecting and presenting the material that follows. The act of making space for *child-informed* documentation of the experiences of performers of Black and global majority heritage, however, deliberately problematises the ventriloquist undertones of 'giving voice' and constitutes a small step towards de-centring whiteness in contemporary performance research with children. In particular, the project's methodological commitment to queering existing research methods, particularly within childhood studies in the global north, intends to position the people we call children as researchers in their own right and sets out to discover how much control and authorship they can have over the ways in which their experiences are both researched and archived within an artistic-academic context, particularly those who may be materially disadvantaged by the intersection of age with both race and class. What accompanies the documentation of material archived by the performers on their experiences of *News News News*, therefore, is some contextual writing and reflections on the questions and methodological concerns I am left with as marginalia.

This commentary, which sits beside the main text, is intended to be read as an acknowledgement of the messy implicated-ness of my interpretive work and decision-making as lead researcher and curator of the pages that follow.

My accompanying commentary includes contextual information as well as autoethnographic notes and reflections that are guided largely by the question: How useful is appropriating both existing approaches to positioning children as researchers in childhood studies (and its related disciplines) and research methods that are commonly reserved for adults in performance studies in the post-performance archival process? To ask these questions through practice, I created a game for the workshop which I share below, which adopted and reworked existing methods of research drawn largely from disciplinary approaches that are well-established within childhood studies as well as activities that are more consistent with approaches to practice research within the field of performance. The game was designed to allow for the performers' self-reflexivity and for them to be positioned and framed as both researchers and archivists, who were offered existing research methods to adopt and use within the game. Positioning children as active participants in research is not new and gained momentum in the 1990s (James and Prout 1997, Qvortrup 1994). However, what is novel here is precisely the application and reworking of existing research methods, outside the framework of education and pedagogy, in the context of creating a post-performance archive of knowledges and experiences of the people we call children, specifically those of Black and global majority heritage.

Whilst the development of the game was guided by existing approaches to research with children both outside and inside of the field of performance, these approaches were deliberately inflected by an overarching motivation to bring children and adults into 'lateral contact', building on the focus of the previous chapter. In comparison with the online one-to-one verbal interviews and written correspondence between myself and older teenage performers, however, the conditions for lateral contact here had to be reconsidered and approached differently to accommodate a school-based context, which involved a greater number of performers who had experienced a shared artistic process culminating in a public performance. The workshop aimed to foster lateral contact in a number of ways: exposing the performers to the idea that research is unfinished and processual, explicitly positioning them as co-producers and archivists of knowledge about the performance they appeared in throughout the research workshop, and creating fruitful conditions to share their findings by supporting them on the second day to generate a manifesto on working with children in performance that they consented to be disseminated both here and with an international audience of other child and adult performers, makers, and pedagogues as part of an ASSITEJ-funded symposium at Fundus Theatre in Hamburg, Germany. In this regard, the research can be situated more as research *with* the people we call children than *by* children, where the latter instead describes 'self-directed empirical research from inception to dissemination' and 'relates to issues that they, not adults, have identified as significant in their lives' (Bucknall 2012: 6). The workshop proceeded instead from the (adult) researcher's assumption that the performance and its process was, at least to some extent, significant to the lives of the children involved and aimed to share the research in a pre-determined artistic-academic context. However, as the documentation attests, the game itself and the manifesto structure created significant moments of self-direction and opportunities to archive issues that are meaningful to and for the performers themselves.

Before introducing the performers' documentation, the framing of the workshop bears some reflection. Emphasis was placed on the process-based nature of research by undermining the 'adult' status of the research/researcher as a complete and finished product/producer from the moment the workshop began. This approach resembles the 'least-adult role' (Mandell 1988) as a positionality for the researcher with children that involves minimising the differences between adult and child, mainly the myth of 'adult superiority based on age and cognitive maturity' (ibid.: 435). However rather than Mandell's call to 'abolish adult-child differences', the workshop was set up not to diminish but to draw attention to any perceived material and imagined differences and instead involved actively dismantling the idea of the authoritative, expert researcher by discussing with the children both my own and my research assistant's positioning as 'not-knowing' and by articulating the processual nature of our own research activities when introducing the workshop. Drawing attention to and aiming to dismantle inherent power imbalances was therefore a significant part of the methodology. The activities in the game were also framed away from leading the performers' responses and towards more of an open, curiosity-driven exploration, with a view to creating opportunities for them to have authorial control over the narratives of *News News News* that they were documenting and, in some cases, investigating. In particular, through the game's activities, the performers were offered a stake in both framing their own experiences of the performance and looking back closely on their experiences through a simple research-based attitude deriving from an etymological origin of 'research' from Old French *recercher* meaning to 'seek out, search closely'. Each activity within the game also derived from a specific research method or methodological commitment that was democratised, shared, and named on each activity card so that the performers were equipped to enact a research process rather than gesturing tokenistically towards their activity as 'research'.

Following the game, the performers were supported to take up a 'researcher as activist' attitude by collectively creating a manifesto on making performance with children. This was, in part, a novel exploration of the genre of the manifesto as a means of doing child-led or collaborative research with the people we call children in performance that would feedback in a meaningful way to the artistic-academic community. It was also a direct response to the dominant association of the manifesto form with adult voices even within the context of children's participation in contemporary performance, despite the appearance of children in recent art manifestoes. In 2018, for example, child performers read to camera theatre director Milo Rau's manifesto 'Manifest Van Gent' for the city theatre of Ghent (NTGent). More recently, between 2021 and 2022, the WhiteChapel Gallery in London has hosted a year-long project by Stanley Schtinter entitled 'Important Books (Or, Manifestos Read By Children) [close brackets]', where the use of parentheses in Schtinter's title unintentionally enacts the regular marginalisation of children from the genre of the manifesto.

This trend towards the people we call children doing the labour of reading out adult-written manifestos further inscribes their position as consumers rather than producers of the manifesto. Ultimately, they are positioned as audiences of, or ventriloquists for, the manifesto rather than authors of it. As conduits for an adult voice, the positioning of the children in these examples problematically re-inscribes the historic separation of children from the political realm. I have discussed this separation elsewhere with reference to Hannah Arendt's claim that children's 'newness' – which for Arendt is tied up in her theorisation of natality as the condition of possibility for political action – needs to be protected from the world and, in turn, the world needs to be protected from their newness (Arendt 1958, Arendt [1961] 1993, Senior 2016). We will see, however, that the manifesto produced with the young performers in Manchester offers a unique form for activist practice to be built within child-informed research in a way that could also contribute to an adult academic world where there is already an acknowledgement that the manifesto genre allows (adult) researchers to 'speak collectively, build consensus, raise awareness, advocate for and accelerate change, speak for and from the margins, disrupt the status quo, unsettle stuck discourse, sidestep conventional modes, expose broken promises' (Ashby *et al.* 2019: 2).

Although critiques of the heroic voice of the manifesto are abundant in the academy (Alvarez *et al.* 2012: 5), with 'some argu[ing] that the manifesto is passé: paradigmatically modernist, unrepentantly masculinist, and thoroughly authoritarian' (Weeks 2013: 216), it is this very 'adult' voice that the manifesto, queered by the people we call children here, seeks to challenge. However, whilst both the game and the manifesto set out to 'make space' (Mitra 2019) in the academy for the voices of those we call children, in the end, I am not convinced that either one makes sufficient space for children of Black and global majority heritage. I go on in the closing chapter to consider instead glitch feminism as a critical perspective and practice that, in dialogue with some of the insights developed throughout the book, has the potential to offer an imagined and material space that is founded on performance strategies born out of experiences of intersecting marginalisation, some of which emerge in childhood. To this end, glitch feminism in practice might offer some useful strategies to nuance the research with the people we call children that follows; from being informed by a decolonisation agenda to being motivated by anti-racism and intersecting disadvantages within performance.

The Game

Audio

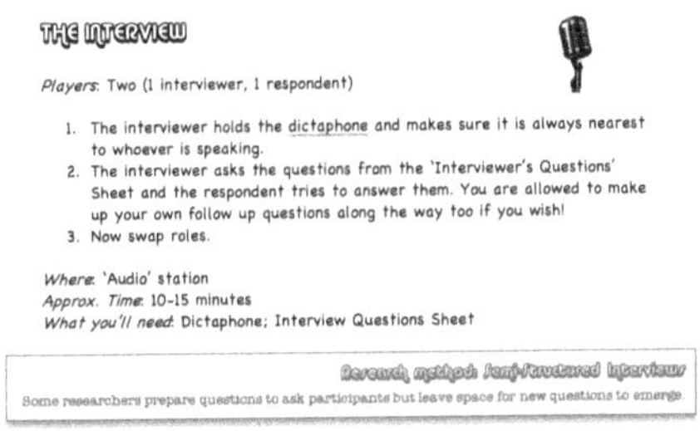

Figure 9.1 'The Interview' research activity card.

We are in an 'attic' classroom during one of the hottest days of the year in Manchester in 2022. Tired, sweaty bodies. The significant heat undoubtedly contributes to the quick pace the children move from one activity to another. We have set up four stations: audio, imaginative, sensory, and visual. They are each invited individually or in pairs to spin an arrow on a wheel board and then choose a card that corresponds to the station the arrow points towards (see Fig. 9.1).

The audio station draws on existing methods of research but in a way that deliberately plays with the absent presence of the adult figures that ghosted the creation of each of the activities: the adult researcher/interviewer who provides the questions (see activity: The Interview), the adult artists whose words are used as found material to create poems (see activity: Chance Methods), and an adult audience member they imagine is responding to a post-performance response: 'Children are [fill in the blank]' (see activity: The Audience).

Aligning with Mary Kellett's argument that the 'barrier to empowering children as researchers is not their lack of adult status but their lack of research skills' (2005: 11), each activity provides an

What's the first image that comes to mind when you think about News News News?

Shams: All the fun
Hannan: The logo of it, how it's, you know, presented.
Anon: The *News News News* logo
AF and BD: A child with a microphone in their hand, speaking into the mic and then holding it up to an adult's face.

What is the first word that comes to mind when you think about News News News?

Shams: Amazing.
Hannan: News. Because that's the main word.
Anon: Andy.
AF and BD: Curiosity.

Can you tell me a story about News News News?

Shams: Well, at the start I was terrible and I thought I was definitely going to laugh in the performance and when I ended up doing the performance just looking at the audience made me do better.
Hannan: So, basically we were in *News News News*, and one time we were playing because it was our break and Eslam brought in pizza.
Anon: We played outside and we got to have pizza because Eslam brought it.
AF and BD: Eslam, Hannan and Kairo's story was on what endangered animals there are in Manchester. As part of that we were lucky enough to go to the – currently closed

opportunity for the children to learn, use, and name a research method or methodology. I make a mental note not to forget that there are systematic and structural barriers that are indeed the result of children's lack of adult status which prevents them from participating in research and contrary to this argument many of the people we call children already possess research skills even if they or the adults around them might not recognise them as such. However, it is Kellett's challenge to the assumption that research is synonymous with adulthood that drives the integration of research skills within the game's activities here.

Two children at a time are invited to conduct a semi-structured interview written by an absent adult researcher (me) through a framework that leaves the children open to make choices around which questions to ask, how to ask them, and to pose new/different questions or open up the conversation. They don't take up the opportunity to ask questions that are not already written down for them.

AF and BD refer to the artists, Andy Field and Beckie Darlington, who were not present during the workshop and were asked these questions on a separate occasion.

The Interview intentionally builds on skills and experiences the performers have already developed as part of the *News News News* creative process where they created filmed content for the performance by interviewing politicians, activists, academics, and members of the public on self-selected topics.

to the public – Manchester Museum to meet the curator of Herpetology there. The curator has discovered and named a whole new species of frogs, and they have a lot of endangered frogs at the museum. They took us and the children into the vivarium there and let the children hold some of the animals. In the moment, Kairo and Hannan were too nervous to touch them, but Eslam wanted to hold everything he could. These frogs are from places like Costa Rica and they're super colourful and amazing-looking, and I felt a real sense of wonder seeing them up close and Eslam was really amazed by them too. It felt like a really special moment, which I would never have had if it hadn't been for their curiosity and their choice of story.

Were there any moments in the process of making or showing News News News where you felt unfinished?

Shams: Probably when I … erm … no, at the end I felt there was something for me to do that I could have done but I felt like I could have done better during my speech and then at the end I felt like I could have done better which made me feel unfinished.

AF and BD: The whole of the first half of the show feels unfinished until the audience are in their seats. There is only so much practising you can do with audience stand-ins and us pretending to be audience members.

Many of the adult-led questions are intentionally informed by dominant perceptions of children as, for example, unfinished, in the making, and 'out of control'. These same questions were asked of the adult artists as a way of queering adult-led approaches to interviewing by drawing attention to and creatively using these biases around children's capabilities and capacities to yield responses generated from questions that are outside of the usual provocations they might asked as (adult) artists.

Were there any moments in the process of making or showing News News News where you became aware of class/gender/race/ability?

Hannan: Yes. When I was [inaudible] reminded me about it.

AF and BD: Working in a school environment that is so diverse, amongst both the children and the teaching staff, made us aware of class and race, and happy that we could be a temporary part of this community and that the show itself could be reflective of the diverse nature of the city of Manchester itself.

There were many inaudible moments on the recordings namely the rustling of papers, a hand over the speaker, or the persistent sound of a toy trumpet from the prop box.

Were there any moments in the process of making or showing News News News where you felt in or out of control?

Hannan: I felt like, out of control, because I get too excited and it goes the wrong way.

AF and BD: The obvious thing that comes to mind is how I don't feel in control during the unscripted moments in the performance. I find that really tense, and I am really nervous during the show in general because the children are holding together the whole thing. Past experience tells me how capable they are, and I also obviously want that lack of control. Afterwards, I always feel amazing, but I feel the adrenaline of not being in control in those moments!

A question about control not commonly asked of adults with responsibility for children yields a moment of vulnerability for the artists. In this moment, a question driven by a normative assumption about the child, makes visible an unfinished adult.

Were there any moments in the process of making or showing News News News where you felt curious?

Hannan: I wanted to discover more about endangered animals because that's what me Cairo and Eslam did.

AF and BD: I am still baffled and fascinated by Roblox, despite various attempts to explain what it is.

Were there any moments in the process of making or showing News News News ...where you rolled your eyes?

Anon: <laughing> No

AF and BD: The third or fourth time that a taxi we had booked to get us to one of our interviews failed to show up on time, or at all.

... where you experienced a transition or transformation?

Anon: No

AF and BD: Stepping into the main theatre at Contact [the venue] with the children for the first time felt like a transformation. Suddenly the idea of the 'show', which had always been somewhat distant and abstract, came sharply into focus.

I later wonder whether I should have offered the children some training in their role as interviewers to tease out these one-word answers. Perhaps gamifying the archival process also created a sense of urgency that did not allow these thoughts to breathe sufficiently.

... where you were confused?

Anon: No. Oh yeh. There was one time where I had to say a line, but I thought Shams was saying it, so I never said it but it was in the practice not in the real show.

AF and BD: When the show has started, we are hidden by the edge of the stage, where we can hear but not see what is happening. So when Daniel and Morgana go into the audience, we can hear the laughter but cannot see why people are laughing. It's a nice moment – to feel like people are having a good time and that D & M were doing a good job but not to know exactly why…!

... where you felt embarrassed?

Anon: Yeh, because in the real show, I messed up.

AF and BD: Throughout the recording of the air pollution story – when the children were interviewing Prof. Hugh Coe, when they were testing pollution levels near their school, when they were interviewing people on the street – I felt embarrassed about our adult failure to make any meaningful change happen, despite knowing how bad things are.

Another moment of adult vulnerability.

... where you made or remade a memory?

Anon: Just making the show was definitely a memory.

AF and BD: One memory I will take with me is from just before the performance. Eslam's dad had wanted to get everyone pizzas and they took absolutely ages to come. Eslam was upset because he thought they wouldn't come in time and then just at the last minute, his dad arrived with the pizzas so we ran upstairs and we all sat on the floor of the rehearsal room, eating takeaway pizza together. It was a beautiful moment of calm before the excitement of the show itself.

Pizza came up frequently in the children's responses too and was a key memory for both children and adults. The peer-to-peer interview format seems to be encouraging moments of shared connection for the children, which are largely based around this key memory and their individual contribution to the performance. However, the questions and/or the peer-to-peer setup is limited in its ability to tease out details of the process. Interestingly, snack times during the workshop ended up being key in enabling the children to reminisce and discuss in a very relaxed way, namely without recording themselves, their shared memories. On reflection, I would like to explore rituals that include eating as part of a future post-performance archival process.

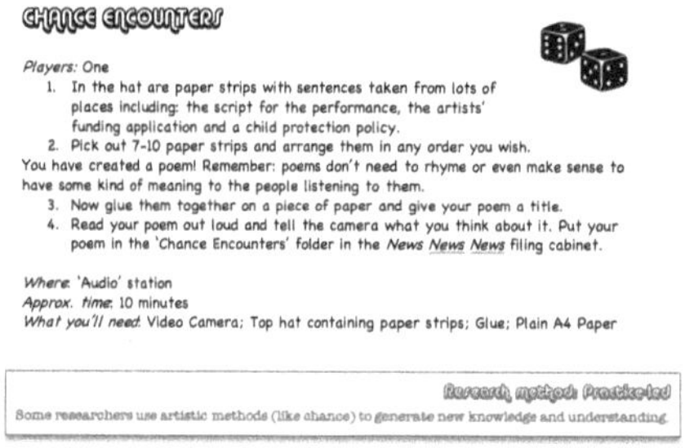
CHANCE ENCOUNTERS

Players: One

1. In the hat are paper strips with sentences taken from lots of places including: the script for the performance, the artists' funding application and a child protection policy.
2. Pick out 7-10 paper strips and arrange them in any order you wish.

You have created a poem! Remember: poems don't need to rhyme or even make sense to have some kind of meaning to the people listening to them.

3. Now glue them together on a piece of paper and give your poem a title.
4. Read your poem out loud and tell the camera what you think about it. Put your poem in the 'Chance Encounters' folder in the *News News News* filing cabinet.

Where: 'Audio' station
Approx. time: 10 minutes
What you'll need: Video Camera; Top hat containing paper strips; Glue; Plain A4 Paper

Research method: Practice-led
Some researchers use artistic methods (like chance) to generate new knowledge and understanding.

Figure 9.2 'Chance Encounters' research activity card.

This activity (Fig. 9.2) echoes established practice-led approaches to research such as arts education research involving found poetry (Prendergest et al. 2008), and more recent attempts to use investigative poetry to potentially capture some aspect of change in audience members following encounters with applied theatre (Prendergast 2020). Chance Encounters more specifically queers recent attempts to generate 'research found poetry' which involves using texts generated by participants as qualitative data from which the researcher then writes found poems to analyse and represent that data (Patrick 2016: 384). It does so, by positioning performers not as research participants as such but more as research poets. This positioning offers some of the creative authorship and ownership that Anna Robinson critiques as lacking in qualitative research which the academic researcher edits and adapts from the found poetry of participants (2022: 74). In this activity, unlike the participant-driven data of 'research found poetry', the data the performers use is based on the found text that they will be familiar with (i.e. the performance script) and text that they will likely have never seen previously (i.e. the child protection policy and the funding application from the project).

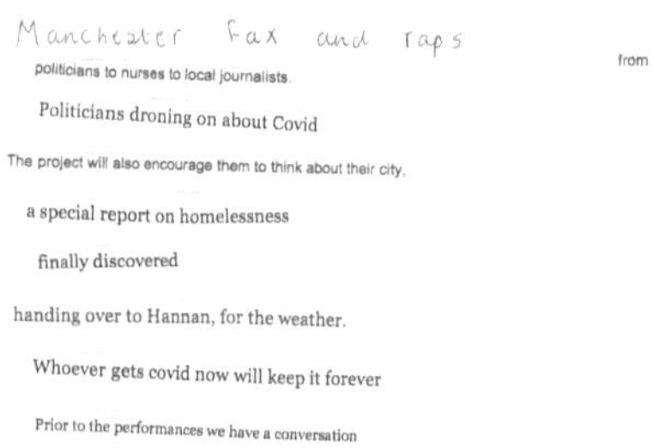
Manchester Fax and raps

from
politicians to nurses to local journalists.
Politicians droning on about Covid
The project will also encourage them to think about their city.
a special report on homelessness
finally discovered
handing over to Hannan, for the weather.
Whoever gets covid now will keep it forever
Prior to the performances we have a conversation

Figure 9.3 Poem entitled 'Manchester fax and raps' by Hareer.

After reading out her poem 'Manchester Fax and Raps' (see Fig. 9.3) Hareer reflects in a video entry: 'I think this poem is boring but it's very political and it has a lot of news'. Hareer's response was the only documented post-poem response. Do the found texts need to be decided by the children rather than the adult researcher in the future?

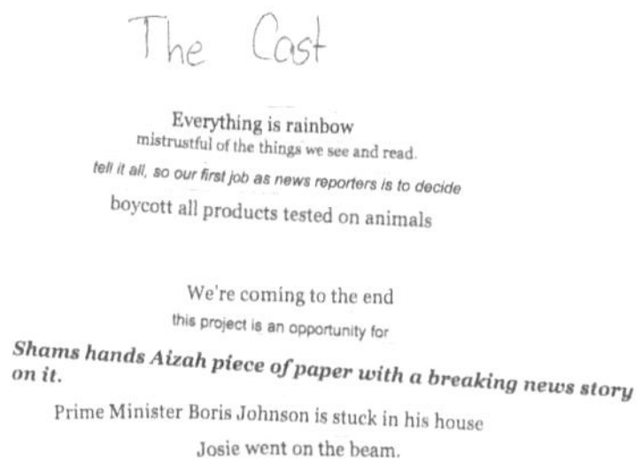
The Cast

Everything is rainbow
mistrustful of the things we see and read.
tell it all, so our first job as news reporters is to decide
boycott all products tested on animals

We're coming to the end
this project is an opportunity for
Shams hands Aizah piece of paper with a breaking news story on it.
Prime Minister Boris Johnson is stuck in his house
Josie went on the beam.

Figure 9.4 Poem entitled 'The Cast'. Anonymous.

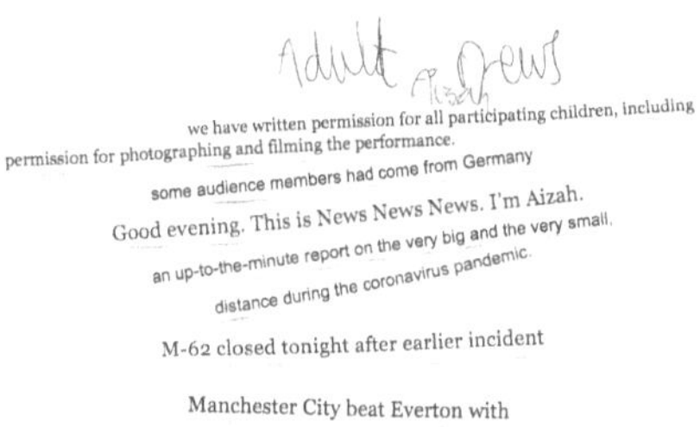
Adult news
Aizah

we have written permission for all participating children, including
permission for photographing and filming the performance.
some audience members had come from Germany
Good evening. This is News News News. I'm Aizah.
an up-to-the-minute report on the very big and the very small.
distance during the coronavirus pandemic.
M-62 closed tonight after earlier incident

Manchester City beat Everton with

Figure 9.5 Poem entitled 'Adult news' by Aizah.

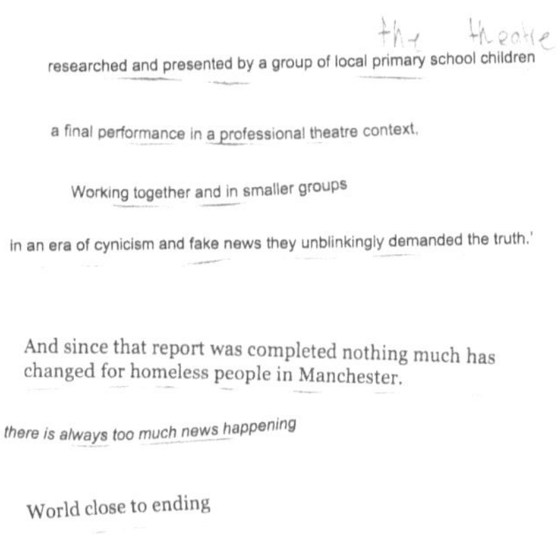
the theatre

researched and presented by a group of local primary school children

a final performance in a professional theatre context.

Working together and in smaller groups

in an era of cynicism and fake news they unblinkingly demanded the truth.'

And since that report was completed nothing much has changed for homeless people in Manchester.

. there is always too much news happening

World close to ending

Figure 9.6 Poem entitled 'the theatre'. Anonymous.

An interesting slippage begins to occur in the distinction between 'researcher-voiced' research poetry and 'participant-voiced' found poetry (Prendergast 2004: 74) because the performers are arguably both researchers and participants simultaneously. In this respect, the activity has some value within a post-performance research and archival process if analysed with further contextualisation to fully exploit the performers' shift between researcher and participant in the creation of archival poems (see Figs. 9.4, 9.5 and 9.6) and also to explore the potential of poetic representations to both document and investigate contemporary performance with people we call children.

Below I write three Haiku inspired by Richard Furman *et al.*'s use of poetry 'as data, as a means of data representation, and as a process of inquiry' in their study on adolescent identity (2007: 301).

The Cast declares end of days
Bookended by hope
From their rainbow perspective

Aizah begins backstage so
The rules are crystal
No, this is not children's news

The world is ending again
What good is Theatre
In the face of homelessness

I am left wondering whether these haiku foreground the performers' researcher-voice or my own.

Imaginative

Deleted Scenes

<Hareer presses record on the AV camera and walks over to the desk where Kairo sits. There is a replica of the red rotary dial phone and a laptop on the table. They look at the camera smiling>

Hareer: We wish that in *News News News* they had fake news

Kairo: Like, Boris Johnson coming back to parliament

Hareer: And also we don't want to hear about politics. We want to hear about things that we like. Real news are boring and we would like to see fake news

Kairo: Like 'new robots are coming to destroy the world!'

Hareer: Or fake news about a game

Kairo: Like new cheat codes

Hareer: We just don't want anything about politics or anything boring. We want fake news if you have to. That's the end.

The imaginative station is largely driven by research methods specific, but not exclusive, to performance studies. One of the activities, 'Replay', involves the children engaging in embodied practice and invites them to film and enact a scene from *News News News*, but change an element of it in any way the performers wish (i.e. script, characterisation, narrative, using direct address to step out of character etc.). 'Repeat' similarly involves the children physicalising a selected still image from the performance but introducing a new prop into their newly composed image, followed by verbal reflection. As such these activities align with embodied archival practice research methods within the fields of theatre and performance. All of these activities are concerned with locating the body and embodied experiences in research with children. The activities emerge in response to a key concern following the childhood studies' paradigm shift from thinking about children as biologically defined category towards children as social actors that are constructed, which 'leav(es) little room for the body/child as physical or corporeal entity' (James et al. 1998: 146).

The 'Deleted Scenes' activity is framed for the children as a 'deconstructionist' research activity that seeks out the missing, hidden, or forgotten and involves composing a short scene that they wish could have been in *News News News*.

<Anon picks up the red phone and speaks into it>

Anon: Oh, we've got some breaking news. Dwayne Johnson died because of ligma (laughs). Ligma is a disease. Ok, that's all for today, ba-bye.

I google 'ligma' and decide to anonymise the performer, should the content be considered challenging for readers who know them. A 'pop culture dictionary' entry via Dictionary.com reads: 'Ligma is a made-up disease and internet hoax claimed to have killed popular Fortnite video game streamer Ninja. When people not in on the joke ask "What is ligma?" pranksters reply with the crass pun "Ligma (lick my) balls" or other such slang term, like nuts.' I'm amused that the author draws on a gaming and largely young people's cultural reference which may not be immediately obvious to the adults who hear or read this scene. The author also allows an element of taboo, particularly within the school context, to be introduced to their 'deleted scene', which highlights the subversive potential of this embodied activity to draw attention to how the performers might develop the performance given the chance. The author is even enacting the 'fake news' Kairo and Hareer call for above, which is both fictional but may have some material impact (knowing cheat codes gives you an advantage as a gamer), which suggests some shared desire to explore 'fake news'.

Sensory

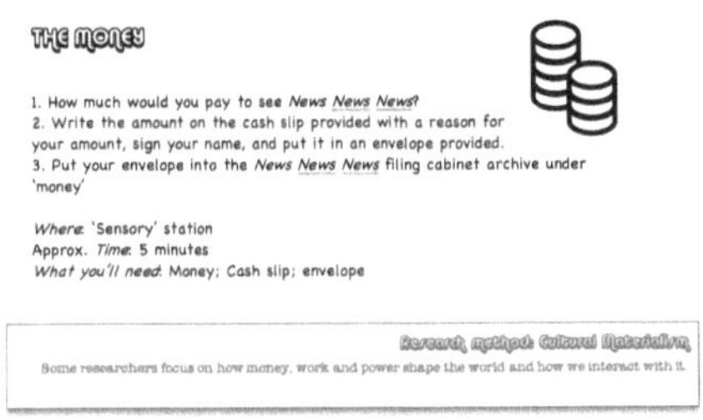

THE MONEY

1. How much would you pay to see *News News News*?
2. Write the amount on the cash slip provided with a reason for your amount, sign your name, and put it in an envelope provided.
3. Put your envelope into the *News News News* filing cabinet archive under 'money'

Where: 'Sensory' station
Approx. *Time*: 5 minutes
What you'll need: Money; Cash slip; envelope

Research method: Cultural Materialism
Some researchers focus on how money, work and power shape the world and how we interact with it.

Figure 9.7 'The Money' research activity card.

The sensory station seeks to capture the children's phenomenological experiences of participating in *News News News*, namely the olfactory, haptic, and taste sensations with which they associate the performance. The station included activities with scented items and different coloured textures for the children to choose from as a way of recording their experiences of both the creative process and the performance itself.

The activity 'The Money' (Fig. 9.7) uses play money to explore the potential financial value of *News News News* for the performers.

"£5 Comfortable seats are given to the audience. A great show from kids Very funny scenes. 3 ~~movies~~ films to watch" (Shams).

A diversity of rationales for the imagined cost of a ticket demonstrates the performers' complex relationships to the financial value of their performance and/or process.

"£8 Because it is really good and a long time to prepare and it's worth it" (Mariam)

Good Value For Money.

"£50 I think it's a reasonable price and it's very affordable" (Josie)

Remuneration for labour.

"£7.50 It is hard for children to learn a show in 1 week" (Aizahali)

Payment that takes into consideration equity.

"Free for kids. £4 for an adult' Kids should pay less because this is a show for kids" (anon)

Economic logic that considers who the work is for.

"£100 for being kind" (Hannan)

Is the performance kind? Are the performers kind? Or is this an appeal for the audience to be kind? I'm not sure.

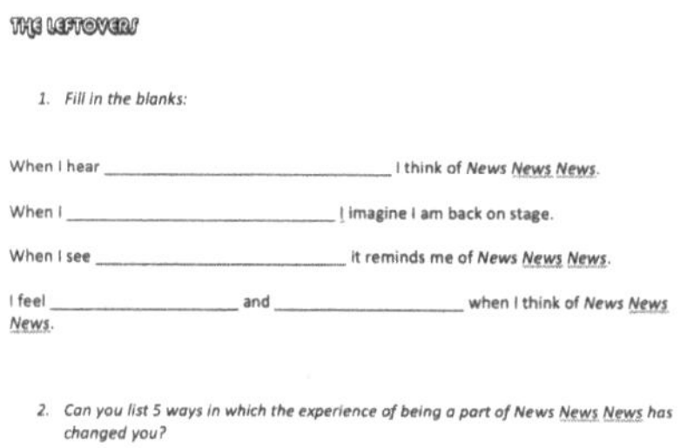
THE LEFTOVERS

1. *Fill in the blanks:*

When I hear ______________ I think of *News News News*.

When I ______________ I imagine I am back on stage.

When I see ______________ it reminds me of *News News News*.

I feel ______________ and ______________ when I think of *News News News*.

2. *Can you list 5 ways in which the experience of being a part of News News News has changed you?*

Figure 9.8 'The Leftovers' research activity card.

1 Happiness. Confidence. Bravery. Courage. Nostalgia. Maturity. Experience. Future. Gratitude. Inspiring.

The performers responses to The Leftovers (Fig. 9.8) are important and valuable experiences. We might ask to what extent are we hearing the 'consumer' voice (Bragg 2007) in these responses citing confidence and happiness etc. or what Arnot and Reay identify as the 'pedagogic' voice (2007), 'a voice that is literally schooled, that is, created by the experiences of being educated within particular kinds of pedagogic, curriculum, and assessment regimes' (Thomson 2001: 5)? The evaluative regimes common to consumer culture, which are also present within the education system, are as much a part of children's culture and it is not uncommon to hear the people we call children echoing stock answers, as anyone familiar with children being interviewed on mainstream TV will know. Do I need to re-frame the exercise to shift away from encouraging the consumer and pedagogic voice towards prompts that will generate unexpected, unanticipated responses?

2 'It changed my opinion on the news'
'Children news is better than adult news'

Does this response suggest a more politically-inflected voice identified by Hadfield and Haw (2001)? That is, what they refer to as the 'authoritative' voice, which claims to represent a group, as well as the 'critical' voice that is resistant to the status quo, seems to emerge in these responses. If the critical voice is one that 'put[s] into the public arena perspectives that are rarely, if ever, heard' then The Leftovers activity has the potential to identify where a performance process has changed a child's perspective on an area of life as significant as the news.

Visual

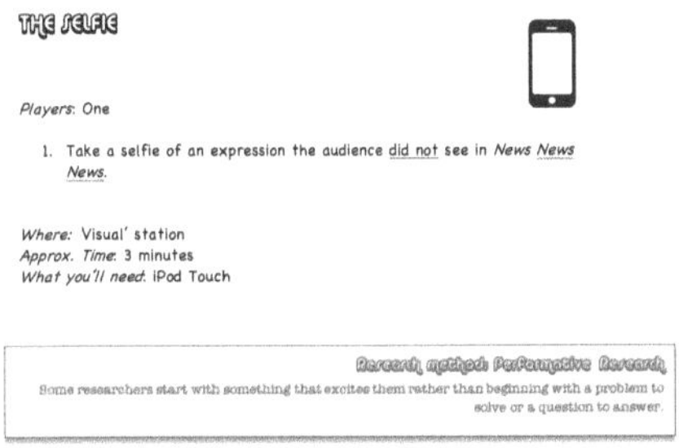

THE SELFIE

Players: One

1. Take a selfie of an expression the audience did not see in *News News News*.

Where: Visual' station
Approx. Time: 3 minutes
What you'll need: iPod Touch

Research method: Performative Research
Some researchers start with something that excites them rather than beginning with a problem to solve or a question to answer.

Figure 9.9 'The Selfie' research activity card.

The visual station includes prompts for the children to draw something that connects one or more aspects of their identity with the performance, to record in written text a moment they would choose to photograph from the process or the performance, and to write a letter to a future performer. Activities within this station are largely driven by research methods such as autoethnography, photo-elicitation, and performative writing. As with the other stations, the activities are largely self-directed to remove (at least some of) the adult-centric focus of established visual methods such as photo-interviewing (Collier and Collier 1986) and instead create the conditions for performers to exercise agency in making their own connections between self and performance.

Figure 9.10

Figure 9.11

Figure 9.12

A side-eye expression shot from below
A look of feigned surprise with a ghost of a smile
A smile
A creative use of props not included in the show
A playful use of landscape mode

It's difficult to know how to read these images (see Figs. 9.10, 9.11, 9.12, 9.13, 9.14). I deliberately don't build in any other invitation for the children to discursively frame their selfies into the research design as I am interested in what the images alone might suggest, but later I crave the performers' interpretative frameworks. While visual research methods with children and young people are not new, this selfie task is novel to the extent that it is queered by sitting between and outside of these established approaches to using visual methods as outlined by Pat Thomson (2008): adult researchers analysing images they themselves have captured of young people's activities; adults using existing images to elicit the perspectives of children; analysing found images by or of interest to young people; images made by adult researchers to capture research findings from young people. Rather than using a found image, these selfies are authored by the children in response to a shared experience. Although a smiling expression is consistent across most of the photos, it is the playful and diverse approach to the task that is noteworthy here (rather than taking the responses at face value and assuming that in response to the prompt there was an absence of playfulness or diversity in what the audience saw).

Figure 9.13

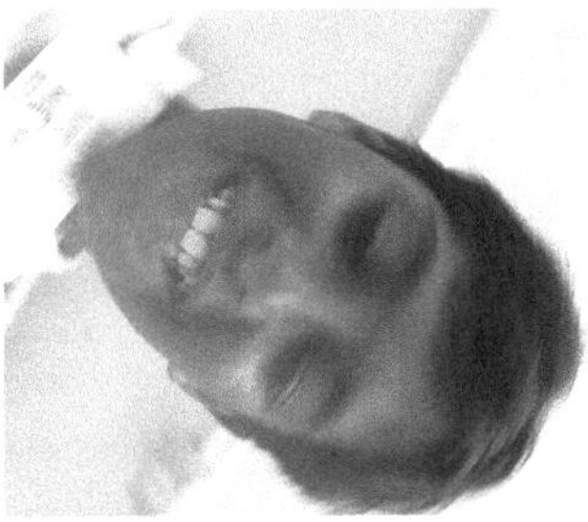

Figure 9.14

On reflection, this activity highlights the importance of further contextualisation from the performers themselves to clarify their decision-making in this activity and to capture something of the multi-layered, complexity of their creative approaches here. A more systematic approach to the elicitation aspect of photo-elicitation is needed as a means of 'mobilizing the agency' of performers who may be intersectionally marginalised by age, race, gender etc. This could, following Laura Azzarito, include 'lay[ing] out a visual infrastructure from which the voice of the subaltern can be amplified, legitimated, and expressed (Azzarito 2023: 42)', although Azzarito's focus is largely on non-Western participants within the context of social justice in education. Nevertheless, the opportunity for photo-elicitation to offer a 'different visuality' beyond a Western colonised frame (Spivak 2006) has potential if adult researchers recognise the various ways in which othering intersects with age to create marginalised positions and barriers to the performers 'being seen and represented on [their] own cultural terms' (Azzarito 2023: 51). The selfie is arguably a step towards meeting the performers 'on their own cultural terms', but whether it creates the 'third space' (Soja 1996) to generate an image that is consistent with how the performers want to be represented and/or identified remains to be seen.

A Children's Manifesto on Making Performance with Children

Ch-Adults Manifesto

As we begin the second day of the workshop, which, unlike the game, involves the more collaborative activity of generating a manifesto, it becomes immediately clear that the school environment is inadvertently in tension with my methodological commitment towards the kind of lateral contact that attends to 'the width of a person's experience or ideas, their motives or their motions' (Stockton 2009: 11). In their study on the importance of spatiality in child-centred research, Barker and Weller note that while schools are 'highly significant spaces and times in the geography of children's lives', schools are also 'spaces over which children have little or no control' (2003: 211). This is keenly felt when, in an attempt to support the completion of the manifesto, a well-meaning member of teaching support staff, who actively wants to help, frequently regulates the children's behaviour, trying to keep them on task by preventing play and making an appeal to the children to be serious. Despite creating a space where play, distraction, and loss of concentration are welcome, the hierarchy has been re-established, notwithstanding my attempts to undo the reinstatement of normative adult/child power relations. Later, I scold myself for not preparing the adults better prior to the workshop.

Ch-adults was coined by Daniel as a joke, and then the term was incorporated into the manifesto's title during its development. The adult researchers were asked to write it on a whiteboard where the final manifesto was composed. Perhaps the term un/intentionally captures the imbricatedness of adults in the manifesto, both in terms of marking the expected adult voice of the manifesto form more generally and/or highlighting the challenge of neutrality for the particular adults (the research assistant and I) supporting the manifesto's development towards something meaningful for the audiences it was destined for.

YES TO BEING PAID IN MONEY, SOMETIMES FAST FOOD OR SUSPICIOUSLY GOOD SOUP

NO TO INEQUALITY, **NO** TO RACISM, SEXISM, OR ANY OTHER ISM, AND **NO** TO BEING TREATED AS IF WE'RE ALL THE SAME

MAYBE TO BEING TRUTHFUL

YES TO BEING QUIRKY, SILLY AND SENSIBLE

NO TO TRYING TO TAKE OVER

MAYBE TO TAKING RISKS

YES TO BEING KIND

NO TO BEING ARROGANT

MAYBE TO BEING SELFLESS AND MAYBE TO IMPROV

YES TO BEING COMMITTED

NO TO WANTING IT ALL

MAYBE TO STEALING OR BORROWING

YES TO VALUING OUR OPINION

Aware of the tendency of adult researchers to 'be guilty of misunderstanding, misrepresenting and sometimes disregarding children's perspectives, particularly when these conflict with the researcher's own experiences, interests and interpretations' (Bucknall 2012: 5), the manifesto becomes a performative means for the performers to both document their experiences and to manifest a call to action on making performance with children with the structure and purpose a manifesto offers but on their own terms. After introducing the performers to some examples of adult-authored and adult/child collaborative art manifestos, Yvonne Rainer's 'No Manifesto' inspired the performers' creation of the 'yes, no, maybe' format, with the 'maybe' being intentionally added by the children to account for a diversity of opinion that was emerging within the group.

Sara Ahmed argues that 'a manifesto is required when a struggle is necessary to give expression to something' (2017: 252). In addition to the challenges that this child-authored manifesto gives expression to – lack of payment, inequality, favouritism, undervaluing children's opinions – I am reminded that, to echo Ahmed's words, a 'struggle is necessary' because:

- The voice of 'the manifesto' is often assumed to be adult, further legitimising the historic separation of children from the realm of Politics
- Artistic and political manifestos are still written about children, without children.
- The rise of the term 'youth activism' often excludes younger children and reifies the idea that children are neutral, apolitical, and not capable of instituting political or social change.

NO TO FAVOURITISM

'A manifesto not only causes a disturbance, it aims to cause this disturbance. To make something manifest can be enough to cause a disturbance' (Ahmed 2017: 252).

MAYBE TO COMMUNISM, WHICH MIGHT MEAN SHARING

YES TO FUN

The use of the manifesto as a research method is concerned not only with creating space for the people we call children's informed experiences of professional performance practice but also exploring the potential of the form to mobilise children's political action and institute change based on their unique knowledge and understanding of intergenerational collaboration. If, as Mary-Ann Caws suggests, '[a]t its peak of performance [the manifesto's] form creates its meaning' (2001: xx) then the very act of a manifesto produced by children for adults (and other children) potentially causes a disturbance. A change has already been instituted, especially as the idea of a child-authored manifesto has been taken up by Fundus Theatre in other contexts following the sharing of this research and dissemination of the Ch-Adults manifesto. It is the ability of the manifesto to cause a disturbance which leads me to turn to another manifesto in the next and final chapter, the Glitch Feminism manifesto by Legacy Russell (2020). It is the potential of the glitch as a performance strategy in dialogue the insights of a child-authored manifesto and the performance and research strategies identified throughout the book, which I want to argue offers an imaginable yet unknowable response to the questions I am left with below. Although driven by concerns about the potential reception of a manifesto (as a public declaration of aims, a call to action, an invitation to revolution etc.) that is written by the people we call children, the questions that remain have wider significance for thinking about future performance practice with young people, because they are symptomatic of relentless dominant perceptions about children and young people's status and capacity to participate in artistic and political life in any meaningful way:

How can the people we call children publicly declare their aims if adults only see children as not yet fully formed adults-in-the-making?

How can the people we call children call for action if adults see them as outside of the supposedly more 'grown up' arena of politics?

How can the people we call children make a declaration from a position of authority if they have very little power to begin with?

How can the people we call children invite 'revolution' if adults don't take them seriously?

How can the people we call children write a manifesto on behalf of themselves if adults always presuppose that behind such writing is an adult voice or adult ideas?

Note

1 The project was kindly supported by Equality Diversity and Inclusion funding at Leeds Beckett University, with research assistance from PhD researcher Sophie Dixon, and our hosts St Margaret's Church of England Primary School in Manchester. Ethics approval was granted by Leeds Beckett University's Research Ethics Committee. Child participants signed an assent form and parents/guardians and adult artists signed a consent form. Thank you to the cast of News News News, Andy Field, and Beckie Darlington for sharing their experiences and permitting the data to be published here.

References

Ahmed, Sara (2017) *Living A Feminist Life*, Durham: Duke University Press.

Alvarez, Natalie and Jenn Stephenson (2012) 'A Manifesto for Manifestos', *Canadian Theatre Review*, 150: 3–7.

Arendt, Hannah (1958) *The Human Condition*, Chicago: The University of Chicago Press.

Arendt, Hannah ([1961] 1993) 'The Crisis of Education' in *Between Past and Future: Eight Exercises in Political Thought*, New York: Viking Press.

Arnot, Madeleine and Reay, D. (2007) 'A Sociology of Pedagogic Voice: Power, Inequality and Pupil Consultation', *Discourse: Studies in the Cultural Politics of Education*, 28 (3): 311–315.

Ashby Simone, Hanna Julian, Matos Sonia, Callum Nash and Alexis Faria (2019) 'Fourth-Wave HCI Meets the 21st Century Manifesto' in *Proceedings of the Halfway to the Future Symposium*, Nottingham, UK, 19–20 November 2019. New York, NY: ACM Press, pp. 1–11.

Azzarito, Laura (2023) 'Photo-Elicitation to Amplify and Elevate the Voices of Research Participants' in Azzarito, Laura (ed.) *Visual Methods for Social Justice in Education*, Cham: Palgrave Macmillan.

Barker and Weller (2003) 'Never work with children?': The Geography of Methodological Issues in Research with Children', *Qualitative Research*, 3 (2): 207–227.

Bragg, Sara (2007) '*Consulting Young People: A Review of the Literature*', London: Arts Council England.

Bucknall, Sue (2012) *Children as Researchers in Primary Schools: Choice, Voice, and Participation*, Oxon: Routledge.
Caws, Mary-Ann (2001) 'The Poetics of the Manifesto: Nowness and Newness', *Manifesto: A Century of Isms*, Lincoln and London: University of Nebraska pp. xix–xxxi.
Collier, J., & Collier, M. (1986) *Visual Anthropology: Photography as a Research Method*. Albuquerque: University of New Mexico Press.
Field, Andy and Beckie Darlington (n.d.) News News News, https://www.andyandbeckie.com/work/newsnewsnews (accessed 23 May 2024)
Furman, Rich, Carol L. Langer, Christine S. Davis, Heather P. Gallrado and Shanti Kulkarni (2007) 'Expressive, Research and Reflective Poetry as Qualitative Inquiry: A study of Adolescent Identity', *Qualitative Research*, 7 (3): 301–315.
Hadfield, Mark and Haw, Kaye (2001) '"Voice", Young People and Action Research: Hearing, Listening, Responding', *Educational Action Research*, 9 (3), 485–499.
Jackson, Alecia Y and Lisa A Mazzei (2009) *Voice in Qualitative Inquiry*, London: Routledge.
James, Allison and Alan Prout (1997) *Constructing and Reconstructing Childhood: Contemporary Issues in the Sociological Study of Childhood*, London and New York: RoutledgeFalmer.
James Allison, Jenks Chris, Prout Alan (1998) *Theorizing childhood*, Oxford, England: Polity Press.
Kellett, Mary (2005) Children As Active Researchers: A New Research Paradigm for the 21st Century? ESRC, UK. https://oro.open.ac.uk/7539/1/MethodsReviewPaperNCRM-003.pdf
Kwakye, Chelsea and Ore Ogunbiyi (2019) *Taking Up Space: The Black Girl's Manifesto for Change*, Penguin Random House.
Mandell N (1988) 'The Least-Adult Role in Studying Children', *Journal of Contemporary Ethnography*, 16 (4): 433–468.
Mitra, Royona (2019) 'Making Space in Dance Theatre and Performance Studies: An Act of Decoloniality', *Decolonizing Theatre, Dance and Performance Studies panel*, Theatre and Performance Research Association, University of Exeter, 5 September 2019.
Patrick, Lisa D (2016) 'Found Poetry: Creating Space for Imaginative Arts Based Literacy Research Writing', *Literacy Research: Theory, Method and Practice*, 65 (1): 384–403.
Prendergast, Monica (2004) '"Shaped Like a Question Mark": Found Poetry From Herbert Blau's The Audience', *Research in Drama Education*, 9: 73–92.
Prendergast, Monica (2020) 'Anecdotal', *Qualitative Inquiry*, 26 (6): 674 –676.
Prendergast, Monica, Lymburner, Julie, Grauer, Kit, Leggo, Carl and Gouzouasis, Peter (2008) 'Pedagogy of Trace: Poetic Representations of Teacher Resilience/Resistance in Arts Education', *Vita Scholasticae: The Journal of Educational Biography*, 25: 58–76.
Qvortrup, Jens, Marjatta Bardy, Giovanni Sgritta, Helmut Wintersberger (1994) *Childhood Matters: Social Theory, Practice and Politics v.14*, Aldershot: Avebury.
Robinson, Anna (2022) 'Found Poems and Creative Editing', *Textual Cultures*, *15* (1): 71–78.
Russell, Legacy (2020) *Glitch Feminism: A Manifesto*, London and Brooklyn, New York: Verso.
Senior, Adele (2016) 'Beginners On Stage: Arendt, Natality and the Appearance of Children in Contemporary Performance', *Theatre Research International*, 41 (1): 70–84.
Soja, Edward (1996) *Thirdspace: Journeys to Los Angeles and Other Real-And-Imagined Places*, Blackwell Publishing.
Spivak, Gayatri Chakravorty (2006) *Conversations with Gayatri Chakravorty Spivak*, Stockton: Seagull Books.
Stockton, Kathryn Bond (2009) *The Queer Child or Growing Sideways in the Twentieth Century, Durham and London*: Duke University Press.
Thomson, Pat (2008) *Doing Visual Research with Children and Young People*, London: Taylor and Francis Group.
Weeks, Kathi (2013) 'The Critical Manifesto: Marx and Engels, Haraway, and Utopian Politics', *Utopian Studies*, 24 (2): 216–231.

Conclusion

The Glitch: Child Activism in Performance

Me (40 years old): *What's a glitch Arthur?*
Arthur (10 years old): *It's a system overload that can cause an error so the game crashes*
Sam (5 years old): *<interrupts>it's like in Go Jetters. So so where Grand Master Glitch [pause] he just he makes, he makes, he makes a jelly machine and it's out of control so it makes jelly all around, somewhere. That is a glitch.*
Me: *Why is that a glitch?*
Sam: *It's because, it's because he has not made things right. So, so what I'm saying is erm a glitch is something that that that makes something not where it should be.*

Children glitch. Many children know how it feels to glitch. Many children know what it means to glitch. Glitching is present in both their gaming language and their lived experiences, as Arthur and Sam – the people who I birthed – attest above. In a moment where form happily meets content, the glitch even ghosts the way in which Sam repeats, interrupts, and brings into being a shared understanding of the glitch through language. Arthur goes on to explain that in one of his favourite games, *The Legend of Zelda: Breath of the Wild,* glitches help him to creatively deviate from limits set by the game designers. When he inhabits the role of the main character Link, for example, Arthur has found a glitch which allows Link to roam outside of the boundaries of the game, exploring his own diversions and curiosities. In addition to the technical glitches in *Zelda*, the character Link offers their own glitch to the gender binary with their gender non-conforming appearance. Link might serve as an important glitch in a context where the people we call children are assigned a binarised gender at birth and handed a script to follow, or else face the sometimes-harmful and even violent consequences of not conforming to normative gender expectations. Namely, Link represents in-between, non-binary, neither female nor male, or both female and male experiences simultaneously and yet, something more expansive. In Arthur's wider gameplay, he has even sought out information from other gamers known as 'glitch-hunters' who help to disseminate glitches so that players can gain an advantage, offer a character a new world to explore, or simply just glitch for fun. As I draw this book to a close, I wonder what potential this

DOI: 10.4324/9781003043072-13

idea of the glitch might hold for performance makers and scholars working with the people we call children as we navigate their worlds and cultures.[1]

In the opening to her book *Glitch Feminism: A Manifesto*, Legacy Russell locates the power of the glitch in her early encounters with the digital realm as a 12 years old Black, femme, female-identifying queer, searching 'for those sites of experimentation where I could explore my true self' (2020: 12). She notes that these were sites that her 'Away From Keyboard' or AFK world did not permit:

> My prepubescent body was exhausted by social mores, tired of being told to take up less space, being seen and not heard, systematically erased, edited out, ignored. All I wanted to do was move. But in the light of daytime, I felt trapped, always shifting uneasily under the weight of incessant white heteronormative observation.
>
> (ibid.)

It is within this digital context that Russell identifies the glitch as a form of disruption and refusal against the restrictions to physical movement that are faced by many female-identifying, queer, and Black people. Whilst Russell does not focus on children in her study, it is notable that the glitch is nonetheless situated in her early play as a child and a teenager online:

> I found new landscapes through being borne and carried online, those early days where I flexed as a digital Orlando, shapeshifting, time-traveling, genderfucking as I saw fit. I became myself, I found my body, through becoming, embodying, a glitch.
>
> (2020: 151)

By bringing a conversation with Arthur and Sam into dialogue with Russell's reflections, I want to highlight that the people we call children and their bodies are already glitching and that the glitch is fundamentally a part of many children's cultures, especially their online worlds. Having identified some strategies for dismantling normative conceptualisations of the child within contemporary performance in this book, I am left wondering about the future of professional performance practice with children in a wider context where children's 'glitches' are often policed, denied, ignored, or actively hidden. How might performance nourish children's existing glitches or spawn new ones to create 'a fissure within which new possibilities of being and becoming are manifest' (Russell 2020: 11)? This question is driven by the recognition that how we conceptualise the child as a discursive figure, has material consequences for actual children: that is, as a homogenised category, children are still assumed to be in a state of becoming and yet as bodies they are simultaneously subject to the same gendered, sexist, classist, ableist, racist cultural scripts as 'adult' bodies in a world that attempts to fix their fluidity. Dominant narratives of children, for example, deny them sexuality and yet simultaneously fix them as heterosexual, otherwise, why would the gay child need to 'come out' (Stockton 2009: 158)? Furthermore, the people we call children, like adults, are encouraged to be legible and readable, and yet their material presence – including the bodies of children that adhere to white, cisgender norms – are often considered 'disruptive'. This tension between the legibility and illegibility of the bodies of those we call children is both a strength and a problem for performance as a place where bodies can be reimagined and re-categorised, but where, historically, the framing and reception of such bodies have also been shaped by hegemonic perceptions of the child.

In this final section, then, I want to end by proposing that we can employ glitch feminism as a critical lens and practice for thinking through not only possible futures of contemporary performance with children but for imagining the potential for *activist* performance futures with the people we call children within this context. Whilst Legacy Russell's study focuses on the work of adult artists, glitch feminism offers a language, both to describe how children's bodies in performance have withstood 'flattened readings' as 'historically othered bodies' like the adult bodies Russell references and to look forward to a future performance landscape where bodies of the people we call children are instead acknowledged as 'intersectional bodies who have travelled restlessly, gloriously through narrow spaces' (2020: 18). In her book, Russell is predominantly, although not exclusively, attending to the bodies of Black and global majority heritage and queer-identifying people in the context of work by Black, queer, trans, and non-binary adult artists. Her development of glitch feminism, however, is useful at this particular moment where activism by children is becoming more visible and yet simultaneously children are being weaponised by far-right ideologies and used as bait in the so-called 'culture wars'. In addition to highlighting the glitchiness of (1) the strategies of age play already identified; (2) audience-based encounters with performers we call children; and (3) the practice of doing research with children documented in this book, we can also turn to glitch feminism to consider future performance and research strategies with young people. I want to suggest it is through the glitch that the people we call children emerge in performance as intersectional and multiple selves, who have the potential to practise political agency.

The Child as Empty Signifier

As we have seen, children's bodies are historically othered both on and off stage. However, I want to nuance this observation through the lens of glitch feminism by proposing that the bodies of the people we call children glitch and their glitching bodies are often treated like 'empty signifiers' (Russell 2020: 147), yet they are simultaneously layered with heteronormative imagery and policed by majority culture's expectations. We know from Lee Edelman (2004), that children are used as symbols for a future that is heteronormative. One of the most recent examples of this symbolism being put into practice is that children's 'innocence' and 'vulnerability', particularly in the US and the UK, has been appropriated by Conservative Christian, far-right and anti-LGBTQA+ groups to politicise Drag Queen Storytime events. Claiming to want to 'protect' children, such groups pit children against a discourse that ideologically frames 'nonconforming gender identities as "deceptive"' (Ellis 2022: 94). Yet materially children also have bodies that glitch, that is, bodies that are, as Russell would say with regard to adults, 'fluid, insistent… refuse to stand still: [they] slip, [they] slide' (2020: 145).

Whilst some performance and live artworks such as *The Hamilton Complex* and Fundus Theatre's *Playing Up Gender* (2021) offer space for children to play with gender – and as we have seen in the case of the former to challenge intersecting gender and age stereotypes – we are yet to imagine a more diverse performance landscape in which the people we call children are able to safely explore and inhabit, without consequence, their multiple selves beyond the patriarchal adult gaze that would seek to police this play in the name of 'protecting' children. The absence of professional performance practice with and about the people we call children who are also trans, for example, is evidence of the lack of recognition of children as human beings, with perceptions, opinions, and experiences of their own bodies beyond or in a different relationship to gender than the binarised one assigned at birth. The recent cancellation of Lies Pauwel's show with trans teenagers (Trueman 2018) signals that in the UK, in particular, there is a lack of material support for creating space for underrepresented and marginalised individuals and groups of young people. This lack of support implies that 'protection' is largely reserved for gender-conforming children, which creates problems for 'trans-inclusive and trans-affirmative voices struggling to find a way to protect trans children that does not imagine them as deserving of protection because they are, finally, the property of adults[…]' (Gill-Peterson 2018: vii–viii). This colonising type of protection – which I have discussed in terms of patriarchal protectionism operates to regulate certain bodies and experiences to maintain the status quo in line with cisgenderism as a 'cultural and systematic ideology that denies, denigrates and pathologizes self-identified gender identities that do not align with assigned gender at birth' (Lennon and Mistler 2014: 63).

The language of protection also appears in Russell's frustration that 'gender circumscribes the body, "protects" it from becoming limitless, from claiming the infinite vast, from realizing its true potential' (2020: 12). There is no question that children, like all people, need to be safe from violence, harm, and abuse, but the 'protection' on offer for many children, which undoubtedly shapes the contemporary performance landscape too despite small pockets of resistance, follows a patriarchal lineage. This lineage is concerned with protecting the world from children and children from the world, as Hannah Arendt (1958, 1961) would have it, in a way that mobilises protection as a means of control and social discipline in favour of hegemony. Such patriarchal protectionism takes different forms depending on the context and to further problematise the issue 'protection' is afforded to some people we call children more than other people we call children. For example, innocence is a category often denied to children of colour with research showing that 'Black children may be viewed as adults as soon as 13, with average age overestimations of Black children exceeding four and a half years in some cases' (Goff *et al.* 2014: 541). Within contemporary performance contexts, patriarchal protectionism arguably plays a part in framing and dictating children's access to and/or participation (or lack thereof) in professional performance for a number of reasons. For example, venues might not programme work with young people that does not adhere to hegemonic representations of children for fear of risking their funding streams or receiving negative publicity; parents, families, authorities, and other stakeholders might anticipate concerns around safeguarding or the appropriateness of 'adult' content; and assumptions driven by a childhood developmentalist perspective, which call into question children's ability to comprehend certain themes and to exercise agency, can work to maintain a protectionist perspective.

Whilst these concerns are valid, they often close down rather than open up opportunities for children and other young people when approached from this limited patriarchal protectionist perspective. The performance landscape this perspective motivates is, therefore, one in which the people we call children are sometimes given tokenistic, non-performative permission to exercise 'agency' but in very limited terms. In such contexts, they can be addressed as activists as long as it is 'safe' activism, because when the people we call children actually mobilise, they become a problem for patriarchal interests. If agency is something one does rather than something one has, then glitch feminism helps us to recognise the space adults can give up for children to glitch and to become glitch. This giving up space is not about 'including' children on the basis of the narrow terms of an 'inclusion' which risks re-centring already powerful adult voices. Instead, it is about creating space for children to collectively and anonymously (should they wish or need to) refuse the cultural scripts that structure the ways in which their bodies are (mis)read, made visible, invisible, or hypervisible both in performance and beyond. Creating such a space is not an easy task as all the barriers cited above suggest, but it can be particularly difficult for an embodied practice like performance where hierarchies of children's visibility are always already being negotiated both on and off stage by an historically entrenched patriarchal protectionist gaze. So how can we create space for children to author their own hyper/in/visibility within professional performance, against the backdrop of assumptions that they lack the 'ability' to self-identify, self-represent, and make legible or refuse legibility of their own bodies without false claims of hidden adult ventriloquism?

I would argue that glitch feminism offers at least two useful invitations to support the creation of this kind of space for children's future participation in contemporary performance. First, embracing glitch feminism offers the performance community an important opportunity to recognise online worlds and their interaction with the AFK world as potential safe spaces of possibility for the people we call children to embody glitch (if they wish to) and to glitch anonymously and, importantly, without consequence. For many children, from primary school through to high school, their subjectivities are already entangled with the technological selves that shape and are shaped by their own embodied knowledges. So, I would argue that approaching participation with the people we call children as *subjects who are Away from Keyboard* has the potential to foster a safe space that works with their existing 'knowledges' of glitching. By safe space, here, I mean one that is not dominated and dictated by patriarchal protectionism. Secondly, we can take away from Russell's manifesto its call to action and learn from its artistic examples of glitch feminism in practice, where activism meets performance. From Russell's examples and her conceptualisation of glitch feminism as a series of performative strategies, we can begin to imagine what an activist performance practice with children might look, sound and feel like: namely, a space for ghosting, refusal, error, remixing, encryption, and throwing shade. Before we imagine this space, let us briefly summarise where glitch has already shown up in the AFK world within the performance examples and performance research discussed so far.

Glitching Age

This book has identified some AFK examples of strategies that contribute to a glitchy future performance practice with children. These include what I am calling trans*-age practices that reveal age-based norms as socially constructed, show children's bodies to be culturally mapped, raced, and gendered and subject to change, and work to dismantle an adult patriarchal protectionist gaze. Whilst age-crossing that works with metatheatricality, defamiliarisation, and the interplay between the live and the virtual has some political potential in generating a glitch between the anatomical age of the performer and the presumed age of the character or persona they play, we have seen how age-crossing sometimes reinforces normative age representation and reaffirms age-based norms that are constructed around assumed differences between 'adult' and 'child'. I have suggested that age transvestism, as it is often described in theatre history, is not inherently politically subversive and is not always operating to denaturalise age signs. This limitation of age transvestism, or age-crossing as I prefer to call it in order to distinguish it from other possible strategies of age play, is a reminder that there must be space within a performative environment for the performers we call children to have the capacity to meaningfully comment on and/or work against normative expectations of their age that are destructive. We might call this: the capacity to glitch. In other words, there needs to be the possibility for glitching in both performance and research with the people we call children.

Other AFK trans*-age strategies that use glitch include gender-specific age play that performs heteronormative patriarchal femininity to excess. We have seen that gender-specific age play has the capacity to demonstrate that the same gazes and material conditions that sexualise work that demands emotional labour in the form of compulsory heteronormative femininity, are intimately imbricated with those that objectify, eroticise, and romanticise the people we call children and specifically girls, even in the name of innocence and protection. The kind of gender-specific age play we witnessed in *The Hamilton Complex* is particularly useful in its capacity to glitch the scopophilia and/or ocular-centrism of theatrical performance and other art practices that demand emotional labour within the wider consumption economy. Through glitching normative practices of visibility, gender-specific age play puts into practice what Claudia Castañeda, following Gayatri Spivak (1990), calls for in relation to theories of the subject. That is, a practice that 'accounts for alterity, for the heterogeneity of situated processes at work in the realization of differentiated bodies' (Castañeda 2002: 169).

The female-girl-child-teenager identified in *The Hamilton Complex* temporarily affirms a position of alterity, always in tension with and drawing attention to the close relationship between gender-conformity and expectations, perceptions, and stereotypes of age. The glitchiness of this diverse subject position, and its refusal to be fixed or made fully legible within the context of expected gender and age norms, signals the political potential of intersectional trans*-age play within contemporary performance of the future. In particular, by performing innocence, and marking it as performance through the glitched figure of the female-girl-child-teenager as a more nuanced identification than that of simply 'children', the performers show innocence to be gendered and (albeit to a lesser extent) raced white. Glitch therefore becomes a way of drawing attention to and disrupting how age ordinarily intersects with race, gender, sexuality, and ability, allowing for more of the 'material specificity' Jo-Ann Wallace (1995) argued is missing from theoretical conceptualisations of the child by drawing focus towards the materiality of the bodies onstage.

This materiality was also felt as a disorienting embodied experience in *Blind Cinema,* in a way that glitched what, drawing on Sarah Ahmed's queer phenomenology (2006), I identified as a heternormatively-oriented audience encounter with children in performance. In particular, the anonymity afforded by the audience's blindfolds, the performers' whispering, and the funnel through which the performers' communicated, extended the bodies of the people we call children in a public space where their bodies are ordinarily policed. Experiencing this performance, instead, offered a live, physical example of glitching as refusal, with the anonymity of the whispering echoing the online, digital version of refusal that Russell identified in her gameplaying youth. Glitching in *Blind Cinema* is the unapologetic facilitation of a disorienting embodied, affective encounter with performers called children and, as such, it elicits recognition of them as embodied subjects in a way that refuses the colonising, consuming adult gaze of the visual economy through which we often encounter them in performance more generally.

The glitch also lives in the metaphor of the teen, as explored with Zina and Sorrel, and in my approach to queering established methods of research on/with/by children alongside the cast of *News News News*. Indeed, Russell makes clear that '[t]he glitch is for those selves joyfully immersed in the in-between' (2020: 11), and it was in growing sideways (Stockton 2009) together through the lateral contact of our dialogue and a research-led game respectively, that our shared in-between selves could find a mutual expression. There is scope to glitch further by remixing the 'adult' genre of the manifesto and exploring how the game's activities like 'The Selfie' could build on performance scholar Claire Hampton's claim that selfies have potential as 'a practice through which hegemonic norms and subordinating ideologies can be resisted and subverted' (2021). Through these intentional and accidental glitches, the book has echoed the roots of glitch feminism as a feminist practice which 'dissents, pushes back against capitalism' and 'inject[s] our positive irregularities into these systems as errata' (Russell 2020: 11, 13). Indeed, the book's offer of a new way of reading age is the result of the ghostly glitching of age onto Judith Butler's well-known theorisation on gender (1990), which irreverently inserts the term age where gender has always resided, thus drawing attention to how age arguably always ghosts gender.

Whilst the glitchiness of the approaches taken in this book do not facilitate Russell's call for 'an occupation of the digital as a means of world-building' (2020: 12), they nevertheless reveal something of the AFK world of live performance and its capacity to glitch in the form of trans*-age play that is fluid, crosses, bends, reverses, disguises, intersects, queers and refuses to conform. So, whilst turning to the digital is an important component of glitch feminism and hopefully will grow through future performance practice with young people, this book attempts to capture how contemporary performance and performance research already have the potential to create 'a fissure within which new possibilities of being and becoming manifest' for *both* the people we call children *and* the people we call adults.

Throwing Shade

I want to propose that the futures of contemporary performance that offer hope for a meaningful artistic-activist practice with the people we call children, will make space for more opportunities to glitch, where glitch embraces its etymological origin from the Yiddish '*gletshn*' meaning to slide, glide or slip 'between new conceptions of bodies and selves' (Russell 2020: 28, 30). One example of glitching as a form of activism is ghosting the binary body (ibid.: 63), where ghosting is used in a colloquial sense to refer to the act of cutting off contact with someone. Ghosting them. Glitching raises a number of productive questions for considering an as yet unknowable future of performance-making with children. How can we create performance environments where children can ghost not only the binary body that they, like adults, are expected to assimilate to, but also where they can ghost related hegemonic representations of the child that are harmful and limiting? What online, AFK, or online-AFK looped worlds can performance generate for children to refuse to perform within hegemonic structures and systems that only address them through narrow figurations of the child that are reductive and disempowering? How can performance create the conditions for the people we call children to celebrate failures and errors within systems that celebrate the avoidance of failure and fail to recognise them in all their complexity as humans? What might encryption and remix look, sound, or feel like in collaborative processes with children that actively embrace glitch?

Let us consider a specific strategy for glitching to anticipate its potential in promoting activist practice: throwing shade. What would it mean for 'throwing shade' to become part of a performance practice with children, specifically the meaning of the term as *publicly* criticising someone or something, as it emerges from Black and Latinx working-class New York ball culture in the 1980s (*Paris Is Burning*, 1990) and as defined by Black transwomen (Davis 2019: 58).[2] In the AFK world, child-activist Greta Thunberg already throws shade in speeches where she turns the narrative of maturity back onto the adults she addresses: 'You are not mature enough to tell it like it is. Even that burden you leave to your children' (2019a: 15).

She throws further shade by drawing attention to adult virtue signalling and non-performative statements that are wrapped up in the idea of adult responsibility for children's well-being:

> Adults keep saying: 'We owe it to the young people to give them hope.'
> But I don't want your hope.
> I don't want you to be hopeful.
> I want you to panic.
> I want you to feel the fear I feel every day.
> And then I want you to act.
>
> (Thunberg 2019b: 24)

We also see examples of children throwing shade, again verbally, at adults in contemporary performance contexts. In *That Night Follows Day* by Tim Etchells and Belgium-based arts organisation Victoria (now known as CAMPO), performers between the ages of 8–14 begin by chanting in unison basic activities that adults do for them 'You feed us. You dress us. You choose clothes for us' before then moving on to shout adults' words back at them: 'You tell us to shut up … You tell us to shut our big fucking mouths'. This script was created through a collaborative process with children that began with a draft text written by Etchells to which 'new material was added, developed, structured and refined in a workshop process with the 16 young people who perform the piece' (Etchells 2008). However, the extent to which these examples of 'throwing shade' allow for glitchy slippages between new notions of bodies and subjectivities is up for debate. It is worth noting, of course, that neither Thunberg nor *That Night Follows Day* intend to 'throw shade' in alignment with glitch feminism but as an audience member for *That Night Follows Day* it is jarring to hear these words being spoken by a group of children, even glitchy, in that children's voices remix 'adult words' in a public forum to a largely adult audience. However, even though we can learn much about the potential of children's political appearance in the public space in which the performance takes place (see Senior 2016), there are no explicitly new subjectivities or bodies on offer for the audience to perceive or the performers themselves to slip and slide between.

Differently, Thunberg's glitching does offer a new kind of in-between subjectivity as child-teenager-activist-female-autistic, as we have never witnessed before with her action, which specifically depends on the looping of both AFK and social media-based action. Her AFK and online action is still met with adult attempts to undermine the threat of the in-betweenness she occupies in the form of accusations that she 'sound[s] and write[s] like an adult' to which she shadily responds 'Don't you think that a sixteen-year-old can speak for herself?' (Thunberg 2019c: 31). Perhaps activism by the people we call children will always be met with claims that there is a hidden adult puppeteer behind the scenes. If we suspect that glitch has activist potential though, it is worth exploring existing examples of 'throwing shade' in performance practice alongside the knowledges that children themselves bring to the collaboration as AFK authors and experts of the content and form of their own shade.

The work of Sin Wai Kin (formerly Victoria Sin), a non-binary and queer drag artist who Russell identifies as glitching by means of throwing shade, can offer some nuance here. Sin, who was assigned female at birth, develops a highly-stylised drag persona based on exaggerated femininity via both Instagram and in AFK settings where they use gender as a prosthesis. The constructedness of Sin's persona is achieved via prosthetics such as breast and buttock inserts that are visually available to be seen *as* prostheses. Sin's prosthetic reveals reinforce gender as an 'assemblage', especially when read alongside their exposition of the usually hidden, backstage labour of gender being fabricated and constructed in the form of makeup tutorials, etc. (Russell 2020: 56–60). The shade of Sin's act, for Russell, is that 'their body shatters the shallow illusion of any harmony or balance that might be offered up within the suggestive binary of male/female' (ibid.: 59). What if performance could work with online-AFK worlds to give space for children to explore throwing shade as Sin does, by finding freedom in errors beyond (but not excluding) gender that are both accidental and intended? A performance practice that would invite the people we call children to create assemblages of 'the child' and 'the adult' could deconstruct the apparent simplicity and normativity of the adult/child binary within majority culture and open up the possibility to reconstruct, slip, and slide between identities that are meaningful to them.

With careful framing and appropriate safeguarding, the use of online, digital, and virtual spaces could (paradoxically, from a patriarchal protectionist perspective) provide a 'safe' space for children to anonymously explore the activist, shady possibilities of assemblage. I am referring to the use of the term safe space as it is employed by Fereshteh Nouraie-Simone (2005) whose study is focused on the web as a liberating territory for young Iranian women, namely as 'a place to resist a traditionally imposed subordinate identity' (Nouraie-Simone cited in Daniels 2009: 108). What if Nouraie-Simone's observations informed the evolution of a performance environment for children that allowed for 'the textual process of self-expression without the prohibition or limitation of physical space' (ibid.: 108–9)? Futures of performance practice that embrace glitch, for example, would allow for children to re-perform and reimagine age-related and intersecting identities. Such an endeavour feels urgent at a time when proposed legislation in the United States, for example, is limiting children's physical access to the potentially glitch-generating art form of drag. As of July 2023, 'at least twenty states have introduced bills aimed at limiting, eliminating, or otherwise suppressing drag performances' (Satta 2023).

Offering the people we call children opportunities for assemblage through which they can explore their multiplicities in performance is also becoming more urgent in the UK context within which the performances I focused on throughout this book were shown. This is not just about creating space for multiplicities that challenge the 'deficit conception' of childhood (Matthews 2008) that has been perpetuated by theories that emphasise children's perceived lack, depending on their stage of development (Piaget 1971). It is also about the current political context, where recent draft guidance to schools issued by the conservative party's education secretary and equalities minister advise that teachers have no 'general duty' to recognise young people's 'social transitioning', that is, requests to change their name, preferred pronouns or change uniforms. The guidance also 'stresses that parents should be involved in any decisions except where it would endanger the child' (Adams and Adu 2023). Teachers are advised to apply 'watchful waiting', a term which is used in the medical community to describe an approach to waiting to see how an illness develops, and to 'ensure [social transitioning] is a sustained and properly thought through decision' (cited in Adams and Adu 2023). Such guidance pathologises trans children's identities and experiences, following a legacy of pathologisation of trans children and their families in the UK (Horton 2022), regardless of the World Health Organization's recent removal of transgender identities as a mental health disorder (WHO 2021). The guidance also fosters a culture of surveillance over the bodies of the people we call children, which is contradictory to the protections for 'gender reassignment' under the Equality Act (2010), and has the potential to contribute to growing global evidence of trans children experiencing bullying, harassment, discrimination, and prejudice (Bower-Brown *et al.* 2023, Horton 2020, McBride 2020). Within this wider context of transphobia, glitching becomes an important strategy of resistance for the people we call children whose bodies are the site of adult surveillance and pathologising at the expense of the rights and protections afforded to them by the Equality Act.

Who can Glitch?

Russell's claim that 'one is not born, but rather becomes, a glitch' (2020: 145) is a reminder that to suggest there is a specific age when one begins to glitch – or to propose that a certain level of 'maturity' or 'ability' needs to be reached in order to experience, embody or otherwise perform glitch – is both reductive and ableist. Indeed, what it means to 'become glitch' may have already happened for the 5-year-old (Sam), may just be starting to occur for the 10-year-old (Arthur), and is only in the process of being named for the very first time for the 40-year-old (Mum) whose dialogue opened this chapter. What is interesting for the future of performance practice with children, beyond the narrow perspective that glitch might only be reserved for adults, is the question of how the performance landscape can create the conditions for glitching to occur, freely and consensually, at any age. Working in school settings, for example, may facilitate but can also limit the creation of such conditions, as an earlier chapter demonstrated when the regulation of bodies and minds to stay productive was reiterated by a member of staff during a primary school workshop. If glitch is concerned with 'celebrat[ing] failure as a generative force' (Russell 2020: 30) then the neoliberal context of education in the UK is undoubtedly in tension with this modality of the glitch.

Since adults are often the people who have the power, privilege, and resources to create the conditions for glitching to occur, adults must start from a position that glitching is a possibility for everyone, beyond the exclusionary rhetoric of maturity that is shored up by the well-established perspective of developmentalism as well as other dominant narratives of the child that are founded on normative ideas of ability and linear progress. Adults who research and/or make performance might instead create the conditions for glitching to occur by adopting a neuroqueer orientation that deliberately challenges dominant expectations of the capabilities of the people we call children. Neuroqueering is particularly fruitful as it describes the intersection between queerness and neurodivergence and is a term that was first used by Nick Walker in a 2008 graduate school paper and also independently coined by Athena Lynn Michaels-Dillon and Remi Yergeau (Walker 2021). Justine Egnar helpfully summarises neuroqueering as:

> a crip project of disidentification (Muñoz [sic] 1999) co-created by academics, activists, and members of online neuroqueer communities that rejects both oppressive dominant and counterculture identities that perpetuate destructive medical model discourses of progress and cure.
>
> (2019: 124)

Normative expectations of children's capabilities I would argue are similarly shaped by the neurotypical standards with which neuroqueering takes issue, constructing dominant identities for young people that are problematic because these standards are also 'complicit in ableism through compulsory able-bodiedness/able-mindedness' (Egnar 2019: 141). To begin from a neuroqueering perspective therefore is to actively disidentify and create opportunities for the humans we call children to disidentify from the neurotypical norms that determine such expectations, especially where they are harmful and reductive. Indeed, by recognising that 'hegemonic and medicalized discourses [...] describe disabled (especially autistic) people as asexual and childlike' (Egnar 2019: 139) we might also draw attention to the way in which 'childlike' is an oppressive and minimising descriptor that ignores, undermines and/or marginalises the rich and complex lived experiences of people called children.

Neuroqueering and glitch feminism share an interest in dismantling and disidentifying from the normative binaries associated with gender, sexuality, race, and other aspects of identity from the perspectives and embodied experiences of neurodivergence and feminism respectively. What is most useful about exploring the opportunities that glitch affords performance from a neuroqueer perspective, however, is that the neuroqueer project is as suspicious of attempts at counterculture identification as much as it is concerned with challenging dominant hegemonic identities determined largely via the medical model of disability. According to Egnar, this is because 'counteridentity groups often reify binaries and construct identities around solidarity that does not recognize the complexity and fluidity of experience' (Egnar 2019: 139). A neuroqueer approach to glitching in performance practice and research then would avoid the trap of creating a counteridentity community for the people we call children that ends up reifying binaries of adult/child. For example, this could be a counteridentity group that simply reverses the binary by positioning or facilitating the counteridentification of the people we call children with the masculine and rational subject that already shapes the dominant perception of the child as a social actor within childhood studies (Burman and Stacey 2010). We might, instead, take the lead from the glitchy 'female-girl-child-teenager' of *The Hamilton Complex* that emphasises interrelationality with special regard from the audiences' perspectives. Importantly, this is not fixed as a counteridentity by the performance. Instead, it is a temporary subject position that generates a sense of solidarity between performers and personas who occupy it (and potentially audience members) and simultaneously points towards intersecting multiple and complex identities that are contained within, but also exceeded by, the figure of the female-girl-child-teenager.

What does this neuroqueer warning about counteridentification mean for future performance practice and research with children then? To some extent counteridentification that reifies norms can be resisted by prioritising neuroqueer as a verb (Walker 2021), that is, as one something does rather than something one is. This involves deliberately practising neuroqueering as a disidentification project rather than being invested in counteridentification and so strategies of trans*-age play and research that facilitate disidentification would be useful for a future practice of glitching that begins from a neuroqueer positionality. Furthermore, we might turn to the idea of assemblage to resist counteridentification when creating the conditions for glitching to occur with the people we call children. What I mean here is not just concerned with using glitchy techniques of assemblage, such as the deconstructive gender assemblage discussed above in Sin's work. Rather, it is about moving beyond a reductive idea of community and instead practising collaboration with young people as an assemblage with the capacity for activism. Assemblage is useful because it resists a limited notion of community that is always already exclusive in its inclusivity or what Chantal Mouffe and Ernesto Laclau have identified as community's 'constitutive exclusion' (1986).

The idea of assemblage I am mobilising here aims to resist the exclusion on which the concept of community depends and that predetermines who glitches, who becomes glitch, and who has permission to glitch. Instead, perhaps in the idea of assemblage, we can locate an approach to collaboration with the people we call children that retains both Butler's notion of 'assembly' as that which constitutes 'bodies in their plurality' (2015: 71) whilst also aspiring to the prospect of a 'community without community' (Derrida 1997). Assemblage, as a way of resisting both conformity that is harmful within dominant culture and also counteridentification, could take its lead from the recent forms of assembly that Butler identifies, namely street protests and occupations of the 21st century that are heterogeneous and necessarily include bodies that are in concert with one another but which do not conform to a predetermined, essentialised sense of identity. Could we create an assemblage in our research and practice with the people we call children that 'imagines a community *yet to come* without normalizing it within the existing community' (Moon 2016)? There is already a desire within Seungho Moon's work for generating such a community without community 'that underscores the interrelationality of self-other' and active citizenship in teaching art-based enquiry and equity pedagogy (Moon 2016: 10) but in terms of research and practice in the field of contemporary performance with children, the activist potential of assemblage as a form of community without community has yet to be fully explored.

Towards an Assemblage of Child Activism

Glitch feminism both facilitates and is facilitated by assemblage and therefore is a fruitful site for creating the conditions for a community without community to evolve. As an approach that works with both the AFK and digital realm, glitch feminism has the capacity to accommodate a plurality of bodies within live, embodied performance practice whilst also exploiting the kind of anonymity that the digital world permits to enable the people we call children to imagine new identities, new worlds and to create avatar bodies that ghost, refuse, remix, throw shade, and survive without fear of punishment or violence. The challenges that the people we call children face in relation to the patriarchal protectionist discourse that seeks to regulate their bodies and experiences cannot be underestimated. Added to these challenges is a gender-critical ideology that works to regulate the bodies of the people we call children by reinstating the gender binary, pathologising trans children, demonising drag performers, and calling into question the motives of scholars and commentators who support a more capacious understanding of children's genders and sexualities and how these might intersect with issues of race and class (Faye 2021, Butler 2023). As Butler argues in their recent lecture 'Who is Afraid of Gender?' at Cambridge University (2023), the anti-gender movement aligns itself with authoritarian promises of a (phantasmic) return of a more 'secure' patriarchal order, which is fuelling right wing, reactionary politics. This anti-gender context makes any attempt to create assemblages for the people we call children to glitch and to imagine new futures as activists in performance both urgent and necessary but also undeniably challenging for all involved.

In making their argument, Butler cites Pope Francis who describes the teaching of gender theory in schools as 'ideological colonisation' and states that 'the same was done by dictators of the last century … think of Hitler Youth' (Butler 2023). This rhetoric from the head of the catholic church is problematic in that it perpetuates the perception that any education that questions the gender binary is akin to fascist brainwashing for sinister ends. Whilst the notion of assemblage I am promoting is not a pedagogical space for 'gender theory', whatever Pope Francis might mean by that, I want to attend to the way in which his statement forecloses the possibility that children are capable of political action without assuming that there is an adult puppet master dictating the terms of an action that is, to him, self-evidently and inherently dangerous. Indeed, Pope Francis leaves us in no doubt as to just how dangerous he considers 'gender theory' to be when he draws a direct comparison between it and the annihilation caused by nuclear arms in order to prop up his alarmist rhetoric (Butler 2023). By creating a fear-inducing image of the people we call children as pawns in an adult's political game, Pope Francis reinstates the historic separation of children from the realm of politics and reiterates a hegemonic positioning of the child as apolitical, ahistorical, and passively ready to be manipulated.

This positioning ignores both historic and contemporary child-led action and the participation of young people in activism outside of, or in tension with, dictatorship and totalitarian rule. To name but a few examples, this includes collective action such as the Birmingham Children's Crusade against segregation in Alabama in 1963, UK-wide school strikes concerning the Conservative government's Youth

Training Scheme (YTS) in 1985, and more recently child-activists who used children's forums and parliaments to stop potential child marriages in Bangladesh and Ghana (Cuevas-Parra and Tisdall 2022). Other examples led by individual young people include Nobel Peace Prize laureate Malala Yousafzai's advocation work for girls' and women's education in Pakistan, Canadian children's rights activist Cheryl Perera who founded a youth-run non-governmental organisation called OneChild that aims to challenge child sex trafficking and exploitation, and Thandiwe Abdullah's activism in setting up the Black Lives Matter Youth Vanguard. The people we call children have been visibly active in recent years in the wider Black Lives Matter movement, protests around gun control in the U.S., and have played a key role in the Arab Spring uprisings as well as on-going participation in political change in the Middle East and North Africa (Watson *et al.* 2015).

Undeniably, all power relations between children and adults must be scrutinised as part of any critical thinking around intergenerational collaborative practice, including work made with people called children for people called adults. However, the same sentiment should also extend to creating the conditions for the people we call children to engage in the activist practices afforded to adults, otherwise, we risk perpetuating the same unequal power dynamics of adult/child relations that Pope Francis evokes in his imagery of Hitler Youth. In other words, rather than using this inflammatory rhetoric of 'protecting' children from fascist dictators (or gender theorists) and in the process framing children's participation in political life in alarmingly negative terms, can we aim instead to create an assemblage that 'protects' the people we call children's capacity to 'speak collectively, build consensus, raise awareness, advocate for and accelerate change, speak for and from the margins, disrupt the status quo, unsettle stuck discourse, sidestep conventional modes, expose broken promises' (Ashby *et al.* 2019: 2)? That is, protect their capacity to engage in activism.

Non-performative attempts to empower children (as if power is something adults own and can gift to children) or well-meaning endeavours to 'give' agency to children which ignores the relational quality of agency (Esser *et al.* 2016, Gallagher 2019) are ineffective. Instead, can we create an assemblage that is led by gloriously glitchy non-neurotypical and neurodivergent skills and experiences that an ableist, capitalist-driven economy often labels as deficiencies? And what is a more equitable way to create an assemblage than by utilising the existing skills and glitchy experiences that the people we call children already possess? Since young people are already negotiating their identities and relationships online (Downing 2013, McInroy and Craig 2020), contemporary performance has much to learn from these lived digital skills and experiences in order to grow, in yet unknown ways, the activist potential of AFK and online worlds of performance. As Russell notes:

> We are not empty signifiers [...] We reject the violent act of naming. We will reconfigure ourselves as we see fit. Modifying and coding, we choose our own names, build our own families and communities, proudly fail in the present as we dream new futures.
>
> (Russell 2020: 147)

Beyond Innocence. Beyond the innocence often ascribed to them through the violent act of naming, can we imagine the people we call children saying, living, embodying, and revising Russell's words, should they wish to? 'Becoming' here would not be envisioned according to the division of child 'human becomings' from adult 'human beings' that shapes the dominant conceptualisation of childhood towards a known destination (Lee 2001: 7). Rather, the people we call children *becoming* (in/through/as) glitch is about embracing what is not yet known. What more imaginative way to dream new futures together than by creating an assemblage that sustains a glitchy activist performance practice that 'speaks for and from the margins'? That is, a glitchy activist practice that acknowledges the real, material, and intersecting disadvantages imposed on the people we call children, specifically young people of Black and global majority heritage, LGBTQIA+, gender minority, and economically poor communities?

Glitch.
Glitch.
Otherwise we are lost.[3]

Notes

1 Glitching has also recently been discussed in performance studies in relation to trans performance in Rachel Hann's scholarship (2022).
2 See also Patrick E. Johnson's scholarship (1995) on 'throwing shade' as defined and used within African American gay culture and how it is subsequently appropriated within North American popular culture, largely in the early 1990s.
3 This line ghosts German choreographer Pina Bausch's well-known phrase 'Dance, Dance. Otherwise we are lost' (cited in Wenders 2011), whose own glitchy repetition simultaneously insists, refuses, and contains within it hope.

Bibliography

Adams, Richard and Aletha Adu (2023) 'Trans Guidance Tells English Schools to Consider Social Media Influence on Pupils Asking to Transition', *The Guardian*, 19 December 2023: https://www.theguardian.com/society/2023/dec/19/no-general-duty-let-children-change-gender-schools-england#:~:text=The%20draft%20guidance%20issued%20by,that%20parents%20should%20be%20involved Accessed 18 January 2024.
Ahmed, Sara (2006) *Queer Phenomenology: Orientations, Objects, Others*, Durham and London: Duke University Press.
Arendt, Hannah (1958) *The Human Condition*, Chicago: University of Chicago Press.
Arendt, Hannah ([1961] 1993) 'The Crisis of Education' in *Between Past and Future: Eight Exercises in Political Thought*, New York: Viking Press.
Ashby Simone, Hanna Julian, Matos Sónia, Callum Nash and Alexis Faria (2019) 'Fourth-Wave HCI Meets the 21st Century Manifesto' in Proceedings of the *Halfway to the Future Symposium*, Nottingham, UK, 19–20 November 2019, New York, NY: ACM Press, pp. 1–11.
Bower-Brown, Susie, Sophie Zadeh and Vasanti Jadva (2023) 'Binary-Trans, Non-Binary and Gender-Questioning Adolescents' Experiences in UK Schools', *Journal of LGBT Youth*, 20 (1): 74–92.
Burman, Erica and Jackie Stacey (2010) 'The Child and Childhood in Feminist Theory', *Feminist Theory*, 11 (3): 227–240.
Butler, Judith (1990) *Gender Trouble*, New York: Routledge.

Butler, Judith (2015) *Notes Towards a Performative Theory of Assembly*, Havard University Press.
Butler, Judith (2023) 'Who is Afraid of Gender?', Public Lecture, University of Cambridge, Wednesday 26 April 2023: https://www.youtube.com/watch?v=yD6UukSbAMs (accessed 18 January 2024).
Castañeda, Claudia (2002) *Figurations: Child, Bodies, World*, Durham and London: Duke University Press.
Cuevas-Parra, Patricio and E. Kay M. Tisdall (2022) 'Investing in Activism: Learning from Children's Actions to Stop Child Marriage', *Childhood*, 29 (4): 529–544.
Daniels, Jessie (2009) Rethinking Cyberfeminism(s): Race, Gender, and Embodiment, *Women's Studies Quarterly*, 37 (1): 101–124.
Davis, Seth E. (2019) 'Shade: Literacy Narratives at Black Gay Pride', *Literacy in Composition Studies,* 7 (2): 56–89.
Derrida, Jacques (1997) *The Politics of Friendship*, New York: Verso.
Downing, Gary (2013) 'Virtual Youth: Non-Heterosexual Young People's Use of the Internet to Negotiate Their Identities and Socio-Sexual Relations', *Children's Geographies*, 11 (1): 44–58.
Edelman, Lee (2004) *No Future: Queer Theory and the Death Drive*, London: Duke University Press.
Egnar, Justine (2019) 'The Disability Rights Community Was Never Mine: Neuroqueer Disidentification,' *Gender & Society*, 33 (1): 123-147.
Ellis, Justin R. (2022) 'A Fairy Tale Gone Wrong: Social Media, Recursive Hate and the Politicisation of Drag Queen Storytime', *The Journal of Criminal Law*, 86 (2): 94–108.
Equality Act (2010) Available online: https://www.legislation.gov.uk/ukpga/2010/15/contents
Esser, Florian, Meike S. Baader and Tanja Betz (2016) *Reconceptualising Agency and Childhood*, Abingdon: Routledge.
Etchells, Tim (2008) 'Natural Is Not in It', https://timetchells.com/natural-is-not-in-it/ (accessed 11 May 2023).
Faye, Shon (2021) *The Transgender Issue: An Argument for Justice*, London: Allen Lane.
Gallagher, Michael (2019) 'Rethinking Children's Agency: Power, Assemblages, Freedom and Materiality', *Global Studies of Childhood*, 9 (3): 188–199.
Gill-Peterson, Julian (2018) *Histories of the Transgender Child*, Minneapolis: University of Minnesota Press.
Goff, Phillip A, Matthew C. Jackson, Brooke A. L. DiLeone, Carmen M. Culotta and Natalie A. DiTomasso (2014) 'The Essence of Innocence: Consequences of Dehumanizing Black Children', *Journal of Personality and Social Psychology*, 106 (4): 526–545.
Hampton, Claire (2021) '*Performing the Self(ie): Performance Studies, Selfies and Feminist Identities*', Ph.D. thesis, Brunel University, London.
Hann, Rachel (2022) 'Producing Trans Performance: 'Transness' Beyond Testimony in *I, Joan*' Glasgow Theatre Seminar Series, University of Glasgow, 18 November 2022: https://www.youtube.com/watch?v=fBnSEBWAfJ8&t=2s (accessed 01 February 2024).
Horton, Cal (2020) 'Thriving or Surviving? Raising Our Ambition for Trans Children in Primary and Secondary Schools', *Frontiers in Sociology*, 5 (67): 1–18. https://www.frontiersin.org/journals/sociology/articles/10.3389/fsoc.2020.00067/full
Horton, Cal (2022) 'Depathologising Diversity: Trans Children and Families' Experiences of Pathologisation in the UK', *Children & Society*, 37 (3): 753–770.
Johnson, E. Patrick (1995) 'Snap! Culture: A Different Kind of 'Reading', *Text and Performance Quarterly*, 15 (2): 122—142.
Lee, Nick (2001) *Childhood and Society: Growing up in an Age of Uncertainty*, Berkshire: Open University Press.
Lennon, Erica and Brian J. Mistler (2014) 'Cisgenderism', *Transgender Studies Quarterly*, 1 (1-2): 63–64.

Matthews, Gareth (2008) 'Getting Beyond the Deficit Conception of Childhood: Thinking Philosophically with Children' in M. Hand and C. Win Stanley (eds.) *Philosophy in Schools*, London: Continuum, pp. 27–40.

McBride, Ruari-Santiago (2020) 'A Literature Review of the Secondary School Experiences of Trans Youth', *Journal of LGBT Youth*, 18 (2): 103–134.

McInroy, Lauren B. and Shelley L. Craig (2020) '"It's Like a Safe Haven Fantasy World": Online Fandom Communities and the Identity Development Activities of Sexual and Gender Minority Youth', *Psychology of Popular Media*, 9 (2): 236–246.

Moon, Seungho (2016) 'The ARtS Community Without Community: Imagining Aesthetic Curriculum for Active Citizenship', *Sage Open*, 6 (3): 1–11.

Mouffe, Chantal and Ernesto Laclau (1986) *Hegemony and Socialist Strategy*, London: Verso.

Nouraie-Simone, Fereshteh (2005) 'Wings of Freedom: Iranian Women, Identity, and Cyberspace' in Nouraie-Simone, Fereshteh (ed.) *On Shifting Ground*, New York: The Feminist Press.

Paris is Burning (1990) Director Jennie Livingston. Miramax.

Piaget, Jean and Barbel, Inhelder (1971) *The Child's Construction of Quantities*, London: Routledge and Keegan Paul.

Russell, Legacy (2020) *Glitch Feminism: A Manifesto*, London and Brooklyn, New York: Verso.

Satta, Mark (2023) 'Shantay Drag Stays: Anti-Drag Laws Violate the First Amendment' *Georgetown Journal of Gender and the Law*, 25 (1): 95–140.

Senior, Adele (2016) 'Beginners On Stage: Arendt, Natality and the Appearance of Children in Contemporary Performance', *Theatre Research International*, 41 (1): 70–84.

Spivak, Gayatri (1990) 'Criticism, Feminism, and the Institution' in Sarah Harasym (ed.) *The Post-Colonial Critic*, New York and London: Routledge.

Stockton, Kathryn Bond (2009) *The Queer Child or Growing Sideways in the Twentieth Century*, Durham and London: Duke University Press.

Thunberg, Greta (2019a) 'Unpopular; UN Climate Change Conference, Katowice, Poland, 15 December 2018', *No One is Too Small to Make a Difference*, Penguin Books.

Thunberg, Greta (2019b) 'Our House is on Fire', *No One is Too Small to Make a Difference*, Penguin Books.

Thunberg, Greta (2019c) 'I'm Too Young To Do This', *No One is Too Small to Make a Difference*, Penguin Books.

Trueman, Matt (2018) '"I Don't Like Acting. I Don't Like Theatre. I'm Too Cynical": Meet Risk-Taking Director Lies Pauwels', *Financial Times*, 17 October 2018: https://www.ft.com/content/b2c8abd4-d08f-11e8-9a3c-5d5eac8f1ab4 (accessed 18 January 2024).

Walker, Nick (2021) *Neuroqueer Heresies: Notes on the Neurodiversity Paradigm, Autistic Empowerment, and Postnormal Possibilities*, Fort Worth, TX: Autonomous Press.

Wallace, Jo-Ann (1995) 'Technologies of 'The Child': Towards a Theory of the Child-Subject', *Textual Practice*, 9 (2): 285–302.

Watson, Debbie, Kristen Cheney and Heba Raouf Ezzat (2015) 'Children and Young People in Times of Conflict and Change: Child Rights in the Middle East and North Africa', *Global Studies of Childhood*, 5 (2): 115–121.

Wenders, Wim (2011) Pina: Dance, Dance, Otherwise We Are Lost. Dir. Wim Wenders. Berlin: Neue Road Movies.

WHO (2021) International Classification of Diseases for Mortality and Morbidity Statistics (11th Revision), World Health Organization. https://icd.who.int/browse11/l-m/en (accessed 8th January 2024).

Index

FSC
www.fsc.org
MIX
Papier | Fördert
gute Waldnutzung
FSC® C083411

Kolibri 360 GmbH
Ferdinand-Jühlke-Straße 7
99095 Erfurt, Deutschland
produktsicherheit@kolibri360.de